The Poet Robert Browning
and his Kinsfolk
by his Cousin
Cyrus Mason

Edited and with an Afterword by
W. Craig Turner

Baylor University Press
Markham Press Fund
Waco, Texas

This volume is the eighteenth volume published
by the Markham Press Fund of Baylor University,
established in memory of Dr. L. N. and Princess
Finch Markham of Longview, Texas, by their
daughters, Mrs. R. Matt Dawson of Waco, Texas,
and Mrs. B. Reid Clanton of Longview, Texas.

Library of Congress Card Number: 81-86286
International Standard Book Number: 0-918954-38-X

The Poet Robert Browning

and his Kinsfolk

by his Cousin

Cyrus Mason

Cyrus Mason; his infant great grandson John Scarlett; his daughter Laura Macdonnell, seated; and his granddaughter Barbara Scarlett pose in the garden of Laura Mason Macdonnell's home in Black Rock on Port Philip Bay (see Introduction, p. xiv). Courtesy of John Scarlett.

Contents

'Fortunately, I am in possession of testimony, written in 1738, amply sufficient to establish the fact that the Brownings of Dorsetshire belonged to the educated class of that County, thus placing me in a position to do justice to the memory of my dead kinsfolk; as a Grandson, to show reverent respect for that same Robert Browning who mi-grated from Dorsetshire; as a Nephew of many Brownings entitled to my warmest esteem; as a Cousin of the man whose genius made the name Browning famous throughout the world; in deference to the wish expressed to me, not long before her death, by my Aunt Sarah Browning, that a correct history of her family should be written, to clear away a mystery surrounding its origin and lastly, to satisfy a pardonable interest manifested, by my own immediate family in regard to its connection with a famous Englishman,

When in London, during the year 1900, I frequently conversed with my Aunt Sarah, the last survivor of the Dorsetshire Robert Browning's children; she was a fine specimen of an educated, well preserved, very aged gentlewoman, with her faculties as clear as her complexion was fresh, her ex-pressive eyes bright as ever, her abundant brown hair arranged really in bands smoothed across the clear unwrinkled skin of her temples; just the same as I

Part One, page 2, of Mason's holograph.

Foreword

It was a July 11, 1955, letter addressed "To the Curator, 'Browning Room,' Baylor University, Waco, Texas, U. S. A." that first brought the owner of the Cyrus Mason manuscript in touch with Mrs. A. J. Armstrong, Director of the Armstrong Browning Library and widow of its founder. Dr. Armstrong had died in 1954, and Mrs. Armstrong had been appointed to direct the activities of the collection.

The writer of the letter was Mrs. Barbara C. Scarlett, granddaughter of Cyrus Mason. A "sample" of five pages of the manuscript (which Mrs. Scarlett mailed to Mrs. Armstrong) arrived at Mrs. Armstrong's office on the morning of August 3, 1955, and on the same day Mrs. Armstrong composed a letter requesting Mrs. Scarlett to send the rest of the manuscript. The remainder was mailed from London on August 8 and was in Waco by August 22. At first Mrs. Armstrong feared that pages 4-8 of Part I were missing, but these pages were later discovered to be collected in the bundle which made up Part V. Thus began the voluminous correspondence which led to the acquisition of the Cyrus Mason manuscript and the publishing rights in the United States and Canada.

Mrs. Armstrong pursued zealously the genealogical questions which the manuscript raised; she was also pointedly concerned to discover whether scholars had had earlier access to the manuscript. Plans for immediate publication were made, but there was an exchange of letters (over a period of weeks) regarding publishing rights; then prior commitments for other publications intervened. The Armstrong-Scarlett correspondence continued until well into 1959.

Various scholars had learned of the existence of the manuscript and had suspected its significance for Browning biographers. Mrs. Scarlett's son, John, had published two newspaper articles (in Melbourne, Australia) utilizing bits of information from the document; but in the present publication for the first time the entire account is provided.

Mr. Craig Turner, while doing graduate work at Baylor, provided an excellent typewritten transcription of the manuscript. For his doctoral dissertation at Tulane University, he accumulated an abundance of historical, genealogical, and biographical data to illuminate the information and implications put forward by Cyrus Mason.

The result is a well-organized and thoroughly-documented presentation of this previously unpublished and highly significant account of several episodes from the life of Robert Browning as seen through the eyes of his cousin.

Mr. Turner has been able to delineate some of Cyrus Mason's eccentricities and prejudices; Turner wisely warns the reader to evaluate Mason's judgments of Browning (and family members) in the light of Mason's own particular and impassioned mind-set. The printed text of the manuscript here provided is an accurate representation of the original; it is also a fresh and insightful review of the career of a poet of great power, a review colored by the personal family feelings of that poet's "cousin."

The manuscript is preserved in the Armstrong Browning Library at Baylor University; Mr. Turner's meticulous work makes Cyrus Mason's insight available to all.

Jack W. Herring
Director, Armstrong Browning Library

Acknowledgments

During the preparation of this edition I have incurred numerous debts which I can only partially acknowledge in this limited way. First, I must thank Professor Jack W. Herring, Director of the Armstrong Browning Library, Baylor University, for the privilege of working with the Mason manuscript and other unpublished materials owned by the ABL and for the professional expertise he has unfailingly contributed to my project. Also, Betty Coley, Librarian of the Armstrong Browning Library, Rita Humphrey, Administrative Assistant, and the entire library staff have rendered invaluable services to my research and have remained patient and congenial in the face of my sometimes unreasonable requests. The staffs and resources of the libraries at Duke University—particularly John Sharpe—and the University of North Carolina at Chapel Hill were also most helpful.

The staffs of the Markham Press Fund and the Baylor University Press have been most receptive and cooperative during the publication of the Mason material, and editor Melanie B. McQuere has been a constant source of aid and encouragement. To Sally Dee Wade, a graduate student at Texas A&M University, I owe thanks for conscientious proofreading and help with the tedious, time-consuming job of adjusting page and line numbers in the Textual Notes. A portion of the research for this project was funded by a grant from the College of Liberal Arts at Texas A&M.

I am also deeply indebted to Browning kinsfolk Elaine Baly and John Scarlett for their generous outpouring of family traditions and for their conscientious responses to my inquiries. I am most grateful to Mr. Scarlett for sending me a copy of a delightful picture of Cyrus Mason, and to Mrs. Baly for giving me a prized locket photograph of Jane Browning.

In addition to Professor Herring's scholarly advice, this edition has also benefited from the insights and the careful reading of Professor Gardner B. Taplin, whom I must thank for his many professional and personal kindnesses. Professors Taplin and Herring have been both mentors and friends: my debts to them and my appreciation of them continue to grow. Finally, I wish to thank my family—my parents, A. C. and Sybil Turner; my in-laws, Dr. S. J. and Ruby Enloe; and my wife and children, Annette, Scott, and Shannon—for their faith, encouragement, and love.

Introduction

Cyrus Mason, the author of "The Poet Robert Browning and his Kinsfolk," held a unique relationship with Browning and his family: Mason's mother was the eldest daughter of Robert Browning, grandfather of the poet, by his second marriage, while his father was the stepson of Reuben Browning, brother to the poet's grandfather.[1] Jane Eliza Browning (1800-1866) was the eldest daughter of grandfather Robert and Jane Smith Browning, and was, therefore, half sister to the poet's father. Her husband, John Mason, was the son of the widow Mason married by Reuben Browning. According to F. J. Furnivall's report of Robert Shergold Browning's account, Cyrus was the fourth of eight children born to Jane and John Mason, and he " 'emigrated to Victoria, and has held a government appointment in Melbourne for many years, and has had a large family.' "[2]

Cyrus was born in London in late 1828 or early 1829.[3] His granddaughter, Mrs. Barbara Scarlett, in a letter to Mrs. A. J. Armstrong, former Director of the Armstrong Browning Library, notes that:

---

1. F. J. Furnivall in his article "Robert Browning's Ancestors," *Browning Society Papers*, Part 12 (London: Browning Society, 1890), pp. 43, 45, on the strength of testimony from Robert Shergold Browning (son of William Shergold Browning and grandson of Robert of Dorsetshire), lists the husband of the widow Mason as Thomas Browning—the son of William Browning, brother of the poet's grandfather. His genealogy further indicates a marriage for Reuben of Dorsetshire, but does not name the wife. I have chosen to follow Mason's identification of his step-grandfather as Reuben (see p. 53).

2. Furnivall's "Ancestors," p. 44; John Maynard, *Browning's Youth* (Cambridge, Mass.: Harvard Univ. Press, 1977), pp. 372-3, lists Cyrus as the fourth of nine children—including Mary Ann Mason who died quite young.

3. I have calculated Mason's birthdate from information received on a photocopy of the "Third Schedule. Deaths in the District of Melbourne in the State of Victoria, Registered by Ernest H. Clarke" sent to me by Leon G. Smith of the office of the Government Statist, Melbourne, Victoria, Australia. The Register of Deaths records Mason's death date as "8th August 1915," while it lists his age as "86 years" and his birthplace as London. Family tradition asserts an 1828 birthdate, according to Elaine Baly, "Talking of the Brownings—Browning's Relations," *Browning Society Notes*, 3 (December 1973).

As a young man, Grandfather (an artist) lived in Paris and in exchange for learning French gave painting lessons. Came out to Aust. on the ship. Met a young widow—Mrs. Montague travelling with her two little girls—great-granddaughters of Lady Mary Wortley Montague who later became Mother's half-sisters.[4]

Cyrus was about twenty-three years old when he emigrated to Australia in 1852 and married the young widow Jessy Montague. Mason and his seventeen or eighteen year old bride "made their first home, virtually in the bush," at a place "called in the aboriginal word, Tynong," according to their great-grandson John Scarlett.[5] "They called the house 'Woodyats' after the name of the Browning house in Dorset";[6] the small edifice was built near the swamp country of Kooweerup in Victoria—probably some sixty to eighty miles from Melbourne. Mason joined the Victoria Railways—"presumably as an office clerk"—and worked with them until he was pensioned off as a draughtsman.[7] Scarlett notes—perhaps as an indication of Mason's success and station—that:

> Cyrus Mason founded the Buonarotti Club in Melbourne and my mother and I used to have a lovely pencil sketch of him—a head study—signed "J. Longstaff." This was later to be Sir John Longstaff, a quite well known Melbourne artist.

An article from the Melbourne *Argus Camera Supplement* of August 10, 1929, describes the Buonarotti Club as "a small coterie" of artistically oriented "persons endowed with the stuff of genius and rare talent."[8] The club name, it explains, was taken

---

4. Mrs. Scarlett to Mrs. Armstrong, August 29, 1955, Armstrong Browning Library, Baylor University. All of the Mrs. Scarlett to Mrs. Armstrong correspondence I have used is at Baylor.

5. John Scarlett to Jack Herring, May 30, 1975, Armstrong Browning Library, Baylor University. All of the Scarlett-Herring correspondence is at Baylor. The remainder of the paragraph—unless otherwise noted—is based on this letter.

6. Scarlett and Cyrus Mason both vary the usual spelling of Woodyates by omitting the "e."

7. The Register of Deaths lists Mason's occupation as "Lithographic draughtsman. Pensioner. Railways."

8. L. T. Luxton, "The Buonarotti Club: Bohemians of the 'Eighties,' " Melbourne *Argus Camera Supplement*, August 10, 1929, p. 3. Included in this full-page

"from Michael Angelo's surname, Buonarotti." Cyrus Mason, "a clever amateur painter," founded the club with several of his underlings, "also talented young painters," in the office of the chief railways engineer. Mason was elected president of the club and was one of its "dominant personalities" until he retired to live in the country about three years after its inception. The club's membership was comprised of a number of names from Australia's painting-literary-musical elite of the late nineteenth century. Among them were Alexander Sutherland, M.A., author of *The Origin and Growth of Moral Instinct*; Sir John Longstaff, painter; and Louis Lavater, musician. Club activities included the sketching from all angles of a "victim" chosen to sit inside a circle of the aspiring artists while musical members provided accompaniment. Also, outdoor painting excursions originating from Mason's Tynong estate—"with a loaf of bread, a bag of tomatoes, a bag of oysters, bottles of beer, and plenty of cigarettes"—were another favorite pastime. Among the most vivid memories of club member Louis Lavater was the marvelous humor of the club. After Mason's retirement to Tynong and the loss of several key members such as Longstaff, the club suffered "a slow 'petering-out' and in a year, or two years—gone!"

In a letter to Mrs. Armstrong of August 8, 1955, Barbara Scarlett remembers that Cyrus "was very much like Robert Browning in appearance." A photograph taken shortly before his death pictures Cyrus Mason seated with his infant great-grand-son, John Scarlett, on his knees; his daughter, Laura, seated to his right; and his granddaughter, Barbara Scarlett, standing behind her mother Laura.[9] This picture shows Mason to be a youthful-looking octogenarian with a full head of white hair, white whiskers, a prominent nose, and seemingly active, bright eyes. Dressed in a black suit with a white shirt and black tie, Brown-

article are three pictures: an 1885 photograph of ten young members of the Buona-rotti (Mason is not among them); a sketch of Mason's daughter Constance made by club member Tudor St. G. Tucker; and the portrait of Cyrus Mason by Longstaff mentioned by Scarlett.

9. Scarlett to the editor, March 11, 1976. I am indebted to John Scarlett for this four-generation portrait. According to Scarlett, the snapshot was taken in the garden of Laura Mason Macdonnell's house in Black Rock, a seaside suburb of Melbourne on Port Philip Bay.

ing's cousin appears to be of short to medium height and of rather husky build; his only slightly wrinkled, seemingly tanned face is solemnly gazing straight into the camera's eye. With his infant great-grandson perched on his left leg, Cyrus Mason holds the child with his left hand around the baby's midsection, his index finger extended horizontally with young John's right hand wrapped around it.[10]

Cyrus Mason's family remembers best his sense of humor and his continued artistic endeavors. Mrs. Scarlett's letter to Mrs. Armstrong reminisces:

> I often think of my Grandfather Mason what a Humorist. he [*sic*] was a delightful man—active and wonderful to the end. He died aged 87—so full of Life and all its interest. I have several water colours of his—all admired by many.[11]

John Scarlett writes that Cyrus—indeed "all the Masons"— possessed "a sense of humor for all seasons and events."[12] Scarlett remembers the story of a particular wake for a family member and Cyrus's "prudently taking sandwiches with him, just in case"; Cyrus was sitting with the surviving sister as mealtime approached:

> When lunchtime came, he mentioned it, which brought a shocked: "Oh, Cyrus, how can you talk of such things, when dear Polly (or whoever it was) is lying there in the next room!" To which my great grandfather replied "Very well, I'll have lunch with the corpse." And presumably he did, having his sandwiches handy for this refreshment.

His appreciation of beauty sometimes led Cyrus Mason into humorous situations. John Scarlett records that his mother, Barbara Macdonnell Scarlett, "being beautiful was a favorite of Cyrus Mason's, who did not take readily to people who were not."[13] Cyrus's forthrightness in evaluating beauty and, more to

---

10. See frontispiece.
11. November 20, 1957, Baylor.
12. Scarlett to Herring, May 30, 1975, Baylor. The funeral anecdote is taken from the same letter.
13. This story is also taken from Scarlett's May 30, 1975, letter to Herring.

the point, lack of beauty often led to embarrassing circumstances when he made use of public transport:

> Before getting into a train he would look around and perhaps say of the nearest woman, "Oh, no—she's *much* too ugly." And he would take my mother's arm and direct them to another compartment. History does not relate the reaction of such offending lady travellers to such a remark. Certainly he never lowered his voice. As my mother, who talked in italics, said, "My dear—he would say these things *right* in their face!"

Mason's interest in beauty was not, however, confined to beautiful people; throughout his life he remained active with his interest and participation in the arts. As we have seen, Mason gave painting lessons in Paris as a youth, and in Australia he founded the Buonarotti Club and continued to paint water colours which, Mrs. Scarlett tells us, were "admired by many."[14] His great-grandson has written that he still has "a little water-colour at home that Cyrus painted of the house [Mason's first house in Australia] as a Christmas card."[15] Mason's artistic inclinations, however, were not limited to painting; his granddaughter has told us that, "after Grannie's death," Cyrus "always seemed to be writing."[16] One result of this activity, of course, is "The Poet Robert Browning and his Kinsfolk," dated July 1908 from Sandringham, Victoria, and signed in Cyrus Mason's own clear hand.

After a twelve-month illness, Cyrus Mason died in East Melbourne, Australia, on August 8, 1915, at the age of eighty-six. The cause of his death has been listed in the Register of Deaths as "senile enlargement of the prostate; Heart failure." His nine children are listed in the same Register as Jessy Harriet, William, Cyrus, Arthur John, Laura, Herbert Reuben, Valentine Frank, Constance Browning, and Theodore.

On July 11, 1955, Laura Mason Macdonnell's daughter, Mrs.

---

14. Scarlett to Mrs. Armstrong, August 26, 1955, and November 20, 1957, Baylor.
15. John Scarlett to Herring, May 30, 1975, Baylor. Mason's choice of the noted Melbourne artist, Sir John Longstaff, to sketch his portrait certainly indicates his appreciation of good portraiture also.
16. Mrs. Scarlett to Mrs. Armstrong, June 20, 1958, Baylor.

Barbara Scarlett, initiated a correspondence with Mrs. A. J. Armstrong—then Director of the Armstrong Browning Library at Baylor University—informing her of the existence of the Mason holograph and offering it for sale. After several months of correspondence across the sea (Mrs. Scarlett, though a native Australian, was living in England at the time), the Armstrong Browning Library purchased the manuscript in November 1955. Mrs. Scarlett writes of it, "My grandfather, an artist, gave some months in writing it."[17] She later informed Mrs. Armstrong that "when Grandfather died he left the MS. to my Mother, then I was left it by her."[18] John R. Scarlett, great-grandson of Cyrus Mason and author of the two Australian newspaper articles in Appendix II, assured Mrs. Armstrong that "Cyrus Mason's manuscript has been in our family ever since he wrote it."[19]

Cyrus Mason's most important motivation in writing this genealogical study is "to attempt the rectification of the 'monstrous fabrication' " that the Browning family history could be traced back to "the laboring class"—almost certainly a slightly veiled allusion to F. J. Furnivall's notorious "Footman Ancestor" theory.[20] He goes to great lengths to trace the Browning lineage back as far as a fourteenth-century "William Brounyng Senior" by means of various county histories and church records, using as a key "the Christian names, William, John, Robert, feeling that the Brownings, bearing those three Christian names, continuously, were the ancestors of the poet Robert Browning."[21]

---

17. Mrs. Scarlett to Mrs. Armstrong, August 8, 1955, Baylor.
18. Mrs. Scarlett to Mrs. Armstrong, August 29, 1955, Baylor.
19. John Scarlett to Mrs. Armstrong, May 5, 1957, Armstrong Browning Library, Baylor University.
20. See Furnivall's "Ancestors," pp. 26-45. Thirty years after Mason's writing yet another kinsman, Sir Vincent Baddeley, was prompted to write an article "in order to dispose of the extraordinary myth which Dr. Furnivall invented about the footman ancestor" (Sir Vincent Baddeley to Mrs. Armstrong, September 29, 1955, Armstrong Browning Library). The article was "The Ancestry of Robert Browning, the Poet," *Genealogists' Magazine*, March 1938, pp. 1-6. Mason's use of "monstrous fabrication" is taken from his Aunt Sarah Browning, below, p. 9.
21. Below, p. 20. Both Furnivall and Baddeley, however, assert that Browning family history, in fact, "goes no further back than [the poet's] great-great-grandfather Robert" (Baddeley, p. 2; see also Furnivall's "Ancestors," p. 35, and below, p. 21, n. 7).

Even though Mason is attempting to disprove the low origins attributed to the Browning clan—in general—by Furnivall, his treatment of the poet and his immediate family—in particular—is certainly not sympathetic. Mason's chief contention with Robert seems to center in "the Poet's aloofness from Kinsfolk," asserting that his development as a poet "obliterated natural affection" towards his family.[22] Robert Senior, the poet's father, appears as a somewhat harmless eccentric who disappeared during his wedding celebration to dissect a duck;[23] Aunt Margaret, Robert Senior's sister, is similarly pictured "mysteriously crooning prophecies over her Nephew" in his infancy.[24] Such idiosyncrasies as manifested themselves in father and aunt, Mason hints, may, through inheritance, be partially responsible for the poet's unnatural "feeling of antagonism" towards his relations.[25]

Despite Mason's claim that he has not relied on material employed by other biographers, he does use two sources cited by Furnivall: John Hutchins's *The History and Antiquities of the County of Dorset* (London, 1774) and Sir Richard Colt Hoare's *History of Wiltshire* (London, 1822-1843).[26] Also, the following works had been published when Cyrus Mason was writing his family history: Edward Berdoe, *The Browning Cyclopaedia* (1891); John Cary, *Cary's New Itinerary* (1826); G. K. Chesterton, *Robert Browning* (1903); "Death of Mr. Reuben Browning," (Liverpool) *Journal of Commerce* (1879); F. J. Furnivall, "Robert Browning's Ancestors" (1890-1891), and "Browning's Footman Ancestor" (1902); Sir Edmund Gosse, *Robert Browning Personalia* (1890); *The Letters of Robert Browning and Elizabeth Barrett Barrett, 1845-1846* (1898); Samuel Lewis, *A Topographical Dictionary of England* (1835); Mrs. Sutherland Orr, *Life and Letters of Robert Browning* (1891); William Sharp, *Life of Robert Browning* (1897); and *The Times* and *The Morning Chronicle* accounts of the Von Müller v. Browning trial. Though he makes direct, indisputable

---

22. Below, pp. 81, 115.
23. Below, p. 65.
24. Below, p. 14.
25. *Ibid.*
26. See Part One, n. 24.

references only to Berdoe's *Cyclopaedia*,[27] Kenyon's volume on Browning and Domett,[28] the *Letters of RB and EBB*,[29] and *The Times* or *The Morning Chronicle* trial accounts,[30] Mason's primary concern—as I have noted—was to counter Furnivall's claims of a servant ancestor.[31]

With the exception of Maisie Ward's *Robert Browning and His World*, John Maynard's *Browning's Youth*, John Scarlett's "Young Robert" and "Lawsuit of the Long Ago" from the *Sydney Morning Herald*, and Elaine Baly's "Talking of the Brownings" in the *Browning Society Notes*, the sources used in preparing this text have not had access to Mason's manuscript and, therefore, could not have been influenced by it.[32]

As editor I have tried to present in the body of this text Cyrus Mason's final intent in the ink copy of his manuscript; in an attempt to reconstruct Mason's *full* intent for the reader who wishes to study the sequence of his writing, alterations made in Mason's own hand are recorded by page and line number at the end of the text. The content notes at the bottom of the pages attempt to clarify the specified material—to shed more light on the episodes under examination—whether in agreement or in contention with Mason's presentation. In these notes I have sought to portray a balanced view of those hazy, uncertain areas of Browning's life and background which Cyrus Mason discusses; in the Afterword I have presented my own analysis of Mason, his manuscript, and its value.

---

27. See Part Four, n. 40.
28. See Part One, n. 16.
29. See Part One, n. 24; Part Four, nn. 22, 37, 38, 49; and Part Five, n. 20.
30. See Part Five, n. 9.
31. G. K. Chesterton's 1903 account, *Robert Browning* (London: Macmillan), also takes note of the "Footman Ancestor" assertion (p. 7), but since Mason refers to his Aunt Sarah's anger about a particular theory in 1900, Furnivall's 1891 publication is the most likely offender. See p. 9 below for Aunt Sarah's reaction.
32. In spite of Maisie Ward's statement to the contrary—"There is probably an allusion to Cyrus Mason's rather spiteful account of the Browning family in Mrs. Orr's biography of the poet" (I, 309, Chapter 1, n. 2)—Mrs. Orr's 1891 biography could not have referred to the unpublished Mason manuscript which was not even written until 1908. Scarlett wrote his 1937-38 articles using the original manuscript as his source while it was still in the possession of his family; Ward used a clerical copy (replete with errors) at Baylor while compiling the 1967 volume of her biography; Maynard relied on an earlier version of this edition in preparation for his 1977

A NOTE ON THE TEXT

The Mason holograph is on 7⅞" wide x 10" long white lined paper with twenty-six lines per sheet. The paper itself is yellowing in spots from age and is ragged around its edges. The sheets are numbered at the bottom beginning with "1" for each of its five sections. Part One contains thirteen handwritten pages; Part Two, eighteen pages; Part Three, thirty-two pages; Part Four, twenty-three pages; and Part Five, twenty-four pages. There is also a Title page (appearing as page 1 in this edition), as well as a Dedication page (page 3) and a Contents page (page 5). Each section is joined in the upper left corner by a roundhead brass paper fastener; each page, except the first of each "part," is indented in the upper left corner to allow for binding—sometimes only the first line, but more often a diagonal slope is formed by the top three lines on the page. The writing begins on the top line of the pages—⅞" from the top of the sheet—and continues through the bottom line; it extends from the extreme left to the extreme right of each sheet with no margins on either side; Mason has written only on the front of each sheet (see p. vi for a photocopy of a page from the Mason manuscript).

The manuscript is written in a clear hand in black ink, now fading, except for the lines calling for insertion of *"fac similes,"* which are in the same hand in red ink. The writer has repeatedly made deletions, insertions, and corrections throughout the manuscript. The majority of his deletions and corrections are marked over by ⚡⚡⚡, while the additions and changes are generally inserted by means of a caret above the marked-out portion. Sometimes, however, a marked-out portion will be immediately followed by a correction. Insertions with no correction involved are made above the line with a caret to indicate proper placement. A second type of black ink is used on The Title and Dedication pages, as well as in making corrections and additions in much of Part Five. This ink is a lighter black, almost gray, but is still in the same hand. The method of marking out used here is a single

---

Browning's Youth; Mrs. Baly cites Scarlett's articles as her source for information regarding the Mason material.

line drawn horizontally through the word or words to be omitted; the caret method of insertions is still employed.

The type of changes which Mason makes generally deals merely with an insignificant change in wording (e.g., p. 7, l. 15: Marked out is *through the career of a*; inserted is *upon occurances during my*) or a change in spelling, but sometimes involves an important softening of language (e.g., p. 106, ll. 2-3: Marked out is *The Poet, blinded to reason, by an overbearing temperament; to stop what he thought fit to conclude was a persecution*; inserted is *Ignoring consequences the Poet*). All of the changes have been recorded in the Textual Notes at the end of the text. When making large-scale changes, Mason several times has neatly cut a portion of paper to fit the dimension of the page and the number of lines to be corrected, written on it the change involved, and glued it over the portion he wished to alter (e.g., p. 113, ll. 15-19). Each of this type of change is noted in the Textual Notes, but the underneath portion is not provided when it is not readable.

Also included throughout the handwritten manuscript are pencil markings making additions, deletions, and corrections. They are in a less steady, seemingly different hand than the ink manuscript itself; they are, presumably, the work of one of Mason's descendants, or perhaps of Mason himself at a later time when his hand was not so stable. They generally consist of rewording and reconstructing, seldom changing the intended sense. The pencil markings have been recorded at the end of the Textual Notes, but have been ignored in the preparation of the text.

Mason's spelling has been maintained throughout the text: it is sometimes very British (e.g., *waggon*, p. 49), other times carelessly done (e.g., *Smollet* for Smollett, p. 49), and still others merely wrong (e.g., *paralels* for parallels, p. 5). In order to assure the reader of textual accuracy in transcription, a list of spelling errors and variants has been included in the Textual Notes. Mason's even more unusual punctuation has been retained as well: this may best be noted in his eccentric and erratic use of commas and his repeated substitution of semicolons for colons. His tendency to omit end punctuation has led the editor, in order to avoid confusion, to supply the appropriate mark in brackets whenever Mason has obviously meant to end a sentence. The only editorial change has been to align Mason's superior letters.

Short-Title Bibliography

Baddeley's "Ancestry": Sir Vincent Baddeley, K.C.B. "The Ancestry of Robert Browning, the Poet." *Genealogists' Magazine*, March, 1938.

Baly, "Talking of the Brownings": Elaine Baly. "Talking of the Brownings—Browning's Relations." *Browning Society Notes*, 3 (December 1973).

Browning's *Memories*: Oscar Browning. *Memories of Sixty Years at Eton, Cambridge, and Elsewhere*. 2nd ed. London: John Lane, 1910.

Chesterton's *Browning*: G. K. Chesterton. *Robert Browning*, English Men of Letters Series. London: Macmillan, 1903.

Columbia Gazeteer: Leon E. Seltzer, ed. *The Columbia Lippincott Gazeteer of the World*. New York: Columbia University Press, 1952.

DeVane: William Clyde DeVane. *A Browning Handbook*. 2nd ed. New York: Appleton-Century-Crofts, 1955.

Furnivall's "Ancestors": F. J. Furnivall. "Robert Browning's Ancestors." *Browning Society Papers*, Part 12. London: Browning Society, 1890-1891.

Gazeteer of the British Isles: *Gazeteer of the British Isles*. 9th ed. 1943; rpt. Edinburgh: John Bartholomew & Son Ltd., 1970.

Gosse's *Personalia*: Sir Edmund Gosse. *Robert Browning Personalia*. Boston: Houghton, Mifflin, 1890.

Griffin and Minchin: W. Hall Griffin and Harry Christopher Minchin. *The Life of Robert Browning*. Rev. ed. Hamden, Conn.: Archon Books, 1966.

Hutchins: John Hutchins. *The History and Antiquities of Dorset*. 2 vols. 3rd ed. Corrected, Augmented, and Improved by William Shipp and James Whitworth Hodson. Westminster: Nichols and Sons, 1861.

Irvine and Honan: William Irvine and Park Honan. *The Book, the Ring, and the Poet*. New York: McGraw-Hill, 1974.

Letters of RB and EBB: Robert Browning and Elizabeth Barrett. *The Letters of Robert Browning and Elizabeth Barrett Barrett, 1845-1846*. 2 vols. London: Smith, Elder and Co., 1898.

Lewis's *Topographical Dictionary*:   Samuel Lewis. *A Topographical Dictionary of England*. 3rd ed. London: S. Lewis and Co., 1835.

Luxton, "The Buonarotti Club":   L. T. Luxton, "The Buonarotti Club: Bohemians of the 'Eighties.' " Melbourne *Argus Camera Supplement*, August 10, 1929.

Marks, *Family of the Barrett*:   Jeanette Marks. *The Family of the Barrett*. New York: Macmillan, 1938.

Maynard's *Browning's Youth*:   John Maynard. *Browning's Youth*. Cambridge, Mass.: Harvard University Press, 1977.

Miller's *Portrait*:   Betty Miller. *Robert Browning: A Portrait*. New York: Charles Scribner's Sons, 1952.

Mrs. Orr: Mrs. Sutherland Orr. *Life and Letters of Robert Browning*. 2 vols. Boston: Houghton, Mifflin, 1891.

Phelps, *Robert Browning*:   William Lyon Phelps. *Robert Browning*. New ed. 1932; rpt. Hamden, Conn.: Archon Books, 1968.

RB and AD: *Robert Browning and Alfred Domett*. Ed. Sir Frederick Kenyon. London: Smith, Elder, and Company, 1906.

RBEBK: *The Letters of Robert Browning and Elizabeth Barrett Barrett, 1845-1846*. Ed. Elvan Kintner. 2 vols. Cambridge, Mass.: Harvard University Press, 1969.

Sharp's *Life*:   William Sharp. *Life of Robert Browning.* London: Walter Scott, Ltd., 1897.

Smith, *History of England*:   Goldwin Smith. *A History of England*. 3rd ed. New York: Charles Scribner's Sons, 1966.

Taplin, *Life of EBB*:   Gardner B. Taplin. *The Life of Elizabeth Barrett Browning*. Hamden, Conn.: Archon Books, 1970.

Ward: Maisie Ward. *Robert Browning and His World*. 2 vols. New York: Holt, Rinehart and Winston, 1967, 1969.

Wheatley, *London*:   Henry B. Wheatley, *London: Past and Present*. London: John Murray, 1891.

A sketch of Cyrus Mason by Sir John Longstaff taken from the (Melbourne) *Argus Camera Supplement*, August 10, 1929, p. 3. (See Introduction, pp. xii-xiii.)

The Poet Robert Browning

and

his Kinsfolk

by

his Cousin

Cyrus Mason

To my
Dear Wife
I dedicate
these Browning Family Memoirs
in the
Fifty sixth year
of our married life
CM

Sandringham
Victoria, July 1908

Part One

Explains why the writer, the only surviving member of the Browning Family possessed of the necessary information, feels it a duty to refute published mis-statements.

Part Two

Traces the Poet's ancestors—"Bruning"—"Brounyng"—and "Browning" by the aid of Christian Names and by writings in existing family Books, up to the period when the Grandfather of the Poet, left Woodyats in Dorsetshire for London.

Part Three

Describes the position of the Dorsetshire Brownings in London, their mode of life and the education of the Poet's Father.

Part Four

Gives, from personal observation, particulars of the Poet's Courtship of Elizabeth Barrett, their Marriage and flight from England.

Part Five

Speaks of Family disappointment—changes in the New Cross Browning Household—the attempt of the Poet's Father to ameliorate his altered position and his banishment from England.

Part One

Authentic particulars of Robert Browning's origin, birth, childhood, education and developement into an acknowledged poetic genius, have never yet been published; being his first Cousin[1] and contemporary, having been in a position to obtain family information relating to those subjects; having associated from my birth with generations of Brownings, I feel impelled to rectify statements which have been published respecting the Poet's forefathers.

My account, drawn from traditions which I have heard related by our kinsfolk, coupled with circumstances that I have personally observed, will I trust furnish the admirers of Browning's writings with interesting matter for reflection; the intrinsic value of his poetry will remain unquestioned by anything which I am able to relate.

Looking back, upon occurances during my long life, by the aid of an unimpaired memory I am drawn to the conclusion that the time has now arrived when the many admirers of Browning should be made acquainted with personal characteristics peculiar to the Poet and his Kinsfolk, especially as I am aware that should I refrain from supplying information within my knowledge, it can never be given truthfully, for I am the only survivor of that generation conversant with the past Browning history.

---

1. Mason's mother, Jane Eliza Browning, was the eldest daughter by the second marriage of Robert Browning of the Bank of England, grandfather of the poet; his father was the stepson of Reuben, brother to the poet's grandfather. See Genealogy, Appendix III.

Fortunately I am in possession of testimony written in
1738,[2] amply sufficient to establish the fact that the Brownings of Dorsetshire belonged to the educated class of that
County, thus placing me in a position to do justice to the
memory of my dead kinsfolk; as a Grandson, to show reverent respect for that same Robert Browning who migrated
from Dorsetshire; as a Nephew of many Brownings entitled
to my warmest esteem; as a cousin of the man whose genius
made the name Browning famous throughout the world; in
deference to the wish expressed to me, not long before her
death, by my Aunt Sarah Browning,[3] that a correct history
of her family should be written, to clear away a mystery
surrounding it's origin and lastly, to satisfy a pardonable
interest manifested by my own immediate family in regard
to it's connection with a famous Englishman.

When in London, during the year 1900, I frequently
conversed with my Aunt Sarah, the last survivor of the
Dorsetshire Robert Browning's children; she was a fine
specimen of an educated well preserved, very aged gentlewoman, with her faculties as clear as her complexion was
fresh, her expressive eyes bright as ever, her abundant
brown hair arranged neatly in bands smoothed across the
clear unwrinkled skin of her temples; just the same as I
remember seeing it when I was a boy; her shapely head,
uncovered by a cap; I am induced to describe her appearance
circumstantially because Aunt Sarah was an example, of
what I may term, the Browning beauty and physical robustness; I recall her dignified presence, remember with admiration the sound of her soft musical voice, when used,
accompanied by graceful movements of her shapely hands,
adorned with what are known, as "filbert nails" and feel

---

2. Mason further identifies this "testimony" in Part Three.
3. "Aunt Sarah" was the daughter of Robert Browning, grandfather of the poet,
by his second wife, Jane Smith; see Genealogy, Appendix III. For more extensive
genealogical charts see Maynard's *Browning's Youth*, pp. 367-75.

pride in my relationship; though Aunt Sarah was, when I last saw her, 85 years of age,[4] everything surrounding her appearance and manner awakened in me a feeling of gratitude for having been permitted to share the blood of her healthy well born race.

Having been absent from England for many years,[5] I naturally spoke to her at our meeting, of the many Brownings passed away during my absence. Aunt Sarah talked of the poet's fame, his death and funeral, which she had attended in Westminster Abbey, this recollection led her to pathetically deplore the publication, since that event, of very much relating to Browning Family history and concerning the Poet's life, as incorrect; with emotion, the old lady produced one published account, indignantly declaring that most of it was "monstrous fabrication," she pointed out parts of the book which we both knew to be contrary to facts, she then begged me to take the publication away out of her sight, became so agitated that I promptly acceded to her request. Dear honest soul! I only realized later, why her face flushed at the thought of her family being given in print, an origin so different to that which pride in her descent had for years delighted her contemplation.

Unhappily, I only comprehended, after my Aunt Sarah was in her grave, the real meaning of her reference to the incorrectness of much that has been published as Browning family history, indeed, it was only after the death of Sarianna Browning, the Poet's sister and I saw no mention of the intended publication of family memoirs, that the full significance of my Aunt Sarah's pathetic appeal became clear to me.[6] I then realized that as the only surviving

---

4. Sarah Browning was born September 9, 1814: Furnivall's "Ancestors," p. 45.

5. Having emigrated to Australia in 1852, in 1900 Mason would have been "absent from England" for at least forty-eight years.

6. Aunt Sarah died November, 1902 (Maynard's *Browning's Youth*, p. 365); Sarianna died April 22, 1903 ("Miss Browning," *The Athenaeum*, 3940 [May 2, 1903], 564-5).

member of the family, possessed of the necessary information, it was my duty to attempt the rectification of "monstrous fabrication." I would have preferred that one of a previous generation had seen the necessity of taking action, in many respects the result would have been better, more particularly as an earlier account, when published, would have prevented certain inuendoes being circulated as to the cause of the silence observed by Robert Browning's kinsfolk.

My Uncles, Robert, William and Reuben, sons of the Dorsetshire Robert Browning, all personally known to me, were justifiably proud of their birth and the name they bore; all were well able to write a clear and interesting account of the Poet's ancestors; Uncle Robert, the Poet's father, though singularly diffident and inclined to eccentricity, was a man possessed of much learning, he wrote excellent prose with perfect facility, enjoyed the best of health, lived to a great age[7] but left behind him no record of family history.

Uncle William, a great student of genealogy,[8] devoted to literary work as an amusement, neglected furnishing any family notes, yet in his book "Leisure Hours", now before me, published in 1841, had acknowledged his Nephew's genius in "Lines" addressed to the author of "Paracelsus", written on hearing of the success of "Strafford"; the final stanza of this poem written by Uncle William, I quote;

"With joy we heard the praise your talent earned,"
"When *Paracelsus*" opened on our view;"
"The germ of sterling genius was discerned—"

---

7. Robert Senior, the poet's father, was born in 1782 and died in 1866.

8. Mrs. Sutherland Orr's *Life and Letters of Robert Browning* (Boston: Houghton, Mifflin, and Co., 1891), I, 116, records: "It was chiefly from this Uncle [William] that Miss Browning and her brother heard the now often-repeated stories of their probable ancestors, Micaiah Browning, who distinguished himself at the siege of Derry, and that commander of the ship 'Holy Ghost' who conveyed Henry V. to France before the battle of Agincourt, and received the coat-of-arms, with its emblematic waves, in reward for his service."

"And by *"The Earl of Strafford"* we have learned,"
"The augury was just—the judgement true."[9]
The first two lines of Uncle William's poem,
"While a French pencil Strafford's fate displays"
"And De la Roche unfolds his final scene."
refer to two pictures exhibited at the Paris Louvre in May 1837, thus supplying evidence that Uncle William Browning had "discerned" the genius of his Nephew, then 25 years of age, at a time when his published poems were being ridiculed for obscurity and "Strafford" had only been printed by the friendly act of a publisher.[10] Uncle William's "Lines" were written when he resided in Paris, where he had cordially received his Nephew as a guest, had then felt pride in introducing to congenial society, a talented and promising member of his family.[11]

Being a man of considerable literary attainments,[12]

---

9. *Leisure Hours* (London: Whittaker and Co., 1841), p. 307. Uncle William's note regarding the first lines reads: "May, 1837, at which time there were exhibited at the Louvre two splendid pictures by that artist, for the duke of Sutherland and lord Francis Egerton."

10. *Strafford* was the first of Browning's works brought out by the expense of a publisher, having been published by Longmans on May 1, 1837. Browning stated in a letter to Mr. Frank Hill (quoted in Mrs. Orr, I, 174) that he got "it printed in four-and-twenty hours, by Moxon's assistance." Macready wrote that "Forster is trying to induce Longmans to publish it; I doubt his success" (*The Journal of William Charles Macready: 1832-1851*, ed. J. C. Trewin [London: Longmans Green and Co. Ltd., 1967], p. 93). Mason, however, feels that "Longman, the London publisher, printed and published 'Strafford' as an act of friendship" for the Brownings; see pp. 45-6 below.

11. I can find no evidence that Browning visited Paris before his marriage, though he writes to Elizabeth of a proposed trip—as a favor to Uncle Reuben—that never took place: see Elvan Kintner, ed., *The Letters of Robert Browning and Elizabeth Barrett Barrett, 1845-1846* (Cambridge, Mass.: Harvard University Press, 1969), I, 230, 237. Also, Mrs. Orr, I, 9, denies the story that Browning was mistaken for an Italian in Paris in 1837 by a nephew: "He neither had nor could have had a nephew; and he was not out of England at the time specified."

12. In addition to *Leisure Hours* (1841), "A collection of miscellanies" (Mrs. Orr, I, 116), William Shergold Browning also wrote *The History of the Huguenots During the Sixteenth Century*, 2 vols. (London: William Pickering, 1829); the historical novels *Hoel Morvan*, 3 vols. (London: T. C. Newley, 1844) and *The Provost of Paris* (Paris: G. G. Bennis, 1833); *A Flemish Legend* ("no copy found; this title is listed among his publications in *Hoel Morvan*; hence issued before 1844."); and essays for the *Gentleman's Magazine*: see Maynard's *Browning's Youth*, p. 363.

Uncle William must have realized later, when his Nephew's writings were published and praised, that the curiosity of readers would demand in the future some information about a family which had produced an acknowledged poet, but after Uncle William returned to England, to permanently reside, circumstances occurred in the family which met with his disapproval, destroying the inclination he formerly had, to leave a record of the origin of a family which had produced "the germ of sterling genius"[.]

Uncle Reuben, a City of London man, by writing and publishing pamphlets on financial matters, using the *nom de plume* "Brutus Britannicus", proved his capability to produce a clear account of the origin of the Browning family,[13] he had been closely associated with the poet while engaged upon his early writings, had been aware of the struggle made to get them printed; had always showed a keen interest in his Nephew's literary work, as an Uncle, well able, advising and generously assisting when most needed; was I know proud of a kinsman so calculated to feed his family pride, yet, though Uncle Reuben was in possession of all the facts necessary to furnish particulars of the family origin, having reached manhood under his father's roof and lived to be an old man, he also left no record of family history among his papers.[14]

I knew Robert Browning, the poet, as a young man full

---

13. Reuben Browning "was gifted with great literary talents, writing not only upon finance, but also upon poetical and home matters." His pamphlets included "A few Observations on the Stamp Act" (1854) and "The Finances of Great Britain Considered" (1859) while the pseudonymous Brutus Britannicus was used "when writing to the *Daily Telegraph.*" Also, "under his own name he published several works upon 'The Currency,' with regard to the Bank Charter Act of 1844, also upon various other financial matters." This information has been taken from a typed copy of "Death of Mr. Reuben Browning," The Liverpool *Journal of Commerce* (Thursday, September 11, 1879), sent to the Armstrong Browning Library by Captain Robert Browning, grandson of Reuben Browning. Maynard's *Browning's Youth*, p. 364, also lists an eight-page pamphlet entitled *Compulsory Immediate Convertibility of the Bank Note a Failure* (n.p., 1868) as among Reuben's publications.

14. Reuben Browning's dates are 1803-1879 (Furnivall's "Ancestors," p. 45).

of vitality and possessing a strong love of approbation; I find it difficult to imagine him content to pass away without leaving some account of his forefathers,[15] or at the least, supplying particulars of his own early days, when his learned father devoted all his leisure time to his son's education, but such being the fact, it must be concluded that events occurred during the Poet's early career which, having caused his elder kinsfolk to maintain silence about family matters, he deemed it wise to acquiesce.

After the death of the Poet it was discovered that he had left among his papers, no particulars having reference to his kinsfolk; it is known that he had requested his intimates to destroy, when read, the letters which he had written to them, thus any references to his kinsfolk, if made by him, would be lost.

In a small volume,[16] a few of Browning's letters written to his friend Alfred Domett, then residing in New Zealand, have been preserved, in spite of the poet's special request for their destruction; a perusal of these letters, written at a most critical time in the life of Robert Browning, causes a feeling of disappointment, almost regret, that they were preserved, for there is no reference made in them to the kindly assistance being rendered by kinsfolk at the very time that they were written; the poet struggling against adverse circumstances, when opening his heart to a former neighbor, his

15. Mrs. Orr, I, 4, is of the opinion that "so long as he was young, he had no reason to think about his ancestors; and, when he was old, he had no reason to care about them; he knew himself to be, in every possible case, the most important fact in his family history." Oscar Browning, however, records in his *Memories of Sixty Years* (London: John Lane, 1910) that Browning "was fond of tracing his family history, which he did with more zeal than knowledge" (p. 6). Sir Edmund Gosse's *Robert Browning Personalia* (Boston: Houghton, Mifflin, and Company, 1890), p. 6, states that Browning was "annoyed" by the " 'tangle of facts and fancies' " which purported to be accounts of his life, and that he verbally dictated to Gosse his own version of his life. This "life," however, attempts to trace forefathers no earlier than the poet's father.

16. I.e., *Robert Browning and Alfred Domett*, ed. Frederick Kenyon (London: Smith, Elder, and Co., 1906).

intimate friend of congenial tastes, made little mention of those of his family then constituting his chief support.[17]

It would almost seem that governed by Browning pride or dominated by inherited eccentricity, the Poet towards all his relations indulged a feeling of antagonism, though from the time when my Mother took him an infant in her caressing arms, from that day when his eccentric Aunt Margaret was detected mysteriously crooning prophecies over her Nephew,[18] behind a door at the house at Camberwell; though as years passed, Father, Mother, Sister and Kinsfolk had come to regard that child, grown up, as a superior being and implicitly believed in the fulfillment of the future foretold for "Young Robert", he had, when writing to Domett developed a temperament which never evinced much regard for kinsfolk, thus rendering it difficult for anyone outside his family to produce his correct biography.

If my record seems to contradict the saying that a Poet is born, not made; when the particulars are related of the training and teaching given to his father, followed by the training and teaching given to himself, with only the one object in view, it will have to be admitted that his Kinsfolk greatly assisted in the making of the child Robert Browning into a Poet. This part of the family history commences from the time when two brothers, Robert and Reuben Browning, the Grandfather and the Grand Uncle of the Poet, with minds stored with learning, having cultivated tastes for

---

17. The *RB and AD* volume contains two letters written by Browning to Domett before the latter's departure to New Zealand, fourteen letters from Browning to Domett while the latter was in New Zealand, and seven letters from Browning to Domett during the 1872-1877 period after both had returned to London. Of the fourteen letters of the middle group, five letters refer specifically to Browning's "father," "mother," and "sister" as sending their regards or as being well, while five other letters refer to "all here" as either being well or sending regards. One letter from the latter group, dated March 19, 1846, refers to *Luria* and *A Soul's Tragedy*, and mentions "My father having been at the pains of getting them printed, I can send a copy" (p. 124).

18. Mason seems to have been the only one to record Margaret Morris Browning's "eccentric" behavior; other references to her are found in Part Three and Part Five.

literature and indulging then, a love for poetry, about the year 1785,[19] decided to migrate from the County of Dorsetshire, England; when the two brothers were settled in London, these cultivated tastes greatly influenced the character and training of a child, Robert, the son of Robert, one of the Dorsetshire Brothers; it is this country born boy's rearing and educating, until he reached manhood and married, which should engage the attention of all readers of Browning's works and furnish matter for reflection; for when in the year 1812, a Robert Browning, of a third generation, was born at Camberwell,[20] near London, a literary, even poetic atmosphere, surrounded the infant.

Robert, the eldest of the Dorsetshire Browning brothers,[21] gave to his son Robert, robust health, a receptive brain and some eccentricity; the other Dorsetshire Browning brother, Reuben, helped the boy to accumulate knowledge, watched it's developement and at an important time in his Nephew's life cultivated the rich quality of his remarkable intellect, humoured it's literary inclinations and so toned it's eccentricity, that the highly sensitive youth, under his Uncle Reuben's system of teaching, reached manhood with a vast amount of learning and a decided leaning towards poetry.

I can safely state, from family tradition, supported by my own personal observation, that had it not been for the kindly

---

19. The Bank of England's Archive Section records that Robert Browning was appointed to a clerkship on August 24, 1769; in 1784 this Robert was made Principal of the Bank Stock Office; he was pensioned off October 31, 1831, with a £421 annuity. Maynard's *Browning's Youth* (pp. 356-7) states that "Almost certainly Reuben did not come to London until after 1785," thus agreeing with Furnivall's conclusion ("Ancestors," p. 29) that Reuben was appointed Churchwarden of Pentridge in 1781 and in 1782. Perhaps this later removal of Reuben (Mason's step-grandfather) in 1785 has caused Mason to confuse the date of the elder Robert's move; also, possibly Robert's 1784 promotion was the inducement necessary to bring Reuben to London in 1785.

20. The poet was born at Camberwell on May 7, 1812.

21. I.e., the poet's grandfather; "son Robert" is the poet's father; and Reuben is the poet's great-uncle.

natured gentleman, Reuben Browning; a peculiar temperament and eccentric manner would have drifted my Uncle Robert into such an aimless wandering life that his poetic son might never have been in existence; the literary world owes a debt of gratitude never yet acknowledged, to the Dorsetshire learned Reuben Browning.

As one result of the Browning robust health brought from Dorsetshire, it is gratifying to me to be able to record that three generations born in London, have had no instance of bodily or mental deficiency; the only malady overtaking them has been old age, to the days of their deaths, Brownings retain mental activity, great vitality and clear healthy complexions, such as may still be met with amongst the inhabitants of the uplands of Dorsetshire.

The first wife of the Dorsetshire Robert Browning[22] gave black hair to her son Robert and her daughter Margaret, abundant dark brown hair has been the characteristic of succeeding Brownings, excepting the Poet;[23] a bald head being unknown in the family.

The Brownings have always had the habit of looking eye to eye at anyone addressed; a very pronounced pride in their race, kept them from even appearing to tolerate mean conduct; with them integrity was always something more than a sentiment, they demanded that it should be recognised in their outward bearing and resented even a suspicion of the least personal resemblance between themselves and anyone of questionable probity, as shewn by an incident which occurred in my presence. One of my Uncles flushed with indignation upon being casually informed that his face

---

22. I.e., Margaret Tittle Browning.
23. A lock of the poet's hair—cut in his youth—which is part of the Purefoy FitzGerald Collection of the Armstrong Browning Library is dark brown; Mrs. Orr, I, 11, notes that his hair was "dark" but was never "black." William Sharp's *Life of Robert Browning* (London: Walter Scott, 1897) concludes that the poet's hair was "of a brown so dark as to appear black" (p. 74).

somewhat resembled that of a City man of questionable reputation, he replied;

"Like that two ends of a scoundrel! The resemblance must cease at once" and forthwith had his whiskers removed; this conduct, characteristic of the Poet's Kinsfolk, must be remembered when reading of circumstances to be subsequently related.

It is not my intention to use any of the material employed by the Poet's biographers when I endeavor to discover the Ancestors of the Dorsetshire Brownings;[24] I shall trace through English County histories and Church records, the "Brunings"—"Brounyngs"—and "Brownings"; the result of my research may be—regarded by some of my readers, as an assumption [.] all similar research must frequently be founded on assumption. When I remember the Browning pride and native courtesy—their dignified bearing and their small and shapely hands, I feel justified in assuming that their ancestry must be looked for in the history of County families and not among the trading or working classes; especially when I know that for three generations, no Browning has been engaged in trade or followed any occupation requiring manual labor.

In a love letter written by the Poet to Elizabeth Barratt, the assumption that the Brownings, from Dorsetshire, were not belonging to the laboring class, is strengthened, when he tells his sweetheart that he would, if obliged to do so, rub down a horse;[25] in that remark the poet betrayed the Browning instinctive objection to manual labor.

---

24. Despite this statement, Mason in Part Two cites two sources also used by Furnivall—"Hutchin's voluminous history of Dorsetshire" and Sir Richard Colt Hoare's "history of Wiltshire" (cf. Furnivall's "Ancestors," p. 27).

25. The "Saturday morning" letter bears the postmark date September 13, 1845, and contains the following sentence:

So for my own future way in the world I have always refused to care—anyone who can live a couple of years and more on bread and potatoes as I did once on a time, and one who prefers a blouse and a blue shirt (such as I now write in) to all manner of gentlemanly appointment, and who can, if necessary, groom a horse not so

Having exhausted my search through County histories and other records, I shall proceed to use traditions passed on to me by members of the family, the last being furnished by Aunt Sarah Browning; I shall then give my own experience of kinsfolk gained by close association with generations of Brownings.

Tracing back one's ancestors does not always yield pleasure to the investigator, but in my search for records of Brownings long passed away, I have been much interested and must confess to feeling gratified at the result; my endeavors will be appreciated when that result is considered in it's relation to the Brownings of modern times, for it will be demonstrated that the Poet's Grandfather brought from Dorsetshire to London, the same forceful manner as had been exhibited by his ancestors.

---

badly, or at all events would rather do it all day long than succeed Mr. Fitzroy Kelly in the Solicitor-Generalship,—such an one need not very much concern himself beyond considering the lilies how they grow.
The Letters of Robert Browning and Elizabeth Barrett Barrett, 1845-1846 (London: Smith, Elder, and Company, 1898), I, 200. The tone of Browning's letter seems decidedly different from Mason's inference in the next clause.

Part Two

When I decided to endeavor to trace the ancestors of the Poet Browning, I arrived at the conclusion that the Christian names formerly given to the sons of a family would prove a safe guide; particularly the name given to the eldest son; Christian names afford to the investigator of an ancestry, much the same service as mile posts to a traveller, when seeking his way on an unknown road; surnames are altered and changed by circumstances; coats of arms added to and are often at the mercy of those recording them pictorially, but a Christian name given to a son in a family, being bestowed by his parents from three very natural causes, affection, family pride and religious sentiment, remains unchanged.

As a husband feels pride when informed that his firstborn resembles himself, so a wife, when declaring that her son shall be christened with his father's name, betrays affection, family pride and religious sentiment; as some families retain, through generations a feature or physical peculiarity which gives to the possessors a feeling of importance, somewhat similar to that experienced by the owners of a family crest; so a mother when giving to her son, his father's Christian name, as a something unchangeable, feels family pride as she prays that it will become renowned and be borne honorably by a succeeding generation, ever adding lustre to the family history.

The hopes of inheritance or a parent's fancy, may cause deviations in family Christian names, but the custom since the introduction of Christianity, to pass on to the eldest son in a family, his father's baptismal name forms the best known means of family identification.

Being acquainted with the Christian names given to the eldest sons of the Brownings, since they quitted Dorsetshire; when commencing my search in County records for traces of Brownings, I looked especially for those bearing the Christian names, William, John, Robert, feeling satisfied that I should be justified in assuming that the Brownings, bearing those three Christian names, continuously, were the ancestors of the Poet Robert Browning.[1]

My first guide post I found in Hutchin's[2] voluminous history of Dorsetshire—edition 1773—in a "William Brounyng Senior", possessor of the manor of "Beaushin" in the district of Marshwood, Dorsetshire, during the reign of Edward 3rd. Whether the manor was held under a grant from the King, by inheritance or by the law of might, Hutchins does not state;[3] the district of Marshwood contained many manors granted by Edward 3rd to his adherents, it may therefore be assumed that this William Brounyng was granted the manor of "Beaushin" as a reward for some service rendered to the King in France.[4]

---

1. "William" and "Robert" are names quite common among the previously documented ancestors of the poet; "John," however, is a name not found among "Brownings" for at least four generations preceding the poet. See Appendix III and Mason's discussion which follows; "Reuben" and "Thomas" are prominent Browning names to which Mason does not refer.

2. I.e., Hutchins's, an account also referred to in Furnivall's "Ancestors," p. 27; see Part One, n. 24.

3. John Hutchins's *The History and Antiquities of Dorset*, 3rd ed., corrected, augmented, and improved by William Shipp and James Whitworth Hodson (Westminster: John Bowyer Nichols and Sons, 1861), II, 263, describes the transfer of Beaushin:

> Beauchin, or *Bessines Hay*, a manor, lying in Marshwood and Stoke Abbas. 3 Edw. III. William Beaushin of Bradford, co. Wilts, releases to William Browning senior of Dorset all his right in the manor of Beaushin and lands in Marshwood.

4. Edward III (1312-1377) was a popular ruler of England whose "main interest . . . was war." In 1337 he declared war against France, initiating what has come to be

"Beaushin" manor was situated some eight miles from Dorchester, in a pleasant undulating country forming the valley through which the Frome River finds its way to Poole Harbor.[5] Fighting men for the King were constantly sailing from the harbor of Poole, to take part in the frequent wars occurring in France, between the English and the French, during the reign of Edward 3rd; returning after their period of service these soldiers brought french names which were employed on many grants of land conferred in South Dorsetshire. The name "Beaushin" is a corruption from the french words *Beau Chien*; the name "Browning is derived from the french name *"Bruning"*,[6] as written in early records, going far to show that these Brownings had a Norman French origin; "Bruning" was altered to "Brounyng", before becoming the name "Browning", now made famous in literature.

The holder of the manor of "Beaushin" was "William Brounyng Senior," clearly indicating, that in the reign of Edward 3rd, "William" was already adopted as the Christian name for the eldest son of this Brounyng family, a custom of naming followed for centuries and continued by Brownings up to the time of my generation.[7]

---

called the Hundred Years' War. See Goldwin Smith, *A History of England* (3rd ed.; New York: Charles Scribner's Sons, 1966), pp. 131-4.

5. See map of Dorsetshire on end papers.

6. Sir Vincent Baddeley asserts that the source was "Brun," a Saxon name of a local chieftain. He also comments that the "forerunners of the modern Brownings were pure Saxons of Wessex." See Baddeley's article "The Ancestry of Robert Browning, the Poet" in *The Genealogists' Magazine*, March, 1938, pp. 1-6. Sharp's *Life*, p. 15, points out that Browning himself told Moncure Conway that the original name was "DeBruni"; Sharp, however, derives the surname "Bruning" from Teutonic origins. Mrs. Orr's authorized *Life*, I, 2, places the origins in Anglo-Saxon stock. Oscar Browning's *Memories of Sixty Years*, p. 6, indicates that Browning used the "Bryning" family coat of arms. Griffin and Minchin, p. 2, trace the ancestry no deeper than the Robert Browning of the Bank of England, the poet's grandfather. Irvine and Honan also mention no earlier ancestor than the grandfather (pp. 1-2).

7. Such a practice seems not to have been followed in the documented genealogy where "Robert" appears as the prominent name and the name of at least six generations of eldest Browning sons; see Appendix III.

The district of "Marshwood", judging by its name, must have been well suited to shelter deer and other animals fitted for the chase;[8] hunting was absolutely a necessary occupation in the fourteenth century in England, in order to provide daily food for the occupants of manors, the name "Fine dog" given to their manor, shows that the Brounyngs of Marshwood, appreciated a good hunting dog and proclaims their devotion to the chase.

William Brounyng Senior of "Beaushin" when not engaged on military service, must have depended upon his fine dog, his cross-bow bolt, his cloth yard shaft or his fishing net, to supply his manor with food, for there was very little trade, commerce or cultivation in South Dorsetshire then, to enable a family to maintain existence.

The frequent wars carried on in France by the English, caused the seizure of any required vessels of forty tons burthen, for the King's service, with no thought of paying compensation to the owner; this arbitrary power prevented the people from following trading enterprise, in fact tended to compel able bodied men to prefer a fighting career, rather than engage in any industrious calling, especially as the pay of a fighting man in the King's service was three times the amount paid to any artizan and the soldier, as an additional incentive for him to join in foreign war, was permitted to retain all plunder accumulated by him during a campaign.

The habit of plundering contracted by fighting men in France, being brought to England on the termination of the period of service, was intentionally encouraged by the Eng-

---

8. Marshwood "lies four miles N. W. from Whitchurch, now a manor, farm, and hamlet, and tything, anciently an honour, the only one in this county, and the head of a barony . . . . It takes its name from the marshy, woody soil of the vale in which it lies, and to which it gives its name" (Hutchins, I, 327); "a chapelry . . . of the county of Dorset, 4¼ miles (W. S. W.) from Beaminster, containing 536 inhabitants" (Samuel Lewis, *A Topographical Dictionary of England*, 3rd ed. [London: S. Lewis and Co., 1835], III, n. pag. [entries are in alphabetical order on unnumbered pages]).

lish nobles and Clergy in order to ensure their own safety and as the easiest method of keeping bodies of fighting retainers, at the least expense to themselves, to be in readiness for other warlike expeditions into France when ordered by the King.

When the returned fighting men from France had spent their pay and exhausted their stock of plunder, accumulated during foreign service, subsistence was maintained by robbing those countrymen at home unprepared to make a defence, thus the occupants of manors in England could only secure immunity from attack, by being prepared to resist assaults made upon them by roaming marauding bands of returned fighting men, the hope of protection by the local authorities, the King's order or the Clergy was never indulged; William Brounyng Senior, of "Beaushin" must have been a fighting man, assisted by retainers, for he not only maintained his position but increased his importance in the Marshwood district, through making alliance with families occupying manors in South Dorsetshire.

Fish must have been plentiful in the waters running through the Frome Valley or the two religious houses "Milton Abbas" and "Cerne"[9] would not have been established; fasting, that is a fish diet, was in the fourteenth century rigorously enforced as a devotional duty; the Brounyngs of "Beaushin" gained the favor of the Church, extended their holdings, not difficult to effect in the reign of Edward 3rd, boundaries being ill defined and surrounding land unenclosed.

William Brounyng Senior of Beaushin, established a

---

9. Milton or Melbury Abbas: "a parish . . . of the county of Dorset, 2½ miles (S. E.) from Shaftesbury, containing 354 inhabitants"; Cerne, or Cerne Abbas: "Eadwald, brother of King Edward the Martyr, became a hermit at this place; and in the reign of Edgar, Ailmer, King of Cornwall, began to erect a noble abbey, which he completed in 987, for Benedictine monks"—Lewis's *Topographical Dictionary*, III and I, n. pag.

family in the Marswood district, for Leland[10] writes of two
of it's members;

"I lerned there that a saying was that the body of
"one of the Brunings was buried at Melton Abbey
"and the body of the other at Cerne"[.]

The district of Marshwood was not only a place well adapted
for hunting but must have repaid efforts when made, to
reclaim it from being a wilderness, for Michael Drayton
sings in his "second song" when extolling the beauties of
Dorsetshire;

"From Marshwood's fruitful vale my journey on to
make".[11]

I have good cause to gratefully acknowledge Marshwood as
the part of Dorsetshire in which the ancestors of Robert
Browning developed the family career, it accounts for the
remarkable health and robustness of constitution possessed
by the two Brownings who quitted that County for London
and the same good health has blessed the descendants of one
of the brothers through three generations.

The next guide to direct my search for ancestors was a
John Brounyng in the law Courts, he was the son of William Brounyng Senior, inherited "Beaushin", married
Alice Mautravers, one of three sisters, descendants of Thomas de Rodburgh, to whom Edward 3rd granted the manors
of Melbury Sampford and Melbury Usmond.[12] These same

---

10. I.e., John Leland (c. 1506-1552), an English antiquary. Mason here is rendering a partial quotation from Hutchins (II, 677):

"Ther be 2 of the Brounings, sumtyme lords of Melbyrie, that hath tumbes in the
church hard by the manor place . . . These epitaphies," continues Leland, "were
written upon tumbes yn the chirch at Melbury. But I lerned there that a saying
was, that the body of one of these Brunings was buried at Milton Abbey, and the
body of the other at Cerne."

Hutchins's source is *The Itinerary of John Leland the Antiquary*, ed. T. Hearne, III
(London: 1710-1712), 76-7.

11. This is line 21 of "The Second Song" from Drayton's Poly-Olbion; "The
Second Song" is almost completely quoted in Hutchins, IV, lxxxi-lxxxii, but Hutchins has "Marshwood's" italicized and spells the following word "fruitfull."

12. Melbury Sampford: "a parish . . . in the Dorchester Division of the County of

manors had been leased to Alan Cheyngne and his wife, for their lives; on the condition of the payment of one hundred marks in silver and the rendering to de Rodburgh a rose at the nativity of St. John the Baptist.

This pretty idea, when Alan and his wife were no longer alive to pay the annual offering did not deter two of the Mautraver sisters from quarrelling over the possession of the two Melbury manors. Joan and Elizabeth brought a suit to prove that their sister Alice, married to John Brounyng, was illegitimate, therefore not entitled to share any of the properties belonging to the estates of de Rodburgs, Folliets or Mautravers, all situated in the Marshwood District.

John Brounyng possessed a forceful character;[13] he in a law court in 1370 defeated the sisters of his wife Alice, established her legitimacy and proved her rights; after this law suit, one of the sisters, Elizabeth, wife of Roger Cheyngne, whose parents had rendered the rose annually to Thomas de Rodburg, endeavored to make good her rights by law to hold both the manors of Melbury Sampford and Melbury Usmond. John Brounyng, the determined man, scorning compromise, again fought an action at law and succeeded in making good his wife's claim to the possession of the manor of Melbury Sampford, securing the advowson of Melbury Church, confirming his right of connection with the Folliet and Mautravers families, the privilege to use their arms and obtaining for his own family the patronage of the church of Melbury Sampford, which was exer-

---

Dorset, 7½ miles (N. E. by E.) from Beaminster, containing 53 inhabitants. . . . The church is an ancient structure, and contains several monuments to the Strangeways family"; Melbury Usmond or Osmond: "a parish . . . of the county of Dorset, 8¾ miles (S. W.) from Sherbourne, containing 319 inhabitants. The living is a discharged rectory, with that of Melbury-Sampford united in 1750 . . . patron, Earl of Ilchester," Lewis's *Topographical Dictionary*, III, n. pag.

13. Hutchins's discussion of this John Brounyng (or Brunyng or Brouning or Browning—Hutchins spells it four ways) is found in II, 657-8, and IV, 438. Mason, however, seems to stress John Brounyng's forcefulness much more than Hutchins does.

cised by a John or William Brounyng from 1400 to 1489; as disclosed by Melbury Church records.[14]

By these two forceful actions at law, John Brounyng established his position firmly in Dorsetshire, styling himself "Dominus de Legh," a title he claimed for himself, from a property he also possessed, named Legh, situated near Doerhurst in Gloucestershire; this circumstance, connected with property, constitutes another guide in my search, which points to the Brounyngs as a family of importance in that County; in 1399 this same John Brounyng of Melbury was made sheriff of the County of Gloucestershire, he must have been a man of forceful activity, for in that same year, having placed the family property in the hands of three trustees, for safety and to be used for the benefit of his wife Alice and their two sons; John Brounyng "Dominus de Legh", joined the forces of Henry 4th,[15] carried to France his fighting instincts and remained abroad for nine years, campaigning for the King; after his return to England, John Brounyng established himself in a prominent position in the Frome Valley, was a friend of the Church and was the

---

14. See Hutchins, II, 681, concerning church patronage. Furnivall's "Ancestors," p. 35, asserts:

At present no connection is known to exist between these Woodyates Brownings and the knightly and squirely family of Brownings who in early days held the Manors of Melbury Sampford and Melbury Osmond in the northwest of Dorsetshire, and whose last representative disappeared in the time of Henry VIII., their manors going into the line of the Earl of Ilchester, who still holds them.

Sir Vincent Baddeley's "Ancestry of Browning," p. 2, concurs:

This is in fact all that is known of Robert Browning's ancestry. It goes no further back than his great-great-grandfather Robert, who was born sometime before 1700, and married Elizabeth Pethebridge.

Oscar Browning's *Memories of Sixty Years*, p. 6, however, asserts that the poet "believed himself to be descended from a legendary Browning who commanded the ship which took Henry V over to France" (see below). Shipp and Whitworth in a note (Hutchins, II, 656, c) quote "Hutchins, 2d edit. vol. ii, page 235":

"Browning's issue continued here several generations, and the *last* of that family sold Melbury to Henry Strangeways" [italics mine].

15. Henry IV (1399-1413) was better known for his ousting of Richard II and his unscrupulous defense of the throne against his own people; it was his son, Henry V (1413-1422), who renewed the Hundred Years' War against France in 1415.

"Bruning" mentioned by Leland as "buried at Melton Abbey" [.]

The next guide used in my search is a brass plate placed in the wall of the chancel of Melbury Sampford Church, to record the memory of John Brounyng, son of John Brounyng, Dominus de Legh and Alice his wife, daughter of John Mautravers, Knight, with no date mentioned. The Brounyng family, at that time, must have been held in excellent repute in the Frome Valley or the insertion of a brass plate in the chancel wall of Melbury Sampford Church, commemorating a John Brounyng, would not have been sanctioned, by the clergy, in proximity to memorials of the titled dead.

In Melbury Sampford church "a handsome altar tomb of Purbeck Marble" offers the next guide, for me to follow the career of the Dorsetshire Brounyngs; on it's margin, a lengthy latin inscription in black letter upon brass, records the place of burial of "William Brounyng Knight," son of John Brounyng Knight and the date is 1467.[16]

As the John Brounyng, Dominus de Legh, the same who fought in France for nine years, had married Alice Mautravers of Melbury Sampford and as the mother of the William Brounyng, buried in the altar tomb in Melbury Church, appears in the latin inscription as Alianora Fitz-Nycoll, one of the Berkley family of Gloucestershire, it is made evident that this William Brounyng, buried in the altar tomb, could not have been the son of that John Brounyng who styled himself the Lord of Legh.

Such a procession of the Christian names William and John, used by the Dorsetshire and Gloucestershire Brounyngs has rendered it difficult to distinguish one generation from another;[17] the William Brounyng buried in the altar

___

16. The inscriptions for John and William Brounyng are found in Hutchins, II, 676-7; the description of William's tomb begins: "At the entrance of the north transept is a handsome altar-tomb of Purbeck marble. . . ."

17. The confusion of "Johns" and "Williams" is understandable after examining

tomb in Melbury Church, very fortunately introduced into his family the Christian name *Robert*, this son of William Brounyng of Melbury, during his father's lifetime was a leading man in South Dorsetshire; history relates that this Robert Brounyng was elected by Melcumbe Regis, Lyme Regis and Dorchester, to represent those different constituencies in four Parliaments, summonded by Henry the sixth, during twenty years of troublous wars abroad and frequent insurrections in England.[18]

This Robert Brounyng the first, must have been a man of strong personality, possessing great power of domination, for though the Christian name Robert was quite new to the family, its use from his time became recognised, until the name Robert Brounyng was made famous in literature and the same Christian name was given to the son of the poet, the present head of the Browning family.[19]

The position of the Brounyngs as a county family in South Dorsetshire, culminated in that William Brounyng buried in the "handsome altar tomb" in Melbury Church; County records furnish no more guides to enable me to follow the family career.

The Brounyngs having adhered to the struggling fortunes of Henry the sixth—been engaged in fighting against frequent insurrections during the latter part of that King's reign, and involved in "the war of the roses", were unfortunately for them, connected with the losing side; at the termination of the struggle, the family suffered in consequence of their King's defeat; "Beaushin" in the Marshwood district and Legh situated in Gloucestershire, were both sacrificed; then when the family patron Henry 6th was com-

Hutchins. He records, with little or no differentiation, several obviously distinct Johns and Williams.

18. See Hutchins, II, 52, 357, 453. Hutchins (II, 357), however, cites the Robert Bruning as serving Dorchester during the reign of Henry VII; he also lists a William Brouning as serving twice in Parliaments called by Henry VI (I, xlvi).

19. I.e., Robert Wiedemann Barrett (Pen) Browning.

pelled to fly for safety into France and Edward 4th seized the throne of England, though William Brounyng at that time was sheriff of the united Counties of Dorsetshire and Somersetshire and he had endeavored to save his remaining property from confiscation, the Brounyngs as a west of England family suffered considerably.[20]

Edward 4th, when firmly seated on the throne, compelled his Parliament to pass an act of forfeiture of estates belonging to all families which had given support to the cause of Henry 6th, and to include in the list of forfeitures many manors held in the west of England.

William Brounyng, the sheriff, had prepared for this contingency some years before his death; with the hope of securing from forfeiture the manors of Melbury Sampford and Melbury Usmond he had conveyed them absolutely to his wife Anne, the mother of Robert Brounyng, who had for so long a period been connected with the parliaments of Henry 6th [.]

Marriage had brought into the Brounyng family the manors of Melbury Sampford and Melbury Usmond; the marriage of Anne, the widow of the William Brounyng buried in the altar tomb of "Purbeck marble", subsequently to Sir Giles Strangways, passed those two manors into the possession of the Ilchester family.[21]

---

20. Henry VI (1422-1461) was opposed in the Wars of the Roses by Richard, Duke of York, whose son, Edward IV (1461-1483), finally succeeded in deposing Henry VI in 1461. Henry VI; his queen, Margaret of Anjou; and their son, Edward, fled to Scotland, not France, following Edward IV's ascension to the throne. Hutchins's "Introduction" records "William Brounyng's" tenure as sheriff (I, xli). Rev. John Collinson, *The History of Somersetshire*, I (Bath, 1791), xxxiii, notes that "Somersetshire and Dorsetshire had one common sheriff till the year 1566, when they were divided by act of Parliament," and he also lists a William Browning as sheriff in 1463-1464 (I, xxxvi).

21. Hutchins, IV, 438, relates: "1523, Sir William Filiol and others confirmed this manor to Henry Trenchard and Anne his wife, late wife of Sir William Browning, and to the longest liver of them, and after their decease to Giles, son and heir of Henry Strangways. This looks as if William Browning had given this estate to his wife, that she had settled it on her second husband for life, and subject thereto had sold the reversion either to Henry Strangways or his son." Also, Hutchins, II, 660,

Though the name Brounyng appears in Dorsetshire history up to the year 1489 and the family pedigree is brought by Hutchins up to 1529,[22] though a John Brounyng held the perilous position of Sheriff of Gloucestershire during the turbulant years 1648-9; the Brounyngs as a west of England family, worthy of record in history, ceased to be recognised after the death of that William Brounyng commemorated on the altar tomb in Melbury Sampford Church. Atkins in his history of Gloucestershire, published 1712, mentions a;

"John Browning Esq.", employing the modern form of spelling the name, "has an handsome house and seat near the Church

"(Cowley) and a large estate in this parish, and is de-
"scended of an ancient family which have long resided
"in this place" [.][23]

The Dorsetshire Brounyngs for centuries had been associated with Gloucestershire; Legh, the place which gave the title of "Dominus de Legh" is in Gloucestershire; this explains the reference by Atkins to "an ancient family" and identifies the connection.

The Christian names William and John were employed

---

states that Katherine, widow of the William Brounyng who "held the manors and advowsons of Melbury Sampford and Osmond and all the lands in those parishes," married Henry Strangways, while Anne and William Brouning, cousin of the above William Brounyng, were allowed use of the land and were to inherit the land—subject to male issue—upon widow Katherine's death. Since there were no sons, the land reverted to the Strangways according to a 30 June 1500 indenture. Oscar Browning's *Memories*, p. 6, notes:

A branch of the Cowley Brownings was settled in Dorsetshire in the sixteenth century. Melbury belonged to them, and the present Earl of Ilchester holds that property from the marriage of a Strangeways with a Browning. But there is no evidence to show that the family of Robert Browning was in any way connected with that branch, and I am reluctantly brought to the conclusion that there is probably no connection between the poet and myself. . . .

22. Hutchins, II, 659.

23. I.e., Sir Robert Atkyns, *The Ancient and Present State of Gloucestershire* (London: Printed by W. Bowyer for Robert Gosling, 1712), p. 195. This is the Cowley Browning family from which Oscar Browning was descended; see Oscar Browning's *Memories*, pp. 4-6.

by both branches of the Brounyngs for eldest sons, but that branch in Dorsetshire introduced into the family the Christian name *Robert*.

I shall now show positive evidence how other Christian names employed by the Dorsetshire Brownings; the poet's direct ancestors, came to be adopted with *Robert* and demonstrate how that name became fixed as the Christian name for the head of the Browning family.

My next guide is a Browning family book, now open before me, a boy's school arithmetic, used at Woodyats, Dorsetshire in 1738.

I will reproduce later, all the writing placed in this Arithmetic, by a Woodyats schoolmaster and two boys his pupils; this book is not only a safe guide to me in following the Browning family career, but conclusively proves that the parents of the Browning boys, then being educated, must have been settled at Woodyats in Dorsetshire, in the beginning of the eighteenth century and then occupied no subordinate position in society, as other Browning old books in my possession, to be mentioned subsequently, will conclusively prove.

Woodyats in the County of Dorsetshire is, according to Hutchins, a parish "lying near the borders of Wilts and Hants, two miles north east from Handly and a mile east from East Woodyats."[24] The scenery of the parish, in which the Poet's ancestors long resided, is very picturesque and made especially interesting by the presence in the landscape, of Tumili or Barrows, raised above the natural surface, by some very ancient unknown people; the old Roman Road, which enters Dorsetshire near the Woodyats Inn, being clearly defined, greatly increases the interest attaching to the neighborhood; indeed the Country surrounding Woodyats is so especially attractive, that Sir Richard Colt

---

24. Hutchins, III, 607.

Hoare, in his history of Wiltshire,[25] the adjoining County, excuses his trespass into the County of Dorsetshire, by confessing, that he could not resist attempting a description of so interesting and picturesque a portion of England, as he found near Woodyats. In this interesting locality, the Brownings, immediate ancestors of the Poet, I know from books, now beside me and through family tradition passed on to me, resided for nearly a century; the character of these books suggest that one or both the Brothers owning them, followed the educational profession, I mention here my view of their calling in Dorsetshire, hoping to clear away some confusion existing in the minds of the Poets biographers when fixing the position in society occupied by Brownings when they decided, towards the end of the eighteenth century, to leave the County of Dorsetshire.[26]

When Robert Browning's genius aroused a demand for information respecting the origin of the Poet's family and intending biographers could only learn that his Grandfather came from Woodyats in the county of Dorsetshire, they sought for the place named and found, marked upon "Carey's Road Map of England", published 1826, for many years regarded as the best topographical authority; only the words "Woodyats Inn", situated on the main Coach Road, with no reference made to the Browning place of residence in existence on the ancient Manor of Woodyats;[27] the

25. Mason's source here is most assuredly the reference in Hutchins, III, 610, to Hoare's *The Ancient History of South Wiltshire* (London: William Miller, 1812), IV, Introduction: "In my pursuit of the Roman road from old Sarum to Dorchester, I was led into the parish of West Woodyates, where my attention was arrested by the numerous vestiges of British antiquity which surrounded me on all sides. They appeared so novel and interesting to me, that I was induced to trespass upon the antiquities of a neighboring county, and include them in my collections for Wiltshire."

26. The main offender seems to be F. J. Furnivall and his article, "Robert Browning's Ancestors," *Browning Society Papers*, pp. 26-45; Furnivall later published another article exclusively dedicated to "fixing the position in society" of the Brownings: "Browning's Footman Ancestor," *Academy* (April 12, 1902), p. 394.

27. Mason's reference here must be to John Cary, *Cary's New Itinerary; or, an accurate delineation of the great roads . . . throughout England and Wales; with many of the*

intending biographers therefore concluded that they had found the home of the Poet's ancestors in Dorsetshire; this erroneous conclusion was strengthened when in 1835 "The Topographical Dictonary" by Samuel Lewis, was published, for in that book, Woodyats West, that is "Woodyats Inn", is described as having 18 inhabitants and no mention made of Woodyats East, for the name of the Browning real place of residence had been absorbed by Gussich St. Andrews; Gussich All Saints; and Gussich St. Michael, all of them churches belonging to the ancient manor of Woodyats, thus proving that Woodyats East, as a place for residence was of some importance.[28]

As this Topographical Dictionary by Lewis, was a work of great research, was accepted as the standard book on English topography and only mentioned the place "Woodyats Inn"; the poet's biographers concluded that the Woodyats described as having 18 inhabitants, had been the abode of Grandfather Robert Browning.[29]

---

principal roads in Scotland . . . from actual admeasurement, 10th ed. (London: G & J Cary, 1826). I have seen a copy of *Cary's New Map of England and Wales, with part of Scotland* (London: John Cary, 1794), upon which, I suspect, the later work was based, and it does indeed only reproduce the Woodyates Inn on the main road with no reference to or differentiation between Woodyates East and Woodyates West (see map 14, n. pag.) Also, *Cary's Traveller's Companion* (London: J. Cary, 1790) and *Cary's New Map of England and Wales, with part of Scotland* (London: J. Cary, 1794) reproduce only the Woodyates Inn on the main road with no reference to or differentiation between Woodyates East and Woodyates West.

28. Lewis's *Topographical Dictionary*, IV, n. pag.:

Woodyates, West, an extra-parochial liberty, in the hundred of Winborne-St. Giles, Winborne Division of the county of Dorset, 5½ miles (N. N. W.) from Cranborne, containing 18 inhabitants. On the neighboring downs are numerous barrows, also a vast rampart and fosse, termed Grimesditch, crossed by the Roman road from Dorchester to Old Sarum.

Ironically, Mason's description of Woodyates (pp. 31-2) is taken from Hutchins's section on "West Woodyates"; Hutchins records West-Woodyates as "Anciently a manor," and even associates it with Gussich St. Andrew (III, 607-8), while he presents East-Woodyates "where was a noted inn on the London road" (III, 441). In the following discussion, Mason has apparently made Hutchins's "East-Woodyates" into his "West-Woodyates," and vice versa.

29. Furnivall (see "Ancestors," p. 26) seems to have been the first to attribute the lease of Woodyates Inn to Browning's ancestors, while Sharp's *Life*, p. 17, reports

It was making a Dorsetshire roadside Inn the starting point for her father's career which wounded my Aunt Sarah Browning's pride in her family and caused her indignant protest to me against monstrous fabrication for it also produced other errors in the Poet's biography.[30]

The grandfather of the Poet; Robert Browning, came to London from Woodyats, a considerable place, situated one mile from the main coach road; it is described by Hutchins as connected with the ancient manor of Woodyats, and church of Gussich St. Andrew, in north Dorsetshire. At the Dissolution, two manors, the rectory and advowson of Woodyats were granted to Henry Langford.

This is the Woodyats where the Poet's grandfather and his ancestors had been reared and educated, not the "Woodyats Inn",[31] a place, which according to Hutchins contained in 1773—the very time when, as shewn by their books, the Browning brothers, educated young men were residing at East Woodyats[32]—"one house and one family" consisting of nine males and four females, six of the household employed in agriculture, seven in trade. From family tradition I am able to state that neither Robert nor Reuben Browning both living at Woodyats in 1773, had ever been engaged in agricultural pursuits or followed any trade and by the accounts furnished to me by my parents, were in their manner of speech, quite free from the use of the remarkable Dorsetshire common dialect.

The Browning's continued to reside at Woodyats in

that "the poet's paternal great-grandfather . . . was owner of the Woodyates Inn." Mrs. Orr, I, 3, merely mentions Woodyates as the "cradle" where the Browning family of the third and fourth generations preceding the poet held "a modest but independent social position."

30. Probably a reference to the "footman ancestor" assertions by Furnivall.

31. Sir Vincent Baddeley, "Ancestry of Browning," p. 4, writes, " . . . the first known ancestor, Robert Browning, who died at Woodyates in the parish of Pentridge in 1746, occupied a house which was *afterwards* a coaching inn . . ." [italics mine].

32. See Part One, n. 19, and Part Two, n. 28.

1783[33] as proved by that date, the name of the place and the name Reuben Browning, great uncle of the poet, appearing in a book which he brought with him from Woodyats to London; it is near me as a write and I shall reproduce later, a *fac simile* of his hand writing.

The distressful state to which England was reduced in the year 1783, supplies the reason why the two Browning brothers were compelled, like many gentlefolk at the time, to contemplate leaving Dorsetshire to seek employment in London.

The prolonged and disastrous war which had raged in the American Colonies, had set class against class throughout England; the Independence of the United States of America was acknowledged by Great Britain in 1783, producing riots which caused the upper classes to range themselves in two hostile camps, at a time when terrible distress, consequent upon the prolonged war between Great Britain and France had brought many of the County families to the verge of ruin; the excitement throughout the South of England was increased by the startling news brought across the British channel to English Ports, of the approaching French Revolution, which roused the Whig and Tory parties into a state of desperation, English Tories were denounced as "Aristocrats," English Whigs were condemned as "Democrats"; the people generally much excited over party strife and the trading classes suffering from the dislocation of business.[34]

In 1785, two years after the treaty of peace had been concluded with America, the King of England was persuaded,—in the hope that his Majesty's recognition of that Republic would tend to lessen the bitterness of feeling then

---

33. See Part One, n. 19.
34. Signed September 3, 1783, the Treaty of Versailles resolved the American Revolution by granting independence to the United States. For a brief discussion of English affairs and attitudes during and immediately after the war, see Smith, *History of England*, pp. 480-90.

existing between Whigs and Tories—to grant an audience to the Ambassador sent to Great Britain from the United States of America; the Brownings it must be noted, always have been pronounced Tories.[35]

When the Allied European Powers invaded France, resolved to stop revolutions which threatened to sweep away Royalty, the Government of Great Britain was compelled to give assistance to the Powers, but mainly with money, a financial policy which afforded Robert Browning of Woodyats, the opportunity of serving the Tory party, of showing his knowledge of Finance and gave hope to him of recovering former family importance.[36]

Having succeeded in tracing the Browning family from South Dorsetshire through Woodyats on the way to London, by following as my guide, succeeding Christian names, it is with some satisfaction that I now record from personal knowledge, that the Woodyats Robert Browning named his eldest son, Robert, to his second son, born in London 1802,[37] he gave the ancient family name William, this William Browning, gave to his eldest son, the family name William, to his second son the family name John, to his

35. John Adams was appointed as the first American Ambassador to England in March 1785: Allan Nevins and Henry Steele Commager, *A Short History of the United States*, 5th ed. (New York: Alfred A. Knopf, 1972), p. 121. Maynard's *Browning's Youth*, p. 93, says of Robert Senior: "His own sympathies were probably slightly toward Whig or later liberal positions, but his satire ranges broadly from Tory to Radical"; see also p. 134—"the family was 'not orthodox' or at all events was 'very liberal'." Sharp's *Life*, p. 143, calls attention to the poet's "ardent democratic sentiments," while Griffin and Minchin, pp. 289-90, note Browning's liberal politics.

36. France declared war on Britain on February 1, 1793, and, under the leadership of William Pitt the Younger, Britain joined in the formation of the First Coalition which included Prussia, Austria, Russia, the Netherlands, Sardinia, Spain, Naples, Portugal, Tuscany, and the Holy Roman Empire. Pitt followed the policy of primarily "helping the European allies by direct cash subsides." Allied armies combined to drive the French out of the Netherlands while "several allied forces penetrated the French frontiers" (see Smith, *History of England*, pp. 514-26).

37. Elaine Baly, "Talking of the Brownings—Browning's Relations," *Browning Society Notes*, 3 (December 1973), p. 5, lists William Shergold Browning's birthdate as 1797.

third son, the family name Robert,[38] thus, before there was any prospect of the name Browning being made famous, he by instinct or prompted by tradition, preserved in the family, the Dorsetshire ancient Christian names.

This sequence of family names employed for centuries in Dorsetshire, Gloucestershire and continued to be used in London by Brownings, cannot be regarded as mere coincidence but must be considered an inherited and distinctive trait of the Browning family, used in the same way that family arms, first borne to give distinction are retained by descendants to the present day.

I know that the grandfather of the Poet was a gentleman of commanding presence, possessed with the same forceful manner which had enabled his ancestors the William, the John, and the Robert Brownings of Dorsetshire to destinguish themselves in war, in law courts, and in English Parliaments; this same forceful manner was brought to London, employed there and as will be found later, was inherited by Robert Browning the Poet.

---

38. William Shergold Browning had ten children: the eldest was named William Mansir and the next John Wace; the third son (born after the eldest daughter) was called Robert Shergold. See Furnivall's "Ancestors," p. 45.

Part Three

In my eagerness to trace the ancestry of the Poet Browning I have, like a faithful dog when tracking his master's footsteps, been compelled to diverge from a direct course, to investigate and decide upon that clue to follow showing the most hope of success, but now, with my old Browning Books around me, my mind stored with traditions and in possession of knowledge concerning the Browning family, gained personally, I can proceed on my way without hesitation, starting with my account from that time when the Woodyats Robert Browning, accompanied by his brother, Reuben, quitted Dorsetshire for London; Robert taking with him a Wife and infant son Robert, to become the father of the Poet;[1] following on to that time when the Woodyats Robert Browning became my Grandfather, then on to that part of my life when, at New Cross, Surrey, I was associated with Uncle Robert and my cousin the poet Robert Browning, showing in my record, that I have been known to three generations of Robert Brownings.

The Books in my possession, brought with many others, from Dorsetshire furnish evidence that 170 years ago,[2] the Woodyats Brownings were then being well educated and that they belonged to a superior class of society; my intimate acquaintance with their descendants, justifies me in stating that the Brownings born in London retained the family

---

1. The Dorsetshire Robert had no son in 1769 when he removed to London; his son, the poet's father, was born in 1782 in London: see Part One, n. 19.

2. I.e., from 1908 when Mason was completing the manuscript.

characteristics, always conducting themselves as courteous ladies and gentlemen.

My first book, by date, to be considered when establishing the Browning's position in Dorsetshire is W. Webster's "Arithmetick in Epitome: or a Compendium, of all its Rules, both Vulgar and Decimal". Fourth edition 1729, used as a schoolbook by two Browning boys in 1738;[3] another signature, in the same book, written 42 years later, by the son of one of the original owners, proves that the poet's ancestors were long established at Woodyats as a family.

Fac simile reproductions of the various writings in this school book, used by the Poet's great grandfather and grand uncle, have the special interest of supplying an excellent example of the ornamental quill penmanship employed by a country schoolmaster 170 years ago;[4] additional writings exhibit attempts, made in the same year, by the two Browning school boys, to imitate their master's hand writing, each boy endeavoring to make good his claim to the ownership of the arithmetic and an added writing also exhibits the

---

3. William Webster, *Arithmetick in Epitome* (London: n.p., 1715): I have been unable to trace Mason's copy of this book or any of his inheritance of the Browning family library except for a family Bible now at the Brighton Grammar School, Victoria, Australia. It has no publication data, but its Preface is dated 1770. The Bible was donated and signed at Black Rock, Melbourne, 10 December 1926, by Laura MacDonnell and A. J. R. Scarlett, and its inscription reads:

These Bibles are a Gift to The Church of England Boys Grammar School Brighton Melbourne from the Grandmother of an Armstrong House Boy (A.J.R. Scarlett) in memory of her Father and Mother, Cyrus and Jessy Mason.

Cyrus Mason was a kinsman of the Poet Browning.

The Bibles came to Australia seventy years ago, belonged to the Brownings and have been used by the family in Australia for four generations.

Cyrus Mason was brought up with Robert Browning, knew his home life education and family surroundings. These Books therefore possess an historic interest, and are given with deep regard for the traditions and further advance of The Brighton Grammar School.

In spite of the reference to plural "Bibles" and "Books," only one Bible has been located thus far.

4. I.e., from 1908. "The poet's great grandfather and grand uncle" are identified below as Thomas and Reuben Browning of Woodyates, Dorset.

schoolmaster's desire to pacify the boys, by making them joint owners of the book.

Two pages, *fac simile* from Arithmetic "1" and "2"[5]

The "Arithmetick" was first given to the boy Thomas Browning January 20th 1738. Ten months later, Reuben, the younger school boy, it can be noticed, claimed part ownership, by writing his own name surrounded by flourishes in attempted imitation of his schoolmaster, at the end of the book, in such an assertive style, that his elder brother Thomas, two days later, felt compelled to repeat his own name, facing the Title page.

The boy Reuben, when making his claim to the "Arithmetick" in writing, it may be noticed, spelt his own name incorrectly, causing his schoolmaster to place the name Reuben properly spelt, also at the beginning of the book, although want of space compelled him to write it across one of his own flourishes, ornamenting the name Thomas Browning![6]

The two pages of writing reproduced from the "Arithmetick", show either that the Browning boys greatly desired learning or that Reuben played a joke upon his brother by writing the word "good" before his own name on the last page and when, two days later, Thomas had repeated his name at the beginning of the "Arithmetick", Reuben wrote the word "good" so that it should apply to the book and not to Thomas Browning his brother.

The ink used in all this reproduced writing, executed at Woodyats, presents a similar dark brown appearance,

5. This—and all lines calling for *"fac simile"* insertions—is in red ink in Mason's hand; none of the *fac similes* themselves are actually included in the manuscript.
6. It is interesting to notice how often the name Reuben—referring to various Brownings of that name—has been misspelled; Elaine Baly ("Talking of the Brownings," p. 4) has written: "I was always irritated at the frequently varied spellings which Robert and his brother Michael used for Reuben, until I recently saw a letter from his own mother Jane in which she refers to her son: 'Rubin brought me the letter from my dear Louisa'. . . ."

clearly indicating that it was all placed in the "Arithmetick" about the same time. The book, with Title page printed in black and red, its two pages of Decimal Tables engraved upon copper and printed from the plate, the binding in strong leather, must have been expensive 177 years ago;[7] it has been carefully preserved, was first used by two Browning boys in 1738, was afterwards employed in the education of the sons of that Thomas Browning, first given the "Arithmetick", then, after the lapse of 42 years, received the signature of another Reuben Browning, which I reproduce as a specimen of fine bold writing, indicative of the Browning forceful manner and as evidence that the family 128 years back, then occupied a position far superior to that filled by the laboring class.[8]

Fac simile signature Reuben Browning "3"[9]

This is the signature of that same Reuben Browning who accompanied his brother Robert to London, about 1785, taking among his many Woodyats books, this old Webster's "Arithmetick", which in after years was to be used in the education of his nephew Robert, brought when a child from Woodyats.[10]

A second book in my possession also shows by the writ-

---

7. Published in 1729, Webster's fourth edition would have been 177 years old when Mason began preparing to write his family history in 1906.

8. This Thomas is the son of the first known Robert Browning. His sons were Robert of Woodyates (the poet's grandfather), Thomas, Reuben of Woodyates, and William (see Furnivall's "Ancestors," p. 45, and Appendix III). The Reuben here referred to (and further identified below) is Cyrus Mason's paternal step-grandfather who married the widow Mason with a son, John (see Genealogy, Appendix III). Mason's reference to books owned by several generations of Brownings seems to have been a not uncommon family practice. In the Armstrong Browning Library at Baylor University a copy of William Martin's *The Historie, and Lives, of Twentie Kings of England* (London, 1615) has been autographed by five generations of Browning owners: Thomas, Robert of Woodyates, Robert Senior, Robert the Poet, and Robert Wiedemann (Pen).

9. See Part Three, n. 5.

10. Robert, the father of the poet, was born in 1782, thirteen years after his father had initially removed from Woodyates; see Part One, n. 19; Part Three, n. 1.

ing on it's flyleaf that the Brownings were residing at Woodyats in 1783; its Title, "The Young Gentlemen and Ladie's
Monitor", announces the Author's intention to "Eradicate
Vulgar Prejudices and Rusticity of Manners"; the essays
the author supplies with this object, are taken from the
"Spectator" the "Tatler" the "Guardian" the "World"
and he gives "An Historical Account of the Origin of
Nations, Laws, Government and Commerce" all "Divided
into Small portions for the Ease of Reading in Classes"[.][11]

The absence from the pages of this book of the teacher's
usual marks, made in the course of class reading, suggests
that it's owner, Robert Browning of Woodyats, being a man
with a taste for good literature, read and appreciated "A
Collection of Select Pieces from our Best Modern Writers"[.]

The date of the publication of this book is not given, but
as no mention is made in the "Historical Account" of the
war for Independence in America and the last historical
event mentioned, is the then troubled state of France,
deploring "the debility of their late efforts" to restrain an
"ambitious Monarch" and foretells the approaching Revolution; the book must have been published before 1775.

The Browning signature which I reproduce from this
book, was made in 1783, the year in which the Independence of of the United States of America was acknowledged.

Fac simile signature Robert Browning "4"[12]

Such a book as the "Monitor", in the hand which could
write so bold a signature, during a time of great National
excitement, would supply it's owner with food for reflection
on his own position as a Country gentleman and rouse the
forceful Browning manner to consider the advantage of
leaving Woodyats, to seek an opening for his energies in

---

11. I have not been able to further identify "The Young Gentlemen and Ladie's
Monitor."
12. See Part Three, n. 5.

London, he would have been brought, by his reading, to realize that for him to remain in Dorsetshire during the troublous times foretold by the "Monitor" as approaching, the learning possessed by him and his ability would be completely wasted; but some time was required to make enquiries and complete arrangements to carry out successfully the contemplated change, for Robert Browning of Woodyats in 1783 had to consider the support of a wife and his son Robert, then a child, to become in after years, the father of the Poet.[13]

To show that this Woodyats Browning studied literature, particularly poetry, when residing in Dorsetshire, I mention here one of his books, now before me; a volume of "Scots Poems wrote by the Ingenious before 1600"; published in Edinburgh 1761.[14] The name "Rob: Browning" is stamped upon the flyleaf of this book in a manner indicating that it was the owner's custom to employ a stamp when putting his name into his library books; this volume affords good proof that the Poet's grandfather must have been a devoted student of poetry, when he read for pleasure a book of 264 pages printed in the Scot's dialect, most difficult to understand, indeed only made possible to an Englishman, by constantly consulting the "Glossary" supplied at the end of the volume.[15]

Another book calls particularly for consideration; it was

---

13. Robert Browning of the Bank of England journeyed to London in 1769, not 1785 (see Part One, n. 19), and Furnivall's "Ancestry," p. 30, records that he married Margaret Morris Tittle on October 13, 1778. Their first son, Robert also, was born on July 6, 1782.

14. I.e., Allan Ramsay, the Elder, *The Ever Green, being a collection of Scots poems wrote by the Ingenious before 1600*, 2 vols. (Edinburgh: A. Donaldson, 1761); *The Ever Green* was first published in 1724 and was printed by Thomas Ruddiman.

15. Mrs. Orr, I, 5, presents an antithetical view, insisting that Robert of Woodyates was a "worldly man . . . his literary tastes being limited to the Bible and *Tom Jones*, both of which he is said to have read through once a year." Griffin and Minchin, p. 7 (probably relying on Mrs. Orr), concur: "Robert Browning, the grandfather, is said to have mainly confined his reading to the Bible and *Tom Jones*. . . ."

once the property of Reuben Browning of Woodyats; "Salmon's Geography" with title page printed in red and black, contains numerous maps printed from Copper plates and is bound in solid leather; such a book must have been regarded 125 years back as eminently suitable for any gentleman's library.[16] In its quaintness of description of countries—it's pourtrayal of a very different map of Europe, to the present subdivision and it's display of lack of information respecting many parts of the world, now so intimately known, "Salmon's Geography" furnishes some very curious reading, but it's most interesting feature, at this time, is the writing on it's flyleaf as will be seen in the *fac simile* reproduction which I supply; it gives an especial interest to my record of the Browning family history, for it proves that its owner, Reuben Browning, while still residing at Woodyats, possessed a pronounced affection for poetry, with taste to employ it and thus indicates clearly the source from which in after years, flowed the teaching of his nephew Robert Browning, after the Brothers left Woodyats and arrived in London.

Fac simile page from Salmon's Geography. "5"[17]

The touching reference made by Reuben Browning of Woodyats, to his friendship with Wm. Longman, a name at that time connected with educational publications, brings to my recollection, the evidence of good feeling which was exhibited for another Browning, 53 years after Reuben Browning recorded in quoted verse, his friendship for Wm. Longman.

When the early writings of Robert Browning, the poet, on being published, proved quite unsaleable and his father

---

16. I.e., 1783. As with all the family books listed by Mason, I have been unable to locate this copy of Thomas Salmon, *The Geography and History of England* (London?: n.p., 1765).

17. See Part Three, n. 1.

was unable to pay for the printing of his son's manuscript, Longman, the London publisher, printed and published "Strafford" as an act of friendship; this feeling of friendship I know is still maintained between a member of the Longman Firm and Brownings Cousins of the poet. I like to imagine that the friend of the Woodyats Reuben Browning "Wm. Longman of Cobley", was the descendant of that Thomas Longman, the founder of the London publishing house in 1724, for I am led to believe that among the archives of that firm, famed for it's enterprise in publishing educational literature; the name Reuben Browning might be discovered, as one of the writers who assisted to produce a literature greatly to the benefit of Great Britain.[18]

The three books from which I have reproduced writing, placed on their flyleaves at Woodyats by Brownings, prove conclusively that the ancestors of the Poet were no ordinary Country people; to me the nature of the literature conveys the impression, that one of the brothers when residing in Dorsetshire, was associated with educational pursuits; after leaving the country, as will be learnt later, one brother Reuben, educated his nephew Robert, with the books he himself had used as a child and brought with him to London from Woodyats.

I consider it a special instance of good fortune, that my allotment of the Browning family library, was sent by my Mother to me, settled in Australia; for the remaining books, stored in the Pantecuicon building, London, while my family was residing in Germany, were destroyed, when that building was burnt.[19]

The has been exhibited by Browning biographers

---

18. No evidence seems to exist for Mason's claim here. See Part One, n. 10, regarding the Longman publication of *Strafford*; see Part One, n. 12, for Reuben's publications.

19. I have been unable to locate any reference to such a building, though Mason's hand seems clearly to spell out "Pantecuicon." His reference might be, however, to the Pantechnicon "in Pimlico, [which was] a bazaar for the sale of carriages, pianos,

much play of imagination around the nationality of the wife of the Woodyats Robert Browning, Grandmother of the Poet.[20]

Guided by statements made to me by my Parents, from my own observation of and conversation with, both Robert and Margaret Browning, children of the first wife and influenced by tradition, current in the family, I have arrived at the conclusion that the lady married by Robert Browning at Woodyats, came from France; this conclusion is supported by a consideration of the position of Woodyats on one of the chief routes to London, used by French refugees, about the time of Robert Browning's marriage.

Towards the end of the 18th century large numbers of french people, belonging to the upper classes of society, sought safety in England from the commotions preceding the outburst of the French Revolution, making their escape from France in sailing vessels, the only means available at that time for crossing the English channel, they were taken to the nearest Ports on the South Coast of England; harbors on the coast of Dorsetshire were the most familiar to the masters of craft sailing from the french ports of Cherbourg, Barfleur or Havre, much used to embark refugees eager to reach England; if landed at Poole, they would make their

furniture, &c. Furniture and other goods can be warehoused." See Weale (first name unknown), *Pictorial Handbook of London* (London, 1854), p. 265.

20. I.e., Margaret Tittle Browning: In a letter to Elizabeth, the poet speaks of his grandmother's having been born in the West Indies (*RBEBK*, II, 1005); Furnivall's "Ancestors," p. 30, points out that she was "a Creole, born in the West Indies," while his p. 31, n. 2, implies that she was of "dark blood"; on p. 36 Furnivall regards the "dark blood" theory as a "certainty." Sharp's *Life*, p. 18, records Margaret Tittle as "a Creole, born in the West Indies"; Mrs. Orr, I, 5, concurs that she was "born in the West Indies"; Chesterton's *Browning*, p. 4, states that "Browning's grandmother was certainly a Creole." Griffin and Minchin, p. 2, claim that Miss Tittle was "a West Indian lady," and, p. 299, "a Creole only in the sense that she was born in the West Indies." Baddeley, p. 2, notes: "She was born at St. Kitts and was therefore a Creole, a white European born in the West Indies." In the paragraphs that follow, Mason seems to be trying to counter Furnivall's "dark blood" theory. Jeanette Marks, *The Family of the Barrett* (New York: Macmillan, 1938), pp. 102-53, most completely chronicles the history of the Tittle clan in the West Indies.

way north through Dorsetshire, passing Woodyats, to reach
the main road to arrive in London by the stage coach. Some
of these french refugees, it is known, remained in Dorsetshire, and among them the lady who became the first wife of
the Woodyats Robert Browning. I should hesitate to put
forward this assumption, if unsupported by the direct evidence of my own senses, collected during frequent opportunities for observing the dark complexions—the almost
black, wavy, not curly, hair of both Robert and Margaret
Browning the children of the first wife;[21] there was, I well
remember, a slight foreign accent in their voices, such as
can be observed with people who have had one french parent; both of them, when speaking, employed a movement of
the hands, backwards from the wrist, quite foreign;[22] indeed
french mannerisms were very pronounced with both
Robert and Margaret Browning.

As regards Robert Browning, the Poet, whom I met at
his father's house and in the house of grandmother Browning; without hesitation I can state that he markedly displayed these same french characteristics; indeed the Poet in
appearance and in manner of speaking, at the time I knew
him, could have passed as readily for a frenchman as Gambetta,[23] a man he much resembled in face, figure and most
certainly, in his conversational vivacity.

Again, if further support for my assumption, that the
first Mrs. Robert Browning was a french lady be required, it
can be found in the ready adoption by her son Robert, late in
life of french manners in Paris and the fondness of his son,

---

21. Mrs. Orr, I, 10, notes that "The poet's father had light blue eyes and . . . a
clear, ruddy complexion." Ward, I, 5, concludes that Margaret Tittle's "portrait is
almost aggressively Aryan."

22. Sharp's *Life*, p. 74, notes that even as a young man, the poet "had that
expressive wave o' the hand, which in later years was as full of various meanings as
the *Ecco* of an Italian."

23. Leon Gambetta (1838-1882) was a French statesman and one of the founders
of the Third Republic.

the Poet, when in the prime of life, for residing in the south of Europe.

The Browning brothers, in the prime of their lives, left Woodyats for London, about 1785, accompanied by Robert Browning's Wife and Robert, the little son.[24] As the brothers had no intention of returning to Dorsetshire, they took with them their library and personal effects on this journey of about 100 miles through a most picturesque part of England. The means of travelling at that time were primitive; if the Brownings went to London by stage coach, that account given by Smollet, in Roderick Random[25] of a very similar journey, conveys a good idea of the dangers from highwaymen and the personal discomforts suffered by travellers, in a lumbering coach.

If the Brownings went to London in the huge tilted stage waggon, drawn by six or eight horses, at that time in use throughout England, their party would be accomodated on straw in it's hinder part, the driver riding a horse by the side of his team, the time to be occupied on the journey, depending on the state of the weather.

Having traced, from a variety of sources, the career of the Dorsetshire Brownings and I trust demonstrated that the two brothers, Robert and Reuben who quitted Woodyats, were educated gentlemen, I must now place on record their mode of life after their arrival in London and describe their pursuits and occupations.

It will be satisfactory to myself to state first, if only to offer, what is termed, a guarantee of good faith, that I am the Grandson of Robert and step Grandson of Reuben, the two Browning brothers who quitted Woodyats to reside in London, my Mother being the daughter of Robert Browning

---

24. See Part Three, n. 13.
25. Tobias George Smollett (1721-1771) was a British physician and novelist whose first novel, *Roderick Random* (1748), recounts a life of adventure on an English highway and aboard an English ship.

and my Father the stepson of Reuben Browning.[26] This somewhat remarkable relationship placed me in the position to hear and now enables me to use, family traditions. I have already explained how the books which I have used, once the property of both the Browning brothers, came by right into my possession.

I have been singularly well placed to learn the Browning family history, for I have been in actual touch with all the numerous Robert Brownings, with the exception of the Poet's son, Robert Barrett, beginning with my Grandfather the Woodyats Robert Browning; the duty of placing a correct Browning history upon record has devolved upon me; what I have learnt and seen of the family shall be conscientiously related.

The stage coach or stage waggon conveying the Brownings to London, from the west of England, to reach the City, passed through Camberwell, a suburb situated less than three miles south of the River Thames.

The Brownings had made their arrangements to reside at Camberwell;[27] coming from the health giving uplands of Dorsetshire, they concluded that for them to reside in a confined London street would be undesirable.

Robert Browning, one of the brothers, supported by Dorsetshire Tories, soon obtained a good official position in the Bank of England,[28] at the time money was lavishly being poured out to the Continent of Europe for the assistance of Great Britain's Allies. The fighting taking place, becoming disastrous to the allied Powers, the enormous sums of money required by them strained even the resources of the

---

26. See Genealogy, Appendix III.

27. Griffin and Minchin, p. 2, point out that the Brownings first settled in Battersea, where Robert—the father of the poet—was born in 1782; they moved to Camberwell in 1784. Reuben probably settled directly in Camberwell after his arrival from Dorsetshire (see also Part One, n. 19).

28. Furnivall's "Ancestors," p. 30, records that "By the influence of Lord Shaftesbury he [Robert Browning of Woodyates] got a clerkship in the Bank of England before he was twenty. . . ."

bank of England; when the French King was executed by
the Revolutionists, British money, for the support of
Monarchy on the Continent of Europe, was needed to such
an enormous amount that, to prevent a financial catastrophe
in Great Britain and to relieve the pressure upon the Bank of
England, Parliament passed the "Bank Restriction Act",
which stopped the issue of coin, except for small amounts,
business transactions being carried on with Bank of England notes.[29]

Throughout the whole of this financial struggle, which
lasted twenty four years, before cash payments were renewed, Robert Browning from Woodyats was a trusted
Bank of England official, an acknowledged authority on
finance, a well known City of London man;[30] he signed the
City's declaration to uphold the British Constitution, joined
the Defence Volunteers became an Officer, for I remember
as a small boy, handling with pride his military "gorget"—
and wondering at the time, what protection a small metal
shield could have afforded, against foreign soldiers.[31]

This Woodyats Robert Browning, the expert Bank of
England Official, the highly respected citizen of London, a
volunteer soldier when Great Britain was threatened with
invasion by Buonaparte's victorious troops, was the Grandfather of the Poet, Robert Browning.

In 1785, the neighborhood of Camberwell, as a place for
residence, was very attractive, the houses were situated in
well tended gardens, tillage was carried on in the surround-

---

29. The Bank Restriction Act was the direct result of a bank run in 1797: "The
bank was forced to suspend payment of gold for its notes, and the government
authorized the continuance of the suspension." Though the act did relieve the crisis
temporarily, "its ultimate results were unfortunate." Too much paper currency was
issued and the highly inflationary result "produced much inconvenience and difficulty in the transaction of business." (W. E. Lunt, *History of England*, 4th ed. [New
York: Harper and Brothers, 1957], pp. 609-10).

30. See Afterword, section II.

31. Mrs. Orr, I, 5, points out that the poet's grandfather was "a lieutenant in the
Honorable Artillery Company, and took part in the defense of the Bank in the
Gordon Riots of 1789."

ing fields and cattle grazed in meadows bordered by hedges teeming with a profusion of wild flowers.[32]

Many names given to the numerous Railway Stations now dotted over the Country, situated between the River Wandle and the Ravensbourne River, on the south side of the Thames, testify that the hills and woods from which the names were taken, comprised a stretch of picturesque scenery particularly calculated to accord with the Browning taste; the rises and lanes were then something more than names, the atmosphere in 1785 so pure, that to inhale it, well to do City men built themselves country residences in Surrey and were driven to and from London in their chariots.

It is not surprising that from the Browning brothers first arrival, that their liking for Camberwell and its neighborhood increased; at Camberwell the Woodyats born boy, Robert Browning was reared and developed; instructed by his Uncle Reuben, he grew to manhood, finding the surroundings of Camberwell congenial to his sensitive artistic nature; and as proof of increased Browning liking for its neighborhood, it was amidst the same attractive scenery that his own son Robert, the Poet, a generation later was educated, sought inspiration wandering over meadows, sauntering through picturesque lanes, or, as mentioned by himself, meditating in one of the woods then dotted over the gentle hills of Surrey.[33]

---

32. Lewis's *Topographical Dictionary* (London, 1835) describes Camberwell: "a parish, in the Eastern Division of the hundred of Brixton, county of Surrey, 3½ miles (S) from London, containing 28,231 inhabitants. . . . The village is pleasantly situated, and the beauty of its environs has made it the residence of several of the more wealthy merchants in the metropolis. . . ." Griffin and Minchin, p. 2, offer a short description which culminates with their question, "Was not the 'Camberwell Beauty' famous?" In Maynard's *Browning's Youth*, chapter 2, pp. 9-19, is devoted to a detailed discussion of "Camberwell and New Cross." In a famous Browning anecdote, a young admirer remarked to the old poet, "There is no romance now except in Italy." Browning replied, "Well, I should make an exception of Camberwell" (quoted in Chesterton's *Browning*, p. 19).

33. For a more complete discussion of the poet's deep attachment to the outdoors, see Griffin and Minchin, pp. 36-7, and Sharp's *Life*, pp. 28, 96.

When in England lately I was much interested when the last remnant of Dulwich Wood was pointed out to me, it stands near the foot of Gipsey Hill; the cluster of trees now enclosed, is likely to be preserved, for which lovers of Browning should be grateful, as tradition says that it was under the trees which I saw, that the Poet loved to ruminate.

Leaving the quiet life, which for over thirty years, he had passed in Dorsetshire,[34] to associate with jostling crowds of business men in the City of London and performing important duties in the Bank of England, bringing him into daily contact with it's leading officials, rapidly developed in Robert, one of the Woodyats Brothers, a very great change, causing the old Browning forceful manner to assert itself; Robert Browning, the Bank of England official, assumed the importance and what I must term, the pompous characteristics of the prosperous "Cit," easily to be recognised in the numerous examples pourtrayed in the literature of the last half of the 18th century and to be seen humorously satirized by Hogarth's pencil;[35] the other Woodyats Browning brother, Reuben, settled quietly at Camberwell with his books, he was a thoroughly studious man, had acquired much learning and was possessed of knowledge which must have enabled him with his pen or by teaching, to provide a comfortable maintenance, I never heard that the Brownings brought property from Dorsetshire, yet Reuben Browning, after being sometime settled at Camberwell, found himself in a position to marry, choosing for his wife, a widow having one boy, who subsequently became my Father.

A second child, Margaret, had been born to Robert

---

34. The grandfather was born in 1749; at the time of his removal to London in 1769 he would have been twenty years old.

35. William Hogarth (1697-1764) was one of the first great English-born painters and engravers, especially popular for his moral and satirical paintings. An excellent collection of Hogarth's art may be found in Ronald Paulson, *The Art of Hogarth* (London: Phaidon Press, 1975), including a number of the famous "conversation pieces" which are at the core of Hogarth's satirical work (see particularly plates 9-22).

Browning by the wife he married at Woodyats, how long the first Mrs. Browning lived, after the birth of the second child,[36] I am not aware, but a book, near me as I write, from which I reproduce a signature, suggests that she died some years after leaving Dorsetshire.[37]

"The Spiritual Chymist or Six Decads of Divine Meditations", printed 1666, is a book especially designed to bring consolation to the bereaved. The Meditations given embrace, what must seem to modern readers, a remarkable selection of domestic subjects which in the year 1793 afforded comfort to the Woodyats Robert Browning, residing at Camberwell.

Among the meditations offered to the bereaved in the "Spiritual Chymist", there is one "On a Grave newly made" which must have brought consolation to the Widower and another Meditation "On the Breast and the Sucking Bottle" seems most applicable to the infant Margaret, deprived by death of her Mother's care and attention.[38] All the Meditations in "the Spiritual Chymist" are treated by William Spurstow D. D. in a most reverential tone, quaint paralels being drawn, supported by Biblical and Classical quotations, employed to divert and console the reader's mind in a time of tribulation.

The two signatures which I give, made ten years apart in Browning books, now in my possession, one written at

---

36. Margaret Morris Browning was born in London on October 2, 1783; her mother, Margaret Tittle Browning, died April 17, 1789, at Camberwell.

37. Robert of Woodyates married Margaret Tittle in London in 1778 (Mrs. Orr, I, 5); Mason again seems to have assumed erroneously that this Robert came to London about 1785; see Part One, n. 19.

38. William Spurstowe's *The Spiritual Chymist; or, six decads of divine meditations on several subjects* (London: n.p., 1666) offers consolation in "On a Grave Newly Made" for the Christian in that death, which was an enemy, becomes "a *Port* and a passage into life" for believers (p. 124); "On the Breast and the Sucking bottle" (pp. 94-7), however, is a metaphorical piece in which ministers are the *"nursing Mothers"* providing the "Milk of the Word" for "new-bourne Babes" in Christ "that they may grow thereby." At her mother's death in 1789, Margaret was more than five years old.

Woodyats in 1783,[39] the second at Camberwell; when they are compared, exhibit a marked change in the individuality of the Woodyats Robert Browning; the power displayed in the signature of 1793, evidences a man yielding to his forceful character and shows the effect of association with the Bank of England directors and City of London men of business.

Fac simile signature, Robert Browning, 1793 "6"[40]

I have now reached a most significant portion of the Browning family history, it marks a time when the literary training of the lad Robert, brought when a child from Woodyats, was rendered uncertain; the superior education being given to him by his Uncle Reuben at Camberwell, was threatened, fortunately subsequent events occurred which averted consequences that might have prevented the name Browning from becoming famous in literature.

The lad Robert's Mother had been dead some years, his Father, absorbed in official duties at the Bank of England, every week becoming more perplexing to him in consequence of the effect produced on the money market, by the French Revolution and the convulsed state of the whole of Europe, found no time or opportunity to indulge his former taste for literature, Robert Browning of Woodyats had developed, in a few years, from a courteous country gentleman, into a full blooded citizen, his mind completely absorbed in the fluctuations of the World's money market, London; he had left the education of his son Robert entirely to the boy's Uncle, Reuben Browning, both before and after that gentleman's marriage to my Father's mother.

Reuben Browning of Woodyats while residing at Camberwell had watched his nephew's dreaminess of manner, had used great judgement in humouring the boy in his habit

39. See Part One, n. 19.
40. See Part Three, n. 5.

of wandering book in hand about the fields and in the woods;[41] had persistently encouraged his literary and poetic tastes, had comforted the boy when subjected to his father's opposition to an advanced education and to the son excused his father's petulance, arising from heavy Bank of England official responsibilities. For years Uncle Reuben had taught his somewhat eccentric nephew to really love books and had fostered in the lad's mind a desire to acquire knowledge, up to that time when Robert Browning of Woodyats remarried,[42] removed his home to a better house at Peckham, in order to break with all former associations and, though the new house was at no great distance from Camberwell he decided to stop his son's studies being continued under Reuben Browning's guidance.

The retired quiet life passed by the Browning brothers, though so near London as Camberwell, is not easy to imagine in the present day; amusement had to be found with books in the house or by exercise in the garden; outside recreation obtained among neighboring lanes, hedgerows and woods or in crossing the meadows to visit at residences scattered over the undulating country; Lord Brougham's modern schoolmaster had not then been encouraged to go abroad, there existed no Society for the diffusion of useful knowledge or any reading public, as now everywhere recognised.[43]

The Woodyats Brownings were reading men, as is proved by the many books brought to London from Dorset-

---

41. See Part Three, n. 33, for a similar vein in his son, the poet.

42. On April 10, 1794, the grandfather of the poet married Jane Smith, "A well-connected English woman" (Furnivall's "Ancestors," p. 30), as his second wife.

43. Lord Brougham (1778-1868) was a prominent figure in British political life for more than thirty years, serving as Lord Chancellor of England from 1830 to 1834. A great orator and a champion of popular causes, Brougham sponsored the Public Education Bill of 1820; in 1825 published *Practical Observations upon The Education of The People*; in 1828 helped create the nondenominational London University; and helped to found the Society for the Diffusion of Useful Knowledge.

shire; I know by family tradition that they made their houses, on the South side of London, centres for intellectual intercourse between neighbors and also encouraged visits from Metropolitan literary men thus attaining in their houses an intellectual surrounding.

Visiting a theatre in London by travelling in the stage coach was, with the Brownings a rare event, for it entailed a troublesome journey over a road formed by laying rough stones, these becoming worn round on the tops caused vehicles to produce a distressing jolting and rattling to passengers; "Macadamizing" a roadway, was not at that time invented, lighting by gas unheard of and the present substantial London Bridge over the Thames, not even proposed.[44]

Leading such a retired mode of life, it can be easily realized how advantageous to study, such an Uncle as Reuben Browning had proved to Robert Browning, but a change in his nephew's future was made imminent, by the second marriage of his father.

After the removal of the Woodyats Robert Browning to Peckham,[45] it soon became evident that his second wife had no inclination for the society of her step-children, Robert and Margaret; they gladly passed most of their time with Uncle Reuben Browning and his wife at Camberwell, the

---

44. A good, brief discussion of John London Macadam and his manner of "macadamizing" roads may be found in W. T. Jackman, *The Development of Transportation in Modern England*, 3rd ed. (1916; rpt. London: Cass and Co., 1966), pp. 276-81. Macadam first gained public attention in 1810 with his criticism of what he considered unsound road-making. By 1816 Macadam had become general surveyor of an extensive turnpike trust around Bristol, and "by 1819 he had under his care one hundred and eighty miles of turnpike roads in that neighbourhood" (Jackman, p. 278). The first pile of the new London Bridge was driven March 15, 1824, by Lord Mayor John Garrett. Designed and executed by John Rennie and his son, Sir John Rennie, the new bridge was located just 180 feet west of the old London Bridge. See Henry B. Wheatley, *London: Past and Present* (London: John Murray, 1891), II, 424.

45. Peckham: "a hamlet, in the parish of Camberwell, Eastern Division of the hundred of Brixton, county of Surrey, 4 miles (S. E. by S.) from London. . . ." Lewis's *Topographical Dictionary*, III, n. pag.

lad's education therefore was fortunately continued in the same manner as formerly.

It is a pleasure to me, to picture Reuben Browning, a man of leisure, in his quiet house, enjoying the seclusion of his garden at Camberwell, employing the Woodyats books, particularly those of them which now lie near me, in the developement of his nephew's peculiarly nervous class of mind and in the education of his own little step-son; I am helped, by the sight of these old books, to recal how my father always spoke reverently and affectionately of his step-father, as a courteous mannered cultured gentleman; my father, with gratitude spoke of the care bestowed upon his young mind in guiding it to develope a liking for good literature, particularly for real poetry; bringing the result, that I never knew him to start on a journey without taking with him a pocket edition of some poet's works; his favorite author for years, I remember, was Robert Burns.

It can be understood how Reuben Browning's method of teaching good literature, developed at Camberwell in the Robert Browning nervous artistic class of mind, a determination to produce poetry.

As proof of the affectionate regard felt in the family for the Woodyats Reuben Browning and how his memory has been preserved by the use of his Christian name, through three generations, I will mention that my Uncle, my Brother, Cousins and one of my own sons, were all given the name of Reuben.[46] When I look at the same name written by the schoolboy Browning at Woodyats in 1738, I feel supported in my previously mentioned assumption that the continued use of a Christian name in a family, may be accepted as assisting to mark the line of descent.

In the year 1800, a daughter was born to the Woodyats

---

46. See Genealogy, Appendix III.

Robert Browning, she was named Jane,[47] after the second wife and as she developed into girlhood, became a great pet with the household of Reuben Browning at Camberwell; having no children of his own and his nephew Robert and niece Margaret being no longer children, the Uncle's affectionate nature found great delight in his new niece, so that she became a particular favorite, was a playmate with the little son of the house and made much of by Robert and Margaret, until a great change was brought about by the Woodyats Robert Browning;[48] his arrogant City manner made him more than ever disapprove of a high class education being given to his son; the prolonged desperate wars raging in Europe, the constant demands made upon Great Britain for money and the little opening and poor prospect in consequence, offering for a literary career, determined the father to remove his son entirely from the influence of Reuben Browning and destroy the literary aspirations indulged by the Camberwell household.

It is only just to remember, that this feeling against cultivated learning was in accordance with the prevailing notion which guided English parents at the begining of the 19th Century, when choosing their sons' careers; it was customary to look upon all students of literature, art or music, as little better than vagabonds, and to regard the arts as unworthy of consideration, it was a time when City of London men swelled themselves with pride because Napoleon Buonaparte had designated Great Britain as a country, occupied by a nation of shopkeepers; the Woodyats Robert Browning having become a genuine City man, felt himself a part of the greatness of his country's commerce, now that

---

47. Jane Browning later married "the little son of the house" and became the mother of Cyrus Mason.

48. Mrs. Orr, I, 6-8, also talks of "a great change" in the grandfather Robert's life, attributing it to his having fallen "greatly under the influence of his second wife. . . ." She possessed "a more than natural jealousy of her predecessor," and demonstrated her "ill-will" towards her stepson.

his son had reached manhood, his father resolved to thrust him into trade and in his forceful manner arrived at the conclusion that the most effectual way of checking literary aspirations and making his son a business man, was to ship him to the West Indies, to be employed on a plantation, which through family tradition, I have always understood was in some way associated with or belonging to, the family of the young man's mother.[49]

I know from remarks made by my father, that the adoption of such a desperate, if not cruel course, was strongly opposed by the young man's Uncle Reuben, but the forceful manner of his brother Robert swept aside all objections, even ridiculed a literary training; then the child brought from Woodyats, reared in the seclusion of Camberwell, educated by his uncle, in a way suited to his sensative nature and calculated to bring out his best qualities, was shipped to the West Indies by his father to fight a way to the knowledge of trade among slaves on a plantation.

The Woodyats Robert Browning by his financial ability and his forceful manner, had year by year increased his importance in the City of London; in his house, surrounded by a numerous young family he was recognised socially as a substantial resident of Peckham; he had always been and in his prosperity continued to be, a staunch supporter of the Church of England, regarding it as the soundest buttress of the British Constitution. His brother Reuben, since his marriage to my Father's mother, living an uneventful life among his books, having lost regard for forms and ceremonies, had become inclined towards Methodism and attended Chapel meetings.

This difference in the religious opinions of the two brothers for a time had produced no perceptible alteration in their friendly intercourse, but when Robert attained a still

---

49. Robert, the father of the poet, went to live on his mother's sugar plantation on St. Kitt's Island as a young man. See Marks, *Family of the Barrett*, pp. 236-7.

higher official position[50] and through that position was associated with the leading financiers and wealthy citizens of London, it was only natural for him to look with distaste upon his brother Reuben's adopted new style of worship, as one, regarded in the beginning of the 19th century, by those occupying substantial residences, as only suitable to the spiritual wants of petty tradesmen or for the religious guidance of people struggling against poverty, certainly not a class of religious service suited to well placed gentlefolk.

I sometimes think that it was the tendency to Methodism in the Reuben Browning household at Camberwell, which hastened the sending of young Robert Browning to the West Indies, but, as will be found subsequently, the change made in his life came too late to affect his religious opinions.

Jane Browning, the eldest child of the Woodyats Robert Browning, by his second marriage, when a girl, being a great favorite with her Uncle Reuben, heard much of John Wesley and his sermons, while assisting her Aunt with needlework; in those days entirely performed by the ladies of a household; this same Jane Browning, long afterwards, when my Mother, often spoke of happy Camberwell days in the house and garden though passed without the many excitements coveted now by girls filling a similar position in society.

It is only fair for me to state here, that her Uncle Reuben's step-son[51] was approaching that age, when he could make himself an agreeable companion to Jane Eliza Browning; reading aloud to the ladies while the household needlework was being performed, he certainly was undisturbed during the reading or diverted from his pleasant occupation by the whirring of a sewing machine.

I have before me a book with the name Jane Eliza

---

50. Probably his appointment as Principal of the Bank Stock Office in 1784.
51. I.e., John Mason, Cyrus's father.

Browning written on it's flyleaf by her Uncle, the Woodyats Reuben Browning, which shows his household's
adherence to Methodism and affection for his Niece, when
he considered a Methodist magazine volume containing the
required religious teaching, a suitable gift book for a young
gentlewoman; yet another book before me, "The Young
Christian's Guide", bears on it's flyleaf the name of Jane's
sister, Christianna Browning, written by her father, proving that the Woodyats Robert Browning considered that
the Church of England doctrine, as expounded in a printed
volume, furnished the best religious teaching and reading
for his daughter;[52] both these books dispel the idea which
has been insinuated by biographers, that the Poet had Jewish blood in his veins;[53] these gift books show that the
Woodyats Browning brothers were men deeply impressed
with the importance of the Christian faith.

To the quiet literary amusements enjoyed at Camberwell and the pleasant country about the Surrey hills Robert
Browning returned unexpectedly, contrary to his father's
positive instructions. Life on a plantation had so jarred his
sensitive nature, had been so opposed to his artistic tastes
and, I may add, his eccentricities, that he could not resist
quitting the Colony to which he had been banished; it has
been suggested by writers, that the return of the Poet's
father to England, was caused by his abhorence of slavery,
that he sacrificed whatever prospects he may have had on
the West Indian plantation, rather than witness cruelties,
then being perpetrated upon slaves.[54] I never heard from my
father or mother, both of them well acquainted with the
circumstances connected with my Uncle Robert's return to

---

52. I have been unable to further identify "The Young Christian's Guide."
53. For other statements regarding the Jewish ancestry idea see Furnivall's
"Ancestors," p. 26; Mrs. Orr, I, 1-2; Chesterton's *Browning*, p. 4; and Ward, I, 5.
54. Mrs. Orr, I, 7, asserts that Robert Senior's return from St. Kitt's was prompted
by his "disgust at the system of slave labor which was still in force there." Chester-

Camberwell, a suggestion that slavery and its abuses had anything to do with it; he was really impelled to leave the plantation through the effect produced upon his artistic nature, by the early instruction given by Reuben Browning, from him he had imbibed a yearning for study which he had found it impossible to satisfy in the West Indies, his refined instincts craved for something more congenial than plantation life, so, without consulting his father, he took ship and returned home. I learnt at a much later period, from Uncle Robert's own lips,[55] that his return from the West Indies to London, really was occasioned by his love of literary work, when he said;

"I have often given in the West Indies a large pine apple for a sheet of writing paper"[.]

As the price for pine apples in London, at the time this remark was made, ranged from two to five guineas each, the

---

ton's *Browning*, p. 12, insists that "Robert Browning senior destroyed all his fortunes in order to protest against black slavery." Sharp's *Life*, pp. 20-1, comments, "The Creole strain seems to have been distinctly noticeable in Mr. Browning, so much so that it is possible it had something to do with his unwillingness to remain at St. Kitt's." In a letter to E. B. B. of Wednesday morning, postmark, August 26, 1845, the poet himself wrote:

> If we are poor, it is to my father's infinite glory, who, as my mother told me last night, as we sat alone, 'conceived such a hatred to the slave-system in the West Indies,' . . . that he relinquished every prospect,—supported himself, while there, in some other capacity, and came back, while yet a boy, to his father's profound astonishment and rage. . . .

Letters of RB and EBB, II, 474. Maynard—in his *Browning's Youth*, p. 24—surmises that the poet's father "no doubt rejected St. Kitt's as much for its provinciality and isolation as for its immorality." These two objections seem summed up in Mrs. Orr's notation (I, p. 18): "One of the experiences which disgusted him with St. Kitt's was the frustration by its authorities of an attempt he was making to teach a negro boy to read, and the understanding that all such educative action was prohibited." Marks, *Family of the Barrett*, pp. 236-7, also cites this episode, his dark complexion, and his aversion to slavery as well as the murder of an uncle on his plantation as causes for Robert Senior's return to London.

55. The poet wrote to E. B. B. Thursday, postmark, August 27, 1846,

> I have never known much more of those circumstances in his youth than I told you, in consequence of his invincible repugnance to allude to the matter. . . . Thus,—If you question him about it, he shuts his eyes involuntarily and shows exactly the same marks of loathing that may be noticed while a piece of cruelty is mentioned. . . .

Letters of RB and EBB, II, 480.

effect upon my youthful mind was to produce the reflection that Uncle Robert had craved very extravagantly for writing paper when upon the plantation, his statement conclusively proves that he could not have been employed upon clerical work, for that would have given him command of writing paper; to a refined artistic temperament, the superintendance or the management of the working of slaves would certainly supply sufficient cause to hurry Uncle Robert out of the West Indies, without any reference to the emancipation of slaves in the Colonies, which was only carried into effect many years after his return to England.

The good standing in the City of London, of the Woodyats Robert Browning, his close intimacy with Rothschild, who, after the battle of Waterloo, was a man of great influence, when he founded the now famous London House;[56] a father's desire to keep his son away from the study of literature as an unprofitable pursuit, all combined to make it easy to place the father of the Poet, in a clerical position in the Bank of England; but it entirely failed in stopping him from studying a variety of subjects quite outside banking business, the most absorbing, strange to say, at the time he was courting the Poet's mother, being anatomy and the dissection of any dead animal obtainable.[57]

This taste for the horrible, in one possessing a sensitive and poetic nature, cannot be regarded as peculiar to Uncle Robert, for Geothe, the German poet was, about the same

---

56. Son of Mayer Amschel Rothschild (1743-1812), the patriarch of the Rothschild financial empire, Nathan Mayer Rothschild (1777-1836) established himself in London in 1804 after a successful six-year merchant enterprise in Manchester. Generally considered the real financial genius of the family, Nathan established his own bank, N. M. Rothschild & Sons, in 1810. His dealings with and for the British during the Napoleonic period made great his small fortune and left him one of the most important and influential financial figures of early nineteenth-century Europe: see Virginia Cowles, *The Rothschilds: A Family of Fortune* (New York: Alfred A. Knopf, 1973), pp. 30-1, 41-4, and *passim*.

57. Mrs. Orr, I, 71, mentions Robert Senior's "study of human anatomy" in connection with his artistic interests.

time, astonishing his friends and admirers by following similar investigations[.]⁵⁸

Uncle Robert became so absorbed in his anotomical studies that he conveyed objects for dissection into the Bank of England; on one occasion a dead rat was kept for so long a time in his office desk, awaiting dissection, that his fellow clerks were compelled to apply to their chief to have it removed! The study of anatomy became so seductive that on the day Uncle Robert was married, he disappeared mysteriously after the ceremony and was discovered, as told to me by my Mother, busily engaged dissecting a duck, oblivious of the fact that a wife and wedding guests were reduced to a state of perplexity by his unexplained absence.

The love felt by the young couple through having enjoyed Reuben Browning's affectionate nature, been benefitted by his learning and having absorbed his poetic enthusiasm, combined to bring forward an unprecedented resolution, when a boy Browning was born at Camberwell in 1812.

The representatives of two generations of Brownings, born at Woodyats, at the birth of this infant Browning at Camberwell, actually planned that he should be reared and educated to become a poet!⁵⁹ The same system which had developed in the child's father a love for literature, it was

---

58. Goethe (1749-1832) immersed himself in scientific investigations throughout his adult life. His researches included studies in anatomy which led to his independent discovery of the intermaxillary bone. "His friends responded to his scientific pursuits with complete lack of comprehension and recognition" (Rudolf Magnus, *Goethe as a Scientist*, trans. Heinz Norden [New York: Henry Schuman, 1949], pp. 21-2). A shorter discussion of Goethe's scientific interests than Magnus is found in Richard Friedenthal, *Goethe: His Life and Times* (New York: The World Publishing Company, 1965), pp. 233-6, 279-91.

59. Gosse's *Personalia*, p. 19, agrees that Browning was "trained to be a poet," and, pp. 25-6, Gosse goes on to imply the family's ready acceptance of Robert's decision to become a poet. Miller's *Portrait*, pp. 19-21, disagrees, contending:

There is a tradition, sponsored by Edmund Gosse, that this choice received the unqualified approval of Browning's parents. . . . But there is evidence that the acquiescence was by no means as prompt or as willing as Gosse suggests. . . .

Miller proceeds to cite "conclusive proof that the son's mode of life evoked some very

resolved should be employed upon the son; that method of teaching which had been used by Uncle Reuben in educating his nephew, when first brought to Camberwell, was to be adopted in shaping the future of a third Robert Browning.

It was never doubted by the enthusiastic father but that his child would have absorbed the poetic instincts of his two preceding generations or that the human material, capable of being moulded into a poet, had not been vouchsafed to the thwarted Bank clerk! This arranged destiny for the infant son accorded with the imaginative and eccentric brain of the child's father; from his birth at Camberwell Robert Browning's swaddling clothes were wrapped around his little body with a poetic consideration—he was rocked in his cradle rhythmically by his father—his Aunt Margaret prophecied in her dark mysterious manner his brilliant future[60]—my mother, when a girl, lulled her nephew to rest by whispering to him lines of poetry!

This beginning of a poet's life this planning of his future by two generations, must be remembered when a generation later the child had been developed by his father into an acknowledged genius.

When Reuben Browning of Woodyats passed away,

---

real opposition in the family circle." Mrs. Orr, I, 71, calls attention to "an idea of his father's that he should qualify himself for the Bar." Ward, I, pp. 48-51, concludes that Browning's parents readily accepted the prospects of a poetic career for their son, but,

> It seems likely that Reuben and the Silverthornes and Masons disapproved, that it was with aunts and uncles that the battles were fought to which he alludes in the Love Letters.

Robert's own remarks are found in *The Letters of RB and EBB*, I, 199, 207, which refer to "this absolute independence of mine, which . . . I have fought so many good battles to preserve." Phelps points out that "it is interesting to remember that Browning's education was simply the elective system pushed to its last possibility. . . . His education depended absolutely and exclusively on his inclinations; he was encouraged to study anything he wished. His father granted him perfect liberty. . . ." (See Phelps's entire discussion in *Robert Browning*, new ed. [1932; rpt. Hamden, Conn.: Archon Books, 1968], p. 4.)

60. See Part One, n. 13.

beloved by everyone, he surely must have realized that his learning and perseverance employed in educating his nephew, had advanced the family standing and that he had not entirely lived and worked in vain.

When many of the family of the Woodyats Robert Browning had reached the lad and lass stage, whether from a dread of the extension of Methodism into the Church of England home at Peckham, whether from a longing to reside in what was then regarded as a more genteel neighborhood or that the wish to leave Peckham arose from the objection indulged by the second Mrs. Browning to the proximity of her step-son Robert, his wife and her step-daughter Margaret; Grandfather Robert Browning decided to leave the south side of the River Thames; for some reason the Peckham neighborhood had become distasteful, perhaps it was increased by his son Robert's incessant study of subjects perfectly useless in Banking business or his desire for a change of residence may have been occasioned by a wish to check his daughter Jane's liking to pay visits to her Aunt Reuben's house at Camberwell, made attractive by the society of her grown up son; something must have transpired to completely sever happy years of association with Peckham and its neighborhood, for Grandfather Browning took a house in Colebrook Row, Islington, at a distance nearly as far from the Thames on its north side, as the former residence was situated on the South.[61]

Facilities for reaching the City from both suburbs, were the same, people who did not keep a vehicle, travelled by the stage from the Angel Inn,[62] or walked; omnibuses were not

61. Islington is a metropolitan borough about two and one-half miles north of Charing Cross; Peckham is approximately four miles southeast of Charing Cross (Leon E. Seltzer, ed., *The Columbia Lippincott Gazeteer of the World* [New York: Columbia University Press, 1952], pp. 852, 1448). Colebrook Row was most noted in the past century as the London address of Charles Lamb and his sister who established residence there in the summer of 1823 (Wheatley, *London*, I, 442).

62. The Angel Inn stood as an Islington coaching inn for more than two centuries.

invented; all travellers to and from their business places could avail themselves of the opportunity of seeing fraudulent tradesmen exposed in the stocks or the pillory.

One unexpected developement happened after the move to Islington, to the astonishment of Grandfather and Grandmother Browning and rather to the perplexity of their daughter Jane.

Aunt Reuben's son maintained by some secret process of calculation, that going to his home, from the City to Camberwell, by the way of Islington, made little difference in the distance he had to walk! Such a disregard of locality and the doubled journey, caused the parents of Jane to suspect that some special attraction for the young man existed at Colebrook Row, Islington; their daughter then confessed to a mutual devotion which caused her sweetheart to disregard doubling the length of his journey home; then it was discovered that years of affection spent together at Camberwell could not be forgotten by the young people at Islington; the marriage of my father and mother was the result of this attachment and explains how I am enabled, being the recipient of many traditions, to record circumstantially the Browning family history.

Whatever objections Grandfather Browning raised to the planning of his grandson's future, the child's young Uncles and Aunts, paternal and maternal, accepted without question, the announcement that the destiny of "Young Robert", as they designated their nephew, was to be a poet;[63] as he grew, they showed no more surprise when his father measured his little son's brain capacity for holding Latin and Greek, than when "Young Robert's" mother— her son grown too tall to continue wearing petticoats—fitted his legs with trowsers, that he might attend a day school in

It became such a landmark that the name has been retained as a local tube station (Kate Simon, *London: Places and Pleasures* [New York: G. P. Putnam, 1968], p. 132).
    63. See Part Three, n. 59.

the neighborhood, the main purpose being to get the boy away from home during the time that his father was in the City.

When "Young Robert" was better able to comprehend the method of instruction employed by his father, he received no other; when removed from the local school, it was soon discovered that he absorbed all learning readily, that he developed a wonderful power of memory, particularly for poetry, much to the delight of his parents for the little boy astonished his kinsfolk, by repeating strings of ryhming verses, while still at an age when other boys residing near, were playing with toys or absorbing sweetmeats.

It can be understood from these particulars, that "Young Robert" soon came to be regarded by his kinsfolk as a very superior being, as a boy, no way resembling other boys of his age, either in application to studies or in the pursuit of amusement, the exhibition of a precocious brain power justified his father's system of education and Aunt Margaret's prophecy of a brilliant future.

My father and mother resided near my Uncle Robert, therefore had frequent opportunity of observing their nephew's progress in classical learning; when in after years they referred to "Young Robert's" youth, I never heard them say that parents or kinsfolk ever suggested that his superior brain should be trained to do anything else but to write poetry.[64]

From the many traditions garnered in my memory, I arrived at this conclusion; "Young Robert's" father recollecting th[e] check given to his own early poetic fancies by his own father, made the resolve that the vast amount of knowledge which his brain had accumulated, should not be lost and determined, as some atonement for the suppression of his own mental gifts and as some recompense to himself

---

64. See Part Three, n. 59.

for the stoppage of his own literary career, that his son Robert, should be made capable of following the life of a poet; in this determination the father entirely reared and educated his child up to manhood, using the same methods as those which had been employed upon himself, by his Uncle Reuben of Woodyats.

Part Four

After the death at Camberwell of Reuben Browning of Woodyats,[1] my parents removed from the south to the north side of London, the familiar fields and shady woods of Surrey, without the former kindly teacher, though associated with many pleasures, only retained a mournful interest; the new residence taken was in Middlesex;[2] being situated within walking distance of Colebrook Row, Islington, I was, when a child, often taken to my Grandfather's House, and thus am able to say that I have been in touch with four generations of Brownings, commencing with the Robert Browning, who came to London from Woodyats, my Uncles and Aunts, their children and now their children's children.

When at Colebrook Row, on one occasion, my Grandfather Browning,[3] not long before his death put a new half crown in paper, sealed it up, wrote my name upon the wrapper and placed the packet in my childish hand; it is a pleasure now to reflect upon an affectionate action performed by a man whose temper was not always under control, indeed, when he was irritated by an attack of gout, I

---

1. Reuben Browning died January 29, 1827 (Maynard's *Browning's Youth*, p. 356).
2. Middlesex is a south England county consisting largely of a residential area which forms part of metropolitan London (*Columbia Gazeteer*, p. 1198).
3. I.e., the first Robert Browning of Woodyates who died in December 1833; since Mason was born in late 1828 (after August 27) or early 1829 (before August 26), this is a very early memory.

know that his company was not considered desirable;[4] his two elder children Robert and Margaret seldom visited at Colebrook Row, the advanced education being given at Camberwell to "Young Robert" by his father, may have been the cause of estrangement, their absence may have been occasioned from deference to the feelings of their step-mother or the known objection existing at Colebrook Row to their preference for Methodism.

I enumerate here the Christian names of Grandfather Browning's children, to substantiate the fact that there never existed any grounds for the assumption, made by biographers, that Jewish blood flowed in the Poet's veins;[5] the following names are recorded in Church of England Registers; Robert, Margaret, Jane, Christiana, William, Reuben, Mary, Louisa, Jemima, Thomas and Sarah; having known then all, excepting Christiana, who died a young woman, I can positively assert that they possessed none of the characteristics of Hebrew personality, all being tall, singularly robust and exhibited clear pink and white complexions.

One cause for the Jewish blood assumption may perhaps be found in the close friendship which existed for nearly a Century between the Rothschilds and the Brownings; beginning with the first London Rothschild, who placed

---

4. Furnivall's "Ancestors," p. 29, records that the poet described his grandfather as "an old gentleman with his gouty leg tuckt up on a chair, much more anxious that his grandson shouldn't get near his toe, than delighted to see the budding author." Mrs. Orr, I, 5, relates that Grandfather Robert was "frequently tormented by gout; a circumstance which may help to account for his not having seen much of his grandchildren, the poet and his sister; we are indeed told that he particularly dreaded the lively boy's vicinity to his afflicted foot." Mrs. Orr goes on (I, 5-8)—as Mason does—to discuss this Robert's second marriage and the subsequent family difficulties between Grandfather Robert and Robert Senior.

5. Mrs. Orr opens her biography (I, 1) with the Jewish question: "A belief was current in Mr. Browning's lifetime that he had Jewish blood in his veins." Citing Furnivall, she agrees that such a belief was "unfounded" (I, 2). Furnivall's "Ancestors," p. 26, had asserted that "there is no ground for supposing the presence of any Jewish blood in the poet's veins."

Uncle William in the Paris house and gave a position in the London house to Uncle Reuben; he for fifty years remained a well known Rothschild's representative in St. Swithin's Lane.[6]

The fourth son of the Woodyats Robert Browning, Thomas, named after his grandfather, unfortunately inherited his father's irascible temper, he aroused the Browning forceful manner and was shipped in 1827 by his father as a passenger to Van Diemen's Land.[7] When a lad he must have been skilful in the handling of tools, for when I was a boy I remarked upon a delicately fashioned ladder, about five feet in length, resting upon the architrave of grandmother's dining room door, and was informed by her, that it had been made by Uncle Thomas to enable his pet canary to mount rung by rung to it's owner's shoulder; unhappily in an ebullition of anger, he destroyed the bird; ungovernable temper interfered with the success of Thomas Browning all through his Colonial career, family pride, openly indulged, lost him opportunities of advancement; he was at the Swan River settlement Western Australia when founded in 1829,[8] from there, went to Sydney, New South Wales, returned to Van Diemen's Land, where he was employed for many

---

6. Nathan Mayer was the first London Rothschild (see Part Three, n. 56). Though both Reuben and William Shergold Browning undoubtedly worked for the Rothschilds, I can find no evidence of a "close friendship" between the two families. However, while none of the four histories of the Rothschild family which I consulted makes any reference to a Browning, Maynard observes that Robert of Woodyates had business connections with private bankers—"especially Nathan Rothschild"— through his position as Principal Clerk of the Bank-Stock Division, bank-stock then being a "speculative commodity" (*Browning's Youth*, p. 357).

7. Elaine Baly, great-granddaughter of the poet's Uncle Reuben, in a letter to the editor, February 3, 1976, writes of Thomas Browning (1809-1878): "The poet's father's half-brother was, I believe the one who also was put to work in the bank, in the house of Rothschild, but did not like it and went to Australia." Van Diemen's Land has been known since 1853 as Tasmania, and is located 150 miles south of Australia.

8. The Swan River Settlement was the first colonial settlement in Western Australia and was founded in 1829; it is located on the Swan River in southwest Western Australia (*Columbia Gazeteer*, p. 1852).

years in a shipping office; in a fit of temper he relinquished that employment and came to reside in Melbourne, Victoria. Knowing at the time that Mr. Charles Gavan Duffy,[9] then holding a position in the Government, was a great admirer of Browning's poetry, I ventured to ask him to find the Poet's Uncle some government employment connected with shipping; he very kindly appointed a time to see us, at his Ministerial Office; unfortunately Browning pride of race, or some knowledge possessed by Uncle Thomas of the Poet's estrangement from his kinsfolk in England, caused him emphatically to decline accepting any advantage in his circumstances if obtained on the credit of his nephew's fame; after this disregard of opportunity, Uncle Thomas gained his future livelihood in Melbourne, by precarious clerical work; always a gentleman, always sustaining a strange family pride in something incomprehensible to me, up to the day of his death.

Grandfather Browning in his endeavor to eradicate his eldest son's love for literary pursuits, shipped him to the West Indies to associate with slaves; his youngest son was shipped by him, to the opposite side of the world, then only known as a fitting place for criminals; Uncle Robert happily had the courage to return from the West Indies, Uncle Thomas, influenced by pride, refused all offers to enable him to return to England, he died after fifty years of separation from the family and is buried in the Melbourne Cemetery.

Having personally known Uncles Robert and Thomas when elderly men, I venture to state the opinion, that had their father treated their temperaments in a less forceful manner, his eldest son, having a passion for learning, possessing a poetic temperament and artistic taste, would have made the name Robert Browning famous a generation ear-

---

9. Sir Charles Gavan Duffy (1816-1903) was an Irish-Australian statesman who served as Prime Minister of Victoria in 1871-72.

lier; the youngest son Thomas having pride in his race, possessing a reverence for integrity and always displaying gentlemanly instincts; if tolerated in his youth and encouraged to study commerce, would have become a successful and respected Citizen of London.

When a boy I used joyfully to run across the "shepherd and sheherdess" fields on my way to Islington and the Browning house, until to me, its well furnished rooms became quite familiar—no veneering there. the massive tables and sideboards seemed as much fixtures as the fireplaces; the grandparents' portraits, painted in oils, half length, nearly life size, always had an effect upon my young nerves; I remember well how their eyes from the Canvass, followed my every movement; whenever I ventured to look at their faces, they seemed to stare back at me in a faultfinding sort of way; though their very red lips had been given by the painter that mechanically produced smile approved by prosperous citizens, I never felt quite at ease when in the dining room, never dared to be quite myself; those portraits of my well nourished, fresh complexioned, respectably clothed grandparents, in massive frames upon the wall, always kept my naturally high spirits very much subdued, even when I sat beneath them, for in that position, I was haunted by a fear that they were both looking down upon me; I generally escaped into the garden when permitted, there, I ventured to be myself and could practice throwing stones across the New River;[10] that portion of the made stream, forming the southern boundary of grandmother's garden seemed to me actually the property of the family, an idea perhaps strengthened by the knowledge that my Uncle

---

10. The New River is an "artificial cut," or man-made stream, which commences near Ware and runs its thirty-six-mile course southward through Herts and Middlesex until it is "received into reservoirs at Hornsey and Stoke-Newington for the water supply of the metropolis" (*Gazeteer of the British Isles*, 9th ed. [1943; rpt. Edinburgh: John Bartholomew & Son Ltd., 1970], p. 507).

Reuben[11] used the City's drinking water for his morning's swim. I well remember the account given of a thief entering the garden gate, early one morning, while Uncle was swimming—the house stood at the corner of a street—and stealing his clothes; compelling the bather to sit immersed in water up to his neck, shouting to the gardener to bring some sort of covering to enable him to reach the house!

How changed the customs and the neighborhood since my boyhood; a bather in the New River at any part of its course now, would be severely punished, that portion of the stream in Islington, where Uncle Reuben enjoyed his morning swim, has been entirely arched over with brick, a road with ornamental reserve made over the river fronting Colebrook Row and the present inhabitants, in answer to my inquiries for the New River, expressed complete ignorance of its existence.

The Colebrook Row garden, it's urns, it's grass plots, it's free growing grape vines I well remember; as a boy I wondered to myself why urns containing nothing were ranged about, why grape vines, pruned with much labor and carefully trained over the house and trellis work were grown; I think now, that some eighty years back, growing vines in his garden increased a citizen's feeling of importance, his vines enabled him to talk in the City about his grapes, though he never ventured to eat them.—I knew three gardens, owned by members of the family, in all of them grape vines grew luxuriantly, the fruit never ripened, was never worth even a boy's attention, as I often discovered by actual test.

It must have been, I think, a romantic feeling or an instinct created in the family by association with localities connected with days formerly spent at Camberwell by the Woodyats Browning brothers, on first coming to London;

---

11. Mason here refers to the poet's father's half brother—the poet's favorite uncle.

that influenced its members about the time when "Sordello" was being completed by the poet Robert Browning at New Cross, Surrey;[12] to give up their residences situated north of London and return to live on the south side of the River Thames.

Louisa Browning and her sister, daughters of the Woodyats Robert Browning, established at Blackheath, a large boarding school for young ladies,[13] it is to be noted that Brownings instinctively turned to the profession of education; Grandmother Browning, with her son Reuben and remaining daughters, after a very lengthy residence north of the Thames, removed from Islington to Hatcham Terrace, New Cross, Surrey; Uncle Robert, his wife, his son the Poet and daughter had resided for sometime at New Cross;[14] Uncle William with his family had been settled for years in Paris; then, shortly after the publication of "Sordello", my parents also decided to remove their family to a house on the south side of the Thames, for I well remember my father and Uncle Reuben, one day, in our house, north of London, investigating the contents of a newly cut book, laughing heartily, as they said, "trying to make head or tail of 'Sordello' ";[15] one of my sisters, curious to learn the cause of

---

12. *Sordello* was published by Browning in 1840.

13. Elaine Baly's "Talking of the Brownings," *Browning Society Notes*, 3 (December 1973), 5, on the testimony of Mrs. Nora Collings (granddaughter of Jemima Browning) records that Aunts Louisa (1807-?) and Sarah (1814-1902) were "successful in running a school in Dartmouth Row, Blackheath." For a more lengthy remembrance of this school written by one of its former pupils, see Millicent Garrett Fawcett, *What I Remember* (New York: G. P. Putnam's Sons, 1925), pp. 38-47. Blackheath is a common and district six miles south-southeast of Charing Cross (*Columbia Gazeteer*, p. 225).

14. Miller's *Portrait*, p. 5, notes that at "the age of twenty-eight"—i.e., in 1840—Robert moved from Camberwell with his family to Hatcham, New Cross; Maynard's *Browning's Youth*, p. 9, concurs. New Cross is a residential and industrial district in Deptford and is located 4.5 miles east-southeast of Charing Cross (*Columbia Gazeteer*, p. 1308).

15. Mrs. Orr, I, 115, similarly notes: "Uncle Reuben was not a great appreciator of poetry—at all events of his nephew's; and an irreverent remark on 'Sordello,' imputed to a more eminent contemporary, proceeded, under cover of a friend's name, from him."

their merriment, entered the parlor, when my father, notic-
ing her astonishment, exclaimed, pointing at her;

"Yet, Naddo shakes the solemnest of brows!"[16]
That pointed remark increased her wonder, but fixed
"Naddo", as a pet name upon my sister, to the day of her
death.

Shortly after this playful naming from "Sordello", my
parents also removed to New Cross and resided near Uncle
Robert Browning; his house was situated on the south side,
of the main Dovor Road, some three quarters of a mile from
Deptford, at the end of a short lane;[17] a very retired particularly quiet place, the upper rooms of the house overlooking a
delightful stretch of country; a position admirably selected
for study and the performance of literary work.

I will remark here that to me, it seems inconsistent, that
among the many enthusiastic admirers of Robert Browning's early writings not one of them has suggested the pres-
ervation of this New Cross Cottage.

For the guidance of the Poet's admirers to reach the
spot, I furnish a sketch plan of the locality, showing the
Robert Browning House and garden at New Cross, where
the Poet's early works were written. The Railway to Croydon, on the east side of the property, being then worked by
an atmospheric system through a tube, not by locomotives,
caused no annoyance from noise or smoke[.][18]

---

16. *Sordello*, Book II, ll. 10-11: "brother Naddo shook / The solemnest of brows."

17. Deptford is a metropolitan borough on the south bank of the Thames located
four miles southeast of Charing Cross (*Columbia Gazeteer*, p. 505).

18. Such a railway would have been most remarkable in the early nineteenth
century, but I have been unable to find a reference to any such system. Indeed,
London's first enclosed rail system, the Metropolitan, was not opened for traffic until
January 10, 1863, and it still had to contend with the pollution of locomotives. The
"first financially viable tube railway," the City and South London Railway, was
founded in 1884 (Philip S. Bagwell, *The Transport Revolution* [New York: Barnes &
Noble, 1974], pp. 135-6). Croydon is a residential county borough in northeast
Surrey some nine miles south of London (*Columbia Gazeteer*, p. 468).

Sketch plan—position of
Browning House, New Cross.   (7)[19]

I visited Uncle Robert's house, knew the family parlor,
the garden, Aunt Robert's[20] roses, that wicket gate the
Robert Browning family used by favor, opening for them a
ready way to wander in the then beautiful meadows to reach
the Dulwich woods, the College and gallery, to enjoy a
collection of pictures of some renown.[21]

All these pleasant surroundings of the Poet I knew, at
the time when he was describing them in letters addressed to
Miss Elizabeth Barrett, an invalid, generally resting upon
her couch in Wimpole St., London; always yearning for a
glimpse of fields, hedges or trees, until the Poet's descriptive
letters of his surroundings, made her resolve, at all risks, to
venture to leave her couch and visit the Regents Park, to see
trees, again feel grass under her feet and gaze at the sky.[22]
The pleasure of receiving Robert Browning's letters and
answering them, was certainly enhanced by the secrecy
maintained; one poet wrote his letters at New Cross, Surrey,
a pretty country; the other poet, penned her epistles in
Wimpole Street surrounded by the bricks and mortar of
London. The correspondence sent from the New Cross
house, as can be gathered from Elizabeth Barrett's letters to
the writer, had the effect of raising the wretchedly depressed
nervous system of a poet at a very opportune time, for the
production of this beneficial change, the readers of poetry
must remain for ever grateful.

---

19. See Part Three, n. 5.
20. I.e., Sarah Anna Wiedemann Browning, the poet's mother.
21. Griffin and Minchin, pp. 11-12, point out that:
    . . . Dulwich was thus, during the early years of the nineteenth century, the chief
    English public picture gallery. . . . The Brownings lived but two miles from
    Dulwich. . . . It was this gallery, in conjunction with the work of de Lairesse,
    which bred and nurtured in the future poet his intense interest in the sister-art of
    painting.
22. EBB's elated description of this momentous occasion is found in *Letters of RB
and EBB*, I, 144-5.

Both correspondents were especially well placed to ensure secrecy; both being acknowledged poets, when writing, shut within their own rooms, would never be suspected by members of the two households, with carrying on a love correspondence, certainly not by the severely stern father of the invalid lady in Wimpole Street or by the dreamy eccentric father of an idolized son living at New Cross; Uncle Robert walking from his house daily to and from the Bank of England, little dreamt of the change impending over his home; how could such a simple childlike nature as his, suspect that a son whom he had scrupulously educated, had filled with classical learning, had reared with every attention to comfort and provided with a retired home particularly well adapted for the production of the hoped for poetical results, would shut himself up in that retreat to write about dancing the polka and expatiate upon similar trivial matters, to amuse a lady quite unknown to any other member of the New Cross household?[23]

Uncle Robert's house, I must confess, always seemed to me genteely dreary, there was an absence of those softening family influences which I was accustomed to meet with when visiting at other houses; each of the occupants of the New Cross house was constantly self absorbed, Uncle Robert intently studying some learned book or amusing himself by making grotesque drawings; Aunt Robert ever mindful of her garden or busy arranging some household punctillios; Cousin Sarianna absorbed in her own importance or considering matters connected with the chapel she attended; the Poet so pre-occupied, by his love affair, that he found no opportunity to show much attention to Kinsfolk. Uncle Robert's family to me seemed enveloped in a misty

---

23. The Love Letters make it clear that Browning's father, mother, and sister knew of his visits to Elizabeth (e.g., Letter 72, *RBEBK*, I, 142), and, shortly before the elopement, knew of the two poets' intimacy (e.g., Letters 523, 559-60, 573, *RBEBK*, II, 1003ff., 1066ff., 1085ff.; see also Griffin and Minchin, p. 151, and Maynard's *Browning's Youth*, p. 46).

pride, which clung about it's members, overflowing the home and communicating to visitors, a feeling of dampness.

The Poet's aloofness from kinsfolk gave rise at this time, to the belief among them, that to his studious Father should be given credit for some of the praise, then sparingly accorded, to Robert Browning's writings;[24] we really had some justification for our belief, all the family were aware that Uncle Robert was a man possessed of great learning, very fond of literary work, we were also acquainted with Uncle Robert's eccentricity and his great desire to see "Young Robert" distinguished as a poet, hence that belief I often heard expressed in the family that Uncle Robert assisted in the production of the early Browning poems. This household talk may have reached "Young Robert's" ears and naturally caused him irritation, he was very quick to take offence and too proud to offer explanations.

The family learnt that Macready, a London leading actor manager, had requested "Young Robert" to write a play to be produced at Drury Lane Theatre;[25] it was written very rapidly and accepted. During it's rehearsal, at a time when all business connected with a Theatre was regarded by middle class families, with very different feelings to those entertained by a similar class in these days there were many serious discussions on the propriety of "Young Robert's" entering upon affairs connected with the stage.

At the first production of "The Blot on the 'Scut-

---

24. Some biographers have awarded such credit to Robert Senior for the part he played in his son's development: Chesterton's *Browning*, p. 119, refers to Robert Senior as the person "to whom Browning owed more than it is easy to guess, to whom we in all probability mainly owe Browning"; Gosse's *Personalia* records that the poet had even said "that his father had more true poetic genius than he had" (p. 18), and that the younger Robert was, "of set purpose, trained to be a poet" by his sympathetic and talented father (p. 19).

25. Mrs. Orr, I, 125, points out that Macready's famous request—" 'Write a play, Browning, and keep me from going to America' "; and Browning's reply—" 'Shall it be historical and English: what do you say to a drama on Strafford?' "—led to the writing and production of *Strafford* in 1837. William Charles Macready (1793-1873) was a noted actor-manager-diarist in Victorian England.

cheon"[26] the family was represented amongst the audience by another Robert Browning, son of Uncle William and myself.[27] We had been furnished with tickets of admission, not by our Cousin the author of the play, but by our ever generous Uncle Reuben.[28]

We took our seats in the Theatre, feeling ourselves of some importance, fully resolved that in criticising the new play, we would be generous towards it's faults and bestow our applause freely for the sake of the family; unhappily many in the audience were not of our way of thinking and soon expressed dissatisfaction with the dialogue, it being beyond their comprehension;[29] an indescribable something around us soon made it evident that the action of the play was found, by many in the audience to be lethargic; it's plot was certainly unsatisfactory to us; unfortunately the stage business connected with a rope ladder hanging from the heroine's bedroom window, was grotesquely managed; we saw a young lover swinging in a perilous position on the ladder, while singing a serenade, in which at the end of a line, the word "drop" was wailed in a marked, if not suggestive manner, thereby causing tittering around us during a scene meant by the author to be romantically expressive,[30]

---

26. The first production of *A Blot in the 'Scutcheon* was performed at Drury Lane on February 11, 1843, and was the second play accepted by Macready from Browning (*Strafford* was the first); Mason makes the common mistake of "on" for "in."

27. This must be Robert Shergold Browning, Uncle William's second son; see Furnivall's "Ancestors," p. 45.

28. Griffin and Minchin, p. 117, cite Joseph Arnould's 1843 letter to Domett as evidence that Macready gave " 'no orders' [i.e., free orders for admission to the theatre; even Browning himself did not receive any]"; Arnould's letter was first published in *RB and AD*, pp. 60-78. Gosse also reports that "no tickets were sent" to Browning (*Personalia*, p. 66).

29. Arnould's letter to Domett (*RB and AD*, pp. 60-78) presents a somewhat different report: "there could be no mistake at all about the honest enthusiasm of the audience. . . . Altogether the first night was a triumph" (p. 65). He concludes: "With some of the grandest situations and finest passages you can conceive, it does undoubtedly want a sustained interest to the end of the third act . . ." (p. 66).

30. Gosse's *Personalia*, p. 67, records: "Anderson, a *jeune premier* of promise, acted the young lover with considerable spirit, although the audience was not quite sure

the audience exhibited impatience by a shuffling of feet, at this manifestation, the author's Cousins hesitated to applaud the performance, fearing to attract attention to themselves or perhaps create an impression that they were connected with the author or were associated with the proprietor of the Theatre; thus it happened that the family, through us, rendered no assistance to the poet play writer towards renown.

We were not particularly concerned at the non-success of "The Blot on the 'Scutcheon"; had we known, how during it's stage rehearsal, "Young Robert's" exhibition of Grandfather Browning's violent temper must have lessened the chance of sympathetic treatment of involved dialogue by the performers, as representatives of kinsfolk, we would have shewn consideration for a known family failing and been induced to applaud for the sake of Uncle Reuben the provider of our tickets of admission, but particulars of the Browning-Macready quarrel were only made known at a later time.[31]

One ebullition of the Robert Browning temper was witnessed by me most unexpectedly, when walking at midnight from London to New Cross, on the road beside the arches, carrying the Greenwich Railway. I had reached a rather dark part of the road, when a horseman, riding at a furious gallop towards London, would have ridden over me, had I not leapt on one side, as I shouted in my astonishment;

"Are you mad!"

The rider suddenly pulled his horse on to it's haunches, wheeled it round savagely and rode at me with uplifted whip. I stood perfectly still and then recognised in the panting distressed beast, my Uncle Reuben's horse "York"!

whether to laugh or no when he sang his song, 'There's a Woman like a Dewdrop' in the act of climbing in at the window."

31. A lengthy discussion of the Browning-Macready quarrel may be found in Mrs. Orr's *Life*, I, 169-87, including a letter from Browning to Mr. Hill in 1884 explaining the altercation from his point of view.

It's angry rider recognised me, for he lowered his whip, then without deigning to speak a word, he savagely wheeled the horse again towards the City and galloped away.

When I subsequently read poems by Robert Browning, in which the speed and sustained power of a horse are depicted, they recalled to my mind how, on a dark road, long before their publication, my shout "Are you mad?["] to a furious rider, nearly brought me into trouble for interrupting a poet's midnight racing thoughts.

In the poem, "Incident of the French Camp", the lines;
"A rider, bound on bound
    "Full-galloping; nor bridle drew"[32]
pictured to me their author disappearing in the darkness; In the "Boot and Saddle" poem, I saw in fancy, it's author galloping towards London;
"Ride past the suburbs asleep as you'd say
"Many's the friends there, will listen and pray."[33]
That line in the poem "How they brought the good news from Ghent to Aix"
"Called my "Roland" his pet name, my horse without fear"[34]
suggested to my awakened imagination "Young Robert", on that dark night long ago, gratefully patting the neck of Uncle Reuben's horse "York" at the termination of his furious gallop.

In Robert Browning's published letters to Elizabeth Barrett,[35] written when I was visiting at his father's house, I can trace how the writer, a man over thirty years of age,[36] at the time of writing, was entirely dependent for support on

32. Lines 14-15.
33. Lines 5-6 of Browning's poem read: "Ride past the suburbs, asleep as you'd say; / Many's the friend there, will listen and pray."
34. Line 52 reads: "Called my Roland his pet-name, my horse without peer;".
35. I.e., *The Letters of Robert Browning and Elizabeth Barrett Barrett 1845-1846* (London: Smith and Elder, 1898).
36. At the time of the first letter included in this correspondence—postmark January 10, 1845—Robert Browning was thirty-two years of age.

his father and still expecting assistance from relations, but throughout the two volumes of letters, the Poet's kinsfolk are almost ignored; one mode of mentioning a kinswoman I particularly regret.

Uncle William Browning had received the Poet most kindly in Paris and, it will be remembered, had written a poem in praise of "Paracelsus" and "Strafford"; yet in a letter written by the Poet to Elizabeth Barrett, he slightingly refers to a cousin expected in England from Paris, on her honeymoon trip.[37]

This cousin, mentioned as likely to prove irksome, was Louisa Jane, the beautiful and accomplished daughter of Uncle William; a lady much admired for her personal attractions, in very truth I can state from my own knowledge, that she embodied in her appearance all the charms of a fascinating woman, more likely to inspire a poem, than be made the subject of a sneer from a poet, because of kinship!

The hope to re-visit St. Petersburg, mentioned in another letter to Elizabeth Barrett, was expected to be realized in the company of Uncle William, but no reference is made to his intention;[38] the horse "York" referred to in another letter,[39] was Uncle Reuben's Saddle horse, but the

---

37. In a letter with the postmark June 27, 1846, Robert closes with the sentence, Yesterday, the whole day, (after the fire went out) was given to a cousin of mine, a girl, just married, and here from Paris with her husband—these two had to be amused somehow.
Letters of RB and EBB, II, 274; see also Part One, n. 11.

38. In a letter with the postmark February 19, 1846, Browning writes:
I also found a note headed 'Strictly private and confidential'—so here it goes from my mouth to my heart—pleasantly proposing that I should start in a few days for St. Petersburg, as secretary to somebody going there on a 'mission of humanity'— *grazie tante*!
Letters of RB and EBB, I, 485-6.

39. I can find no specific reference to York in the Love Letters; Sharp's *Life*, p. 20, however, provides an explanation of Robert's access to "York," and later, in a footnote on p. 189, cites a letter by Robert—written "in 1881 (*vide The Academy*, April 2nd)"—identifying the horse as the inspiration for his "How They Brought the Good News from Ghent to Aix." Perhaps this is the letter which Mason has in mind; or perhaps he is thinking of Browning's unspecific reference to grooming a horse (see Part One, n. 25).

sweetheart is told little of the ever generous kinsman, who not only placed the animal at his nephew's disposal, but was always ready to perform other acts of kindness.

The Poet's love letters when published, confirmed the opinion of him held by the family at the time they were written, that "Young Robert's" education had so engrafted in him the idea of his own superiority, that any personal assistance or help towards his literary fame, was regarded by him, as mere tribute paid to genius by those whom he objected to consider his kinsfolk; he absorbed his father's varied learning, he enjoyed a mother's loving care for an only son, had been assisted in his career by an ever solicitous sister and been helped financially by affectionate kinsfolk, yet, in love letters, in prose or in verse Robert Browning's writings display no fondness for family ties or a knowledge of the meaning of the word domesticity.

I remember being at Hatcham Terrace, New Cross with Grandmother Browning and the Poet, when she mildly asked her grandson;

"Robert, why don't you write something we ordinary folk can
"understand?"

"I must tell you" he answered petulantly "that what I do write,
"is not intended to be understood by this generation"[.]

This somewhat ungallant reply rather irritated the widow of the Woodyats Robert Browning, for she shook her cap strings when she turned towards the Poet, as he hurriedly quitted the room, leaving a member of a first and third generation staring in astonishment after such an exhibition of superiority. This expressed intention of the Poet, in regard to his own writings, was accepted by the family; his remark to Grandmother became familiar as "household words"; being one of the same generation as the Poet, I humbly accepted his opinion of his kinsfolks' intellect in failing to comprehend, even after I have consulted a volume of 576 pages, published as "a guide to the study of the works of Robert Browning"[.][40]

Uncle Robert, at the time his son was absorbed in his love letter writing, always seemed to me the most agreeable member of the New Cross household; in personal appearance he much resembled the pictures of John Wesley,[41] his countenance carried continuously a sort of sedate cheerfulness, as if enjoying a pleasant little chat with himself; he was an omniverous reader, when not actually reading, he would employ his book as a sketching block, no matter the inconvenience of position; he would use a chair back—the mantel-shelf or his knee, his pencil industrious as his face sedately smiled, though his wife and daughter strongly objected to the indulgence, in the house, of a taste for art work, which more than sixty years back was I know regarded, in select English familes as ungenteel.[42] Uncle Robert's artistic work I can state on the best of evidence, was original in design, free in drawing and often very droll, for I had in my keeping for some months in Melbourne, a large sized thick scrap-book, filled with my Uncle's sketches, made on all kinds of paper, with ink, pencil and in color. One series of drawings represented "old masters"; that, called "After Ten Years", done in color, was very droll; the scene, an interior. A man, evidently the long absent husband, has just entered the room, he looks in astonishment at a group of different sized children taking their dinner, waited upon by their parents; the expression on the face of

---

40. The book referred to is Edward Berdoe's *The Browning Cyclopaedia: A Guide to the Study of the Works of Robert Browning, With Copious Explanatory Notes and References on All Difficult Passages* (London: Sonnenschein and Company, Ltd., 1891).

41. A picture of Robert Browning, Senior, taken in Paris in 1861 is reproduced in Miller's *Portrait*, p. 192.

42. Jack Herring's *Browning's "Old Schoolfellow"* (Pittsburgh: Phi Beta Mu, 1972) is a published reproduction of a series of sketches by Robert Browning, Senior, which are exemplary of his artistic activity.

the doubly married mother, as she recognises the new comer, being especially good; the costumes and details of the room showing close attention to the style and the time of the painter Teniers.[43]

My cousin Robert Browning Mansir took this scrapbook to the diggings at Forest Creek, Victoria and unfortunately left it there.[44]

Uncle Robert was very proud to be recognised as a strictly punctual man, in all things; he told me that the only time he had ever arrived late at "the Bank" was occasioned by his getting into and his inability to get out of, a dense crowd assembled to see fourteen men hanged![45]

In bad weather, Uncle Robert would sometimes join me on my way to Deptford Railway Station, to take the train for the City; in his simple way he would tell me that he had been ordered to ride to town and given the money for a third class ticket; we then journeyed together, as was the custom on the Greenwich Railway, over sixty years ago, standing in a high sided truck; having no seats we had to hold an iron bar, fixed

---

43. Both David Teniers, the Elder and the Younger, were celebrated Dutch painters of the seventeenth century whose works were among those exhibited at Dulwich. Griffin and Minchin, p. 12, assert that with Brouwer and Ostade, they were—according to the poet—among the Dutch artists most "admired" by the father of the poet.

44. I can find no Robert Browning Mansir among Browning relatives in published genealogies. Furnivall's "Ancestors," p. 45, which is basic for most subsequent genealogical and biographical studies, lists no one of that name. He does, however, record a marriage between Mary Browning, half sister to the poet's father, and Robert Mansir, but Furnivall records their only offspring as a son who "died young." Furnivall's source, Robert Shergold Browning, son of William Shergold Browning, states that Mansir and Mary Browning "had one child, a boy, who died some years ago" (p. 43). This must be the Robert Browning Mansir referred to by Mason. If so, he obviously did not die in infancy, but could have lived into adulthood, emigrated to Australia, and still have "died some years ago" by 1890, the time of Furnivall's article. Victoria, of course, is a state located in extreme southeastern Australia where gold was discovered in 1851 (*Columbia Gazeteer*, pp. 2022-3).

45. Furnivall's "Ancestors," pp. 31, 32, note, relates:
    Robert IV. always walkt to and from the Bank, and was only once late—or 'below the line'—during his 40 years' service: and that was on the morning of the execution of Mr. and Mrs. Manning. He couldn't get thro' the crowd in the Borough Road.

a few inches above the side of the truck, to steady ourselves from the effect of jerks and oscillations; in this truck having no roof, we were subjected to the weather and falling ashes from the locomotive; I used to think even then, that such a mode of travelling but ill-accorded with the social position of the elderly gentleman dressed in black clothes, standing at my side, for I knew that the Robert Browning establishment at New Cross, was maintained in some style with my Uncle's salary;[46] long since taking those open truck rides with Uncle Robert, I have learnt from the Poet's correspondence with Elizabeth Barrett, that "Young Robert" at that very time was expatiating for the amusement of his sweetheart, upon pleasant times he was enjoying with newly made fine friends, but deploring having to attend at local private parties.

Uncle Robert was a most loveable old man, I remember that during one of our exposed railway journeys together, a piece of ash from the locomotive lodged in one of my eyes. I shall never forget his tender solicitude and persevering endeavors to remove the cause of my suffering.

During the year when "Young Robert" was laboriously producing his love letters, the writing of poetry was neccessarily neglected,[47] his already published works had brought no money returns, but some fame, which had introduced him into the society of leading literary men and to a style of living hitherto unknown to him, just at a time when he felt discontented with his position and had realized the little

---

46. Furnivall's "Ancestors," p. 30, asserts that Robert Senior's "final salary" was £275 per year; testimony before Lord Campbell in the Von Müller v. Browning trial—as reported in *The Times* (see Appendix I)—established that his salary was "about £320 a year."

47. During the twenty-one months of the love letter correspondence (January, 1845, to September, 1846), Browning published numbers VII and VIII of the *Bells and Pomegranates* series (November 6, 1845, and April 13, 1846). In fact, "it was only the energetic remonstrances of Miss Barrett which at last made him give the public an explanation of his title, *Bells and Pomegranates*," asserts DeVane, p. 89. There is in the Love Letters a great deal of discussion concerning the literary endeavors current with the two poets.

progress that he had made towards his own maintenance; that his published writings afforded him little hope for future support is evidenced by many remarks made in letters to Elizabeth Barrett;[48] towards the middle of his published love correspondence there is evidence that "Young Robert" came to the determination to bring about a change in his mode of life, no matter at what risk to himself or unhappiness produced to others.[49]

Whatever faults "Young Robert" exhibited, resulting mainly from his home training, he was assuredly free from the taint of loose morals, the whole family knew, his writings substantiate this fact, that he regarded all women as pure creatures to be adored at a distance and his published love letters in many passages betray an almost feminine innocence; he was strictly a sober man; the published letters to Alfred Domett, written when his want of position was worrying him, show the simplicity of his tastes; but it must be noted that, though writing to a dear and intimate friend, his letters sent to New Zealand, make no reference to the great change in his life he had in contemplation at the time of writing.

"Young Roberts" hope to marry Elizabeth Barrett could only be fulfilled by both the lovers, assisted by the lady's sister,[50] maintaining perfect secrecy; as poets, consulting poets, the two sweethearts had been left together undisturbed day after day, week after week, by the lady's

48. Browning several times mentions his ability to make money with his writings: see particularly Letter 404, *RBEBK*, II, 780ff. ("why, my own works sell and sell and are likely to sell, Moxon says") and Letter 528, II, 1013ff.—especially Kintner's note, p. 1016: "The indication here that Browning was on the verge of popular success in 1846 is seldom noted, but it tallies with the impression gained by a careful chronological reading of critical notices of his work from 1835 to 1847."

49. Mason is probably referring to statements such as Robert makes in his letters postmarked September 13, 1845, and September 16, 1845, in which he contemplates changing his life (Letters 102 and 104, *RBEBK*, I, 191-4, 197-201); Browning frequently used "change" and "alter" in reference to his "mode of life" beginning with these letters and continuing to the elopement.

50. Though Mrs. Orr, I, 210, points out that "her sisters Henrietta and Arabel had been throughout in the secret of her attachment and in full sympathy with it,"

Father; had that peculiar man been made aware that the visiting poet came to Wimpole Street, as the accepted lover of an invalid daughter, the street door would have been slammed unceremoniously in "Young Robert's" face by Mr. Barrett.

It can be understood that the Poet of New Cross, felt impelled by his sweetheart's wish, to adopt towards his own people complete secrecy as regarded his love making;[51] but why a lady, fully arrived at an age when she could act entirely as pleased herself, an assured income, perfectly secured, at her disposal; why when, as admitted, she was able to walk in the Regent's Park,[52] she did not walk away from a far from comfortable home and be free of the dread she confesses she had, of her father exhibiting violence towards her lover, if discovered; can only be explained as a poet's craving for the mysterious, by the selfish charm to some natures, derived from a secret attachment or from the excitement derived by an invalid in the risk arising from the lover's frequent comings and goings in Wimpole Street.

"Young Robert" possessed a Browning characteristic, loyal devotion to women; his word once given, was chivalrously maintained, as sacred as an oath. Whether governed by sympathy, by devotion to the cause of poetry or by a desire to be of assistance to the helpless, once "Young Robert" had declared his affection for Elizabeth Barrett, his father, mother, sister, kinsfolk and intimate friends; the lady's father and her kinsfolk, all were disregarded, the affection they felt for him or his sweetheart counted as

---

Mason's reference here is probably to Arabella, with whom Elizabeth shared her room at night and to whom she was most closely allied.

51. Though the poet did not relate the particulars of the progress of his courtship—in order to protect Elizabeth and Kenyon (see Letters 401-4, *RBEBK*, II, 773ff.)—he did tell his family the drift of things (see Letter 523, *RBEBK*, II, 1003ff.; Letters 559-60, II, 1066ff.).

52. Regents Park, in northwest London, is a circular enclosure of 450 acres containing the Zoological Gardens and the Botanical Gardens (*Gazeteer of the British Isles*, p. 571).

nothing, when compared with his promise to the almost middle aged invalid who had accepted his love; the frequent absences from New Cross had been with difficulty explained to Mother and Sister, rushing daily to post a stream of letters was accounted for by the necessity of smoothing difficult poetical sentences, this fancy the returning stream of letters from Wimpole Street, confirmed. I remember hearing at the time that "Young Robert" had been most serviceable to Miss Barrett in elucidating an abstruse passage in Greek, greatly to the delight of Uncle Robert, who had been his son's sole teacher; the simple old man little dreamt that difficult love passages had been cleverly elucidated by the poets and a secret marriage arranged.

It is with satisfaction that I recal one courteous and graceful act performed by "Young Robert" in my presence. Grandmother Browning was sitting in calm state one morning, in an upstairs room at Hatcham Terrace, dressed with precision for the day, as was her custom; her face really attractive, her abundant hair smoothed over her temples under her widow's cap, it's broad white strings falling gracefully over the body of her black silk dress; as we chatted together I was thinking what a serene, beautiful picture of age she presented, when the door was suddenly opened, and to our great surprise, "Young Robert" bounded into the room, his face ablaze with excitement as, for a moment he stood admiring Grandmother Browning; she sitting too astonished to speak; then for an instant the Poet regarded her approvingly, advanced, seized one of the old lady's hands with both of his and said cheerily, but not without a sort of catch in his voice;

"A monstrous mistake! according to the Book of Common Prayer A man is forbidden to marry
"his Grandmother! The pity of it."

He then stooped and reverently and impressively kissed the surprised and fluttered old lady. I was astounded, for with him, kissing was an unusual form of salutation. "Young Robert" suddenly released Grandmother's hand, turned briskly to the door, without another word to the old lady and taking no notice of me, hurriedly quitted the room.

The Poet's hysterical entrance and departure, the flattering compliment paid to Grandmother Browning, the fervent kiss given, must, I thought afterwards, have been the result of highly wrought feelings produced upon "Young Robert" by the conclusion of all the arrangements for his secret marriage with Elizabeth Barrett; the bound into Grandmother's room had been prompted by his resolve to make a sort of general family farewell; the jesting reference to marriage, betrayed how that momentous approaching ceremony swayed "Young Robert's" brain; the impressive kiss, given to the oldest member of the family, constituted, to such an emotional nature a poet's farewell to father, mother, sister, all kinsfolk, friends, and native Country![53]

I remember, after the marriage and elopement of "Young Robert" became known to us, that the astounded family could not resist laughing at the expense of ever generous Uncle Reuben, when it learnt that he had, in all innocence, supplied the money required, to defray the expense of his poetic nephew's honeymoon trip to the Continent of Europe![54]

---

53. Mason's anecdote must refer to Robert's kissing Jane Smith Browning, second wife of the Woodyates Robert Browning; since the two poets were wed September 12, 1846, Grandmother Jane Browning (1771-1848) would have been about seventy-five years old.

54. The source of Browning's financial aid has been disputed. Furnivall's "Ancestors," p. 30, n. 3, states that his Uncle Reuben "helpt him at first" financially; Mrs. Orr, I, 114, denies such assistance: "This does not mean that the poet was ever indebted to [Reuben] for pecuniary help. . . ." Sharp's *Life*, p. 20, remarks that the question of whether or not Robert received "an allowance from his then unmarried Uncle Reuben, is uncertain." Letter 523 of the lovers' correspondence seems to point to his father as the source of the £100 necessary for their initial expenses (*RBEBK*, II, 1006). Miller's *Portrait*, p. 117 n., agrees that "the poet was forced to borrow £100 from his father." Griffin and Minchin, p. 151, record: "He discussed the situation with his parents, and his father advanced him one hundred pounds for travelling expenses."

Part Five

I now have to touch upon subjects which the many admirers of the Poet will regret to learn, but my resolve to give all the facts which caused family estrangement, leaves me no alternative.

Uncle and Aunt Robert and their daughter Sarianna were wholly unprepared to learn suddenly that their Robert, the pre-destined poet, the good looking favorite in society, the bright member of the New Cross household, had secretly married a lady poet and with her departed to the Continent.[1]

I was in a position to know that had the two poets, after their union, visited the New Cross home, if only to introduce the unknown bride to her newly made relations, before journeying to Paris, "Young Robert's" Mother's and Sister's profound disappointment, at what they regarded as the termination of his literary career, would have been considerably lessened. As women possessed of sense they would have realized that their darling's wife, though an invalid, was an amiable lady of poetic fame, belonging to a highly respectable family; they would have been impressed by a marriage of affection, which though startling, had secured a

---

1. The Browning family seems to have been aware of the intimate relationship between the two poets (see Part Four, n. 23) though the elopement itself must have been a surprise to them. That Robert wanted to tell his family all (Letters 402-3, *RBEBK*, II, 775ff.), that he wanted Sarianna to call on Elizabeth (Letter 386, *RBEBK*, II, 747-8), and that he wanted Elizabeth to visit them at New Cross (Letter 401, *RBEBK*, II, 773-4) are facts clearly recorded in the Love Letters; in all cases Elizabeth's reluctance prevailed.

comfortable independence for an adored son and an unprovided for brother.[2]

The New Cross house which had seemed to me cheerless enough before the Poet's marriage, became absolutely dismal by the creation of a gap in the family of four; this gap Aunt Robert gazed into day after day, seeing no hope of any alteration for the better, in her embittered life; her Robert settled in a foreign country, at that time regarded as too distant for elderly ladies to visit, made painfully apparent to the mother the unlikelihood of ever seeing her son again; as a fact the whole family soon became aware how little prospect existed of the united poets returning to England; the severance from the closest associations connected with thirty four years was made absolutely complete; "Young Robert" stopped communication with his kinsfolk, old familiar friends and acquaintances, excepting his friend Arnould, a lawyer, useful in arranging the money affairs of the poet's wife.[3]

Whatever surprise my Uncles and Aunts felt at the treatment they had received from "Young Robert", they showed it very little; my father, who had followed with interest, the Poet's career from his birth, never alluded to his disappearance, there must have been an arrangement of silence amongst the elders of the family, on a distasteful

---

2. The "comfortable independence" referred to here is probably an allusion to Miss Barrett's "£8000 in the funds, yielding about £300 a year, besides other sums," which rendered her independent of her father's support: see Griffin and Minchin, p. 150; Taplin, *Life of EBB*, pp. 157-8.

3. Robert continued to correspond with his favorite Uncle Reuben who came to be his financial advisor; also, as Paul Landis has pointed out (*Letters of the Brownings to George Barrett*, ed. Paul Landis with Ronald Freeman [Urbana, Illinois: University of Illinois Press, 1958], p. 321, n. 3), "Browning's passion for destroying all evidence dealing with what he considered his personal life is well known." Browning's own letter to George Barrett (Letter 83, p. 320) reveals the poet's destruction of a large volume of family correspondence: "Two years ago, I spent more than a week in destroying my own letters to my family,—from my earliest days up to the death of my father they had all been preserved." Arnould served as a trustee of EBB's funds along with H. F. Chorley and John Kenyon, who actually managed her financial affairs: see Taplin, *Life of EBB*, p. 189, and Maynard's *Browning's Youth*, p. 102.

subject, for when the poet and his wife were mentioned, Uncles and Aunts cleverly turned the conversation.

Having always been accustomed to consider "Young Robert" as the very superior individual in the family, after recovering from our surprise, we of his own generation, passed little jokes between ourselves, having reference to Greek meeting Greek and the clever elucidation of difficulties; the Poet had, in my hearing announced that all comprising our generation, were incapable of understanding his poetry, but we admitted to each other, that we were even less able to understand the undeserved neglect of worthy kinsfolk, which followed that farewell kiss given by "Young Robert" to Grandmother Browning.

After the poets had settled in Italy, Grandmother announced that she had never expected anything different to result from such training; having the privilege of age, she openly visited the sin of the son upon the heads of his parents and sister; shaking her capstrings at Uncle Robert, when he passed Hatcham Terrace on his way from "the Bank", declaring in decisive words that she did not believe and had never believed, in home-made poets!

Uncle Robert throughout this great change in his hopes, bore himself like a philosopher to and from "the Bank", his face expressing the old sedate smile, so that his City friends should not be able to read the extent of his disappointment; he certainly became less chatty and as if understanding his step-mother's condemnation of the system of education which he had adopted with his son, seldom visited at Hatcham Terrace; for this failure of duty on his part, his daughter Sarianna was blamed by Grandmother stating that the sister's conduct was as heartless as the brother's behaviour towards kinsfolk in truth the Poet's marriage developed in the old lady a sad want of faith in humanity; she quite lost her belief in the existence of affection, I heard her say frequently that no such sentiment as family love existed, inconsistently adding to my mother "morning, noon or night I am always glad to see you"[.]

I remember one Sunday morning, when talking with Grandmother at Hatcham Terrace, we both observed Sarianna Browning passing on her way to Chapel, followed by a maid servant carrying her books. Whether to a churchwoman like Grandmother, it seemed inconsistent for a Chapel goer to have her books carried, or the old lady was pursuing the line of conduct she had laid down towards those whom she made responsible for "Young Robert's" neglect of kinsfolk, I cannot say, she shook her capstrings angrily, called Aunt Sarah's attention to what she termed "stuck up manners", then for my information, added: "Poor Robert" meaning Uncle Robert, "since his son's marriage, dare not call his soul his own."[4]

The old lady, I confess, never evinced much regard for Sarianna Browning and actually expressed her annoyance with my mother for having, through affection for her brother Robert,[5] named one of my sisters Sarianna.[6]

The hopeless condition of the Browning home life at New Cross did not improve as time passed, during two years Aunt Robert patiently bore her trouble and when the disappointed lady died, she was not even aware of the existence of her grandson in Italy.[7]

After her mother's death, Sarianna Browning had entire control of the New Cross house, Uncle Robert's life became even more lonely; I cannot say whether the daughter continued her mother's former custom of shaving the patient old man, but I do know that he was got away regularly to

---

4. Maynard's *Browning's Youth*, p. 35, also says of Sarianna: "There is no doubt that she became something of a petty snob."

5. I.e., her half-brother, the father of the poet.

6. Sarianna Mason was Cyrus's younger sister: see Furnivall's "Ancestors," p. 44.

7. She died at Hatcham in 1849, shortly after "Pen's" birth on March 9, 1849. The news of her grandson's birth arrived in London while she was "still breathing, but in the unconsciousness of approaching death," writes Mrs. Orr, I, 233.

walk to and from "the Bank", spite of his loneliness, advanced age and the distance he had to travel; his modest expenditure was examined and questioned at home, until existence became to him simply mechanical; the daily routine of a breadwinner he sedately performed, his love for books and devotion to study, his taste for art and facility for sketching unheeded or treated with contempt; his simple manner of life severely criticised, until the old man's affectionate disposition impelled him to seek elsewhere than in his home, for sympathy and he found it in the smiles of the widow of a Captain in the Austrian Army,[8] residing in Hatcham Terrace, next door to the house occupied by grandmother Browning.

The result of Uncle Robert's meeting with sympathy outside his own home—the opposing conduct of his son and the consequent unhappiness it brought upon the family, though made public property through the London press, has never been referred to, as far as I am aware, in any biography of Robert Browning.[9]

By a remarkable coincidence, two widow ladies found their amusement in observing passers by from the upstairs windows of two houses, side by side, in Hatcham Terrace, New Cross; Uncle Robert, 68 years of age,[10] on leaving the lane in which his house was situated, crossed the road, on his way to the City, to avail himself of the better footpath in front of Hatcham Terrace, only a plantation of trees, inside a paling fence, being on the opposite side of the main road; in his walk to and from "the Bank", being only separated

---

8. The widow is Mrs. Von Müller, identified below by Mason.

9. No full-length account of Browning prior to 1908 makes any reference to Robert Senior's relationship with the widow and the subsequent lawsuit. Furnivall, however, in his "Ancestors," p. 30, advises the reader to "See the amusing breach-of-promise case, widow Von Müller v. Browning, *Morning Chronicle* and *Times*, 2 July 1852. A letter from the poet is referd to in it." Since then Miller's *Portrait*, pp. 168, 172-4, 180-1; Taplin's *Life of EBB*, pp. 261-2; Ward, I, 197-204; Irvine and Honan, pp. 274, 282-3, 298; have all called attention to it.

10. I.e., in 1850.

from the Hatcham Terrace houses, by a strip of front garden, the old man was daily brought into the view of the two widows watching the traffic from their upstairs windows.

Though Uncle Robert rarely called upon grandmother Browning, the old lady, sitting in state at her window, always looked for her son's return from "the Bank", acknowledging his bow with the greatest interest, to her, his passing was an important part of the day's proceedings.[11]

The other widow also sat at the upstairs window of her house, the one first reached by Uncle Robert on his way home; one afternoon by some mischance, never explained, the bow which should have been directed towards the Browning widow, was made too soon by Uncle Robert, perhaps in absent mindedness, but having been made, it was at once appropriated and graciously acknowledged by the Austrian Captain's widow; from that day, the unknown gentleman's bow was also expected by her as an important part of the day's proceedings and constituted in a short time, a cheerful break in the monotous lonely life of Uncle Robert.

When two people, strangers to one another, make acquaintance across a front garden by facial expression, it's progress must necessarily be rapid, to ripen into affection; Uncle Robert's sedate smile, when he bowed between iron pickets enclosing the front gardens of Hatcham Terrace, expanded day by day into a cheery laugh, the Austrian Captain's widow in return, bowed from her window with such a gratified expression upon her countenance that the simple minded old man, unaccustomed to receive any marks

11. Robert Senior was, of course, grandmother Jane Smith Browning's stepson; Mason's remembrance of the events that follow, obviously influenced by the newspaper accounts of the trial (see Appendix I), is either confused or conjectured. Jane Smith Browning died in 1848, the year before Robert Senior's wife—the mother of the poet—died; the elder Browning, therefore, could not have been waving to his stepmother in 1850-1851.

of affection in his home, prolonged his bowings and greetings through the iron pickets, fronting the road, as if to make evident his appreciation of the kindness shown to him, then following up distant salutations he lost no time in bowing himself into an upstairs room to make personal acquaintance with the Austrian Captain's widow.

This introduction of Uncle Robert to a lady, a stranger, made in an upstairs room in Hatcham Terrace, singularly resembles that accidental acquaintance with a lady, a stranger, begun in an upstairs room by "Young Robert" in Wimpole Street; with both father and son acquaintance rapidly ripened into professions of love, bringing gratification to both the ladies.

Both the gentlemen hastened to declare affection for the lady introduced, one, because he was advanced in life, lonely, neglected and had little time to waste; the other, as can be traced in his published love correspondence, because he had reached an age when he felt that a change in his manner of living had become necessary; both father and son pursued their love making clandestinely and both, when separated from the objects of their affection, soothed their impatient feelings by writing streams of correspondence which flowed continuously through the post office to both their sweethearts! "Young Robert" when obliged to make excuses for his frequent absences from home, had been in a position to gratify his invalid lady love, by offerings of roses and carnations from his mother's New Cross garden; Old Robert, careful to keep his daughter in ignorance of his love making, had to rely upon impetuosity to hasten it's progress; hearing that his sweetheart contemplated leaving England, impetuosity impelled him in December 1850, to send her a letter, without signing his name, declaring his devotion, regretting the prospect of losing her,[12] it was really

---

12. See Appendix I.

written as a test of reciprocity and resulted successfully; Young Robert's forceful manner and resolute management, had triumphed over many difficulties surrounding his secret courtship and had carried off his prize from Wimpole Street; his simple old father, in his eagerness to follow up the success attending his anonymous letter, failed to remember the jealous eyes of his mother watching from her window in the house next door to that occupied by the Austrian Officer's widow, thus bringing disaster to his courtship.

As grandmother Browning sat in state every day, every day she looked in the direction Uncle Robert would come when walking from the City, impatient to receive and acknowledge his bow; to the old lady's surprise the day arrived when she saw her son bowing and smiling through the row of iron pickets fronting the garden belonging to the next door house; such a proceeding by an elderly man, at first was considered eccentric, but when Grandmother Browning subsequently saw Uncle Robert, not only bow and smile when passing the next door iron pickets but, with head turned, continue his bowing and smiling as he passed his mother's garden, the astounded old lady lost all patience, called to her daughter Sarah and informed her that "poor Robert" had lost his senses, for that no sane man would "grin", so she termed Uncle Robert's love smile, through the iron railing enclosing two gardens, without once looking up to his mother's window; she pronounced poor Robert to be mad, insisted that his daughter Sarianna must be informed immediately of her father's extraordinary conduct, adding, that his daughter was the proper person to look after him, but if she neglected to perform her duty, the police must forthwith be communicated with!

Sarianna Browning being informed of her father's conduct, made investigations into the proceedings which had been seen taking place in front of Hatcham Terrace; then Uncle Robert's secret love makings were discovered; his daughter, having no cause to doubt her father's sanity, felt that her self-importance had been ignored, her dignity offended; forgetting that her father was the head of the family, she failed to realize that by discouraging, if not slighting his simple tastes at home she had caused his affectionate nature to seek for sympathy abroad. For more than forty years Uncle Robert had been regarded by his own family, as simply a bread winning machine, travelling from his home to the Bank of England. When Sarianna Browning discovered that the bread winning machine had not only diverged from its routine, to smile at a widow between iron pickets, but had actually courted her, been accepted as a lover and that the couple intended to be married, she so entirely lost control of her forceful manner, that without consulting or considering her father, his feelings or the suitability of the engagement made; felt that her offended dignity could only be soothed by sending to her brother, the Poet, particulars of the disgrace her gentility had to endure at New Cross, begging him to at once take some action to avert disaster; and bring the simple old bread-winning machine back into working order.

The letter sent by Sarianna Browning to her brother comfortably settled in Italy, proved a terrible shock to his nervous susceptibilities; that his father, known from the time of "Young Robert's" earliest recollection as a Bank clerk, in receipt of a salary, which had enabled him to maintain his family in a respectable position, could have even contemplated making any change in his studious mode of life, appeared to the Poet incredible; the idea that his father had himself proposed to re-marry was not to be entertained; his father's unselfish, regular habits forbade the thought; the only possible explanation appeared to be that his father's simple nature had made him the easy dupe of a scheming woman; the son failed to understand how his own love affair, secret marriage, flight from home and the death of his mother, had completely changed all the surroundings of his father's former life at New Cross.

Filial affection failed to suggest to the Poet, that by hastening to his imagined duped father, he might have been able to extricate him from an embarrassing situation; granting that a journey to New Cross might have proved useless and no other way be devised to save his father from the designs of a widow; the son's forceful manner might have influenced the father to at once resign his position in "the Bank", claim his well earned pension, return with him to Italy and live there, free from all risk of being cajoled into marrying anyone. Unhappily "Young Robert's" dominating nature prompted him to take upon himself in Italy, the management of his father's love affair at New Cross. In reply to his sister's appealing letter, the poet ordered her to at once bring their father to Paris, there he would meet them, together they would learn particulars of the duping and after their meeting he would take action against the designing woman.[13]

We never learnt what really transpired in Paris between Uncle Robert and his children; the family felt sure that the simple minded father would never, under any circumstances, employ subterfuge; as we learnt afterwards, he gave to his children full particulars of his courtship and actual engagement to marry the Austrian Captain's widow; in his

---

13. No evidence exists to support Mason's surmises here; for several quite different evaluations of this time period—especially different from Mason's mistaken idea about the poet's ordering his father to Paris—see Miller's *Portrait*, pp. 168, 172-4, 180-1; Taplin's *Life of EBB*, pp. 260-2; Ward, I, 197-204; and Irvine and Honan, pp. 274, 282-3, 298. A brief, general itinerary of this busy period of the poet's life reveals that Robert and Elizabeth began their trip to London, by way of Venice and Paris, in May 1851, arrived in London on July 23, and remained there until September 25. From London they traveled to France and settled into winter lodgings in Paris on October 10. Sometime thereafter, possibly in December, Robert Senior and Sarianna visited the poets for about three weeks. On July 5, 1852, days after the judgment was rendered against Robert Senior, Robert and Elizabeth returned to London. In late July the poet went with his father and sister to Paris to help them establish a new residence there; Browning rejoined Elizabeth in London on July 24.

eagerness to explain how earnestly he had considered his position when proposing marriage, he also confided to his children some doubts he had at one time entertained, respecting his sweetheart's first husband being dead, when she married a second time; his masterful children, seizing upon their father's former doubts, at once took his love affair into their own management; past doubts were revived and magnified, the risk he would incur, by marrying a doubtful widow, must have been forcibly made apparent, arousing Uncle Robert's former religious scruples, for he returned to England determined not to fulfill his engagement to marry the Austrian Captain's widow; as grandmother Browning had formerly said "poor Robert could not call his soul, his own"; the breadwinner departed from Paris instructed by his children to stop all further communication with his sweetheart; his son undertaking to inform her by letter that she must cease pursuing and persecuting his father.

Robert and Sarianna Browning were too anxious to prevent their father re-marrying, to perceive, that a lady sitting at her window in Hatcham Terrace, could not have forced her attentions upon an elderly passer by; had they troubled to inquire at New Cross, it could have been learnt that from December 1850 to September 1851, the Austrian Captain's widow had really been pursued, if not persecuted, from one friend's house to another, by her ardent wooer; that she had been made the recipient of many love letters learnedly written; that she had been made a party to interesting discussions upon religious questions, thereby gaining her esteem, which had ripened into affection and had induced her to consent to marry her courteous lover.[14] In ignorance of these eight months of love making by their father, the brother and sister thought fit to regard the Aus-

---

14. See Appendix I.

trian Captain's widow as a designing woman resolved on persecuting a simple old man. Ignoring consequences the Poet wrote and sent from Paris, to his father's affianced wife, a letter which must be regarded as the greatest blunder ever committed by a highly educated man![15]

To a lady, forty five years of age, moving in similar society to that occupied by the Brownings—a lady, with a well married daughter, who had actually received wedding presents from grandmother Browning's daughters—both mother and daughter intimate friends of the medical man who had attended Aunt Robert Browning in her last illness;[16] to this educated lady, the widow of an Austrian military officer, Robert Browning, the Poet, sent the most insulting letter any honest woman could receive, questioning her respectability, even threatening her with public exposure, if she did not discontinue the persecution of the writer's father.

A poet is permitted great license but the contents of this letter surely exceed the limit.

The Austrian captain's widow received this abusive letter November 1st 1850,[17] with a feeling of disgust, she would have put it into the fire, but her practical son-in-law being present, took possession of it; the lady then, remembering her elderly lover's courteous manner, concluded that he was entirely ignorant of the insults conveyed to her in writing; prompted by affection, she wrote in grief to Uncle

15. Research has thus far failed to locate the poet's letter; references to it, however, have been made in *The Times* and *The Morning Chronicle* reports of the trial (see Appendix I); in a parenthetical remark in Furnivall's "Ancestors," p. 30; in Miller's *Portrait*, pp. 172-3; in Taplin's *Life of EBB*, pp. 260-2; in Ward, I, 197-205; and in Irvine and Honan, pp. 282-3, 298.

16. The lady is Mrs. Von Müller; her daughter is Mrs. Sutor; *The Times* records that Mrs. Sutor testified that one of Robert Senior's sisters "made me a present on my marriage" (see Appendix I); the medical man is Alfred Collinson.

17. Mason has again confused dates as the letter was received November 1, 1851; Mason himself dates the "wooing" from "December 1850 to September 1851" (see above).

Robert "expressing her supreme surprise", but as she received no acknowledgement, her son-in-law, a well to do ship owner and business man, accompanied by two friends, took the Poet's Paris letter to demand an explanation from the elderly lover at the Bank of England; when the widow's son-in-law was seen by Uncle Robert, for the first time, he was greeted joyously by the simple old man with the exclamation; "You are Sutor! I recognize you by the portrait I have seen in your house."

This remark made to the son-in-law, was actually a confession of the courtship which had been carried on by Uncle Robert, with the ship owner's mother-in-law, while she was on a visit to her daughter at Upton,[18] during the absence of Sutor in America; the business man at once produced the letter and asked Uncle Robert if he was aware of its contents.[19]

The old man expressed complete ignorance of the contents of the letter but innocently added;

"I recognise my son's hand writing".

Following this candid admission of the authenticity of the letter, the practical business man at once asked, informed of all the preceding circumstances, promptly enquired;

"Now that you are not under your son's influence, is it your intention to carry out your original views and marry Mrs. Von Müller?"

Uncle Robert still under the influence of his visit to Paris [and the] replied, "certainly not," without giving any reason for the alteration of his "original views".

Such a blunt refusal left only one course open for a practical son-in-law to take to clear his wife's mother from

---

18. Upton is a town and parish in South Yorkshire, six miles south-southeast of Pontrefact (*Columbia Gazeteer*, p. 1987).

19. Robert Senior's recognition of Sutor was in May when the latter conveyed two letters to Mr. Browning from Mrs. Von Müller: see Appendix I.

cruel imputations, made in writing, against her character, that course he at once adopted, by instructing his lawyer to commence an action to recover damages for breach of promise of marriage!

Uncle Robert by following his son's example when pouring a stream of love letters into the house of his beloved, had no doubt furnished grounds to the lawyers to hope for a successful action and the abusive letter sent by his son to a highly respectable lady, made success a certainty.

Both the father's and the son's love letters have been given to the world. It is difficult to decide which series was the most unsuited for publication; in both cases publication was made, without the writer's consent; the father's love letters were made public property when read in a London Law Court; the son's love letters were published in two volumes, after the writer's death.[20]

It can readily be understood that when the family learnt that an action for breach of promise of marriage against old Robert Browning of New Cross, Surrey, had been initiated by a widow, that it's members experienced feelings of astonishment, indignation, and merriment; astonishment that the head of the family could have been drawn into such a ridiculous position, indignation, because his well known simple ways had not been more carefully considered by his daughter and merriment over the idea that lawyers could imagine that a jury would award damages, worth having, against an old man possessed only of a bank clerk's salary. Our sympathies naturally went out to the Poet and his sister, for being ignorant of the abusive letter sent from Paris we

---

20. I.e., *The Letters of Robert Browning and Elizabeth Barrett Barrett, 1845-1846*, 2 vols. (London: Smith and Elder, 1898). *The Times* reported that Sir A. Cockburn, Mrs. Von Müller's attorney, read to the court "upwards of 50 letters" written by Robert Senior to the widow; very little of this correspondence has been preserved in the newspaper reports of the trial (See Appendix I).

regarded the Austrian Officer's widow as a designing woman attempting to extort money.[21]

When the trial was listed in July 1851,[22] City men, also under the impression that the plaintiff in the action was only a designing woman, prepared to make merry with the long respected name of Browning; on the day of the trial, before Lord Campbell, fifty of Uncle Robert's passionate love letters were read, to the edification of those attending the Court; a spirit of fun took possession of business men around the Bank of England and in St. Swithin's Lane, both neighborhoods where the name Browning had long been known and respected; one gushing love letter received by the plaintiff, from Uncle Robert, read to the jury, begged for a glove or some portion of dress which his sweetheart had worn, that it might be treasured as a token of affection; following the reading, Uncle Reuben on reaching Rothschild's, found his office table piled with soiled gloves, old shoes, stockings, crumpled caps and handkerchiefs, with a card announcing that the worn articles were sent by the "old lady of Threadneedle street"[23] as tokens of her affection for "R.B." the initials used in the City by both the Browning brothers.

At the trial, counsel for Uncle Robert attempted no defence, he characirised the letters read in Court, sent by his client, as written by "a poor old dotard in love"; letters to be disregarded by intelligent men and concluded his address, by asking the jury to award to the plaintiff, whose respectability was, he admitted, unquestioned, only "the smallest amount of damages"[.]

The Judge assumed, when summing up the evidence, a

---

21. It is interesting to notice that Mason and the family initially saw Mrs. Von Müller as a "designing woman," while Mason attributes the poet's actions to his assessment of the widow as a "scheming woman."

22. The trial took place July 1, 1852, not 1851.

23. The "old lady of Threadneedle street" is the Bank of England.

very different attitude, he described the love letters sent by the defendant to the plaintiff, as written by "a man of great intellectual powers and of considerable attainments", but characterised the letter sent from Paris to Mrs. Von Müller, by the son of the defendant, making grave imputations against that lady's respectability, as, "a very gross Case".[24]

It was the Poet's blundering letter which really influenced the jury to give a verdict against Uncle Robert; the damages awarded to Mrs. Von Müller, £ 800! The astounding fact about this trial, as made clear by evidence given in the Court, is, that both the plaintiff and the defendant were sincerely attached to each other! No valid reason existed why they should not have been married; they occupied the same social position, their tastes were quite in sympathy, after a close acquaintance extending over many months; but the Poet, forgetful of his own secret courtship, marriage and consequences, yielded to one of his ebullitions of temper, willed otherwise, regardless of results and forbade the marriage of his father; by this display of forceful manner the Poet not only humiliated his kinsfolk but brought his father, towards the close of a life of unswerving integrity, into the position of a defaulter; we all knew that it was impossible for Uncle Robert to pay the awarded damages and costs and deeply sympathised with him in his degraded position; then followed the course of action which the Poet should have adopted earlier, unhappily he only employed it after family humiliation had been inflicted, Uncle Robert was induced to resign his position in the Bank of England, his feelings receiving small consideration from his children, his regard for punctuality and his life long pride in keeping free from debt were ignored, dominant wills took possession of the simple old man, to avoid paying his legal obligations he was exiled, a pension from the Bank of England ensured

---

24. For Lord Campbell's summation, see Appendix I. The November letter seems to refer to the one sent by Robert Senior, not his son.

his maintenance but not with his son in Italy; Uncle Robert was ordered to leave England and reside in Paris; thus suffering during his life, two banishments; the first inflicted by his own father, the second brought about by his own son.

After the evidence given at the trial and it's immediate result, it can be understood why members of the family have evinced little eagerness to be connected with a renowned Poet, who had for years treated kinsfolk as inferiors and had forgotten assistance rendered to him; such unreasonable conduct on his part had had to be tolerated; but when he caused the banishment of his father, the head of the family, a gentleman beloved by everyone, a feeling was engendered which resulted in complete reticence; thus, up to the present time, no correct biography of the Poet, Robert Browning has been possible.

Uncle Robert's temperament, derived, as I have endeavored to show, from a french mother,[25] fortunately accomodated itself to a french climate, the surroundings of Paris and association with it's lively inhabitants. Though he had been for so many years strictly a City of London man, french manners and customs fitted Uncle Robert's nature as easily as the new clothes, purchased in Paris, fitted his body. From relations who met the old man in his exile, I learnt that he retained his sedate cheerfulness; being able to really "call his soul his own", he passed his time, in fine weather investigating old books on the stalls along the quays; in indifferent weather reading in the Paris noble library or conversing with his friends over coffee taken on the Boulevards.

Being amply furnished with the means of living by the payment of his Bank pension, free from his children's interference,[26] simple minded but learned Uncle Robert was able

---

25. For a discussion of Robert Senior's "french mother," see Part Three, especially n. 20.

26. Sarianna, his daughter, accompanied him to Paris and lived there with him until his death in 1866.

to indulge his literary and artistic pursuits; philosophy turning his exile into a pleasure for fifteen years he never
returned to England, then the Robert Browning brought by
his Father from Woodyats to London,[27] his receptive mind
filled with learning by his Uncle Reuben at Camberwell;
having lived to see his son fulfill the destiny he had allotted
to him at his birth; passed peacefully away, a contented man
at the ripe age of 84.[28]

Margaret Browning was as eccentric in her ways and as
simple minded in her behaviour as her brother Robert, we
met mostly at family funerals; whether in the churchyard at
Walworth[29] on the south side of London or amongst the
Browning graves at Islington on the north, Aunt Margaret,
dressed in solemn black, always attended with the family
gathering of mourners; her dark hair and complexion, her
foreign mysterious movements and profoundly expressive
dark eyes always produced a peculiar sensation in the minds
of us young people; the reading of the burial service concluded, she advanced to the edge of the grave, looked down
with shaking head at the coffin, returned to say a few
words mournfully to most of us, then holding her unused
prayerbook upright with both hands, she walked away erect
and stately, only to be seen again by us, after another death
in the family. As Aunt Margaret never appeared at the
house of mourning, she must be exonerated from all suspicion of a desire to receive from the hands of the undertaker,
the black silk scarf and gloves it was, at that time, the custom
to distribute amongst mourners.

My far from congenial task, undertaken as a duty to my
family, draws near a conclusion; I wish that I was able
conscientiously to record any act of consideration, shewn by

27. See Part One, n. 19, concerning the migration to London.
28. Robert Senior died in 1866 (Furnivall's "Ancestors," p. 44).
29. Walworth is a district in South London in the metropolitan boroughs of
Southwark and Camberwell (*Gazeteer of the British Isles*, p. 704).

Robert Browning the Poet, to any of his kinsfolk; having known all of them I can state truthfully, that being gentlefolk, they were certainly worthy of his recognition; I am not aware that any member of the family ever sought monetary assistance from the Poet when prosperous in Italy or after he returned to London; I do know that he was waited upon, as head of the family, when in Italy and in London by kinsfolk, but I cannot find in my memory any evidence that they were induced, by the manner of their reception, to make a second visit; my own Mother, having known the Poet from his birth, nursed him as an infant, fondled and played with him when he was a child; prompted by affection, called upon him after his return from Italy to reside in London, but made aware by her reception that she was not wanted never troubled him with another visit. Other members of the family also called, but being chillingly recognised, a feeling of pride asserted itself and the Poet and his sister became ignored by them, thus explaining the absence of the names of Kinsfolk from London Society Browning anecdotes.

Being aware of his learned fathers eccentricity, it seems to me most charitable to ascribe his son's treatment of kinsfolk as an inherited eccentricity which took an unexpected direction due to his home education & parental over indulgence that led to a settled dislike to his relations irrespective of their attainments or position in life; and could not have been produced by literary success, for I know that it existed long before the name Robert Browning was even recognised by the reading public, it increased during the Poet's courtship and after his marriage became, what I can only designate as a disease.

Antipathy for kinsfolk entertained by Robert Browning, with me, begets regret for the loss it has entailed upon the reading world; his writings, in their learned obscurity, betray an absence of that affectionate sentiment from which flows the purest source of delight found in most poetry.

When I reflect upon Grandmother Browning's question put to "Young Robert", in affectionate sincerity and remember his cold blooded reply, that he did not write for his own generation, I ask myself, will any generation care to unravel entangled words, however learned, only to discover the want of something which makes poetry speak to throbbing hearts of all generations?

In the early days of the Poet's success, I well remember how my generation glowed with pride in the possession of a family genius or flushed with indignation when his writings were ridiculed in the press for their obscurity; I can record truthfully that it was with no thought of a monetary gain or of any hope of advantage to ourselves that made us enthusiastic over the knowledge that our Uncles and Aunts were in a position to forward an ambitious career, not one of my generation ever dreamed that Cousin Robert might have devoted his time and energy in a more lucrative way, we knew that Uncle Robert had always intended to make his son a poet and we loyally wished him every success.

Strangers, even foreigners, are better qualified than kinsfolk to write of Robert Browning's life in Italy—some particulars of his later career in London can be obtained from the columns of Society papers. His son, Robert Barrett Browning, now the head of the family, was seen by his kinsfolk at his father's funeral, after that event, he left England to reside in his palace in Venice and remains as much a strange foreigner to all his kinsfolk as any lighthouse keeper stationed on the shores of the Meditteraenan Sea.

With a distinct remembrance of my early days I have been able to relate how kinsfolk assisted the Poet, Robert Browning, to attain a position of fame; I have recorded that his father's house at New Cross appeared to me genteely dull, yet was a well appointed comfortable residence, standing secluded in a carefully tended garden; in those days long passed away, I could enjoy the perfume of the flowers, could unlatch the wicket gate opening from the garden, a way into undulating meadows divided by hedges from which I gathered honeysuckle and wild roses; now, the Uncle, with one ambition, who so unselfishly maintained the genteel house; the Aunt, who cultivated the fragrant flowers, thinking only of her adored son; the "Young Robert" who in that well kept house, produced his poetry; the Cousin Sarianna, who devoted her life to forward her brother's literary ambition; remain with me but as memories of kinsfolks' disappointments, all that brain power in the child Robert Browning, born at Woodyats developed by his learned Uncle Reuben Browning;[30] all the following intellectual training of "Young Robert" by his father, of a certainty produced a famous Poet, but in the achievement, obliterated natural affection; the family of four at New Cross devoted their lives to attain the one result, success assured; they drifted apart, never to be again together;[31] the Poet of three generations of learned education, lies entombed in Westminster Abbey, his father is buried in Paris, his mother in London and his sister's remains, rest in Venice![32]

Cyrus Mason

Sandringham
Victoria, July 1908

---

30. Robert Senior was born in London; see Part One, n. 19.
31. After the death of Robert Senior in 1866, the poet and his sister were reunited and lived together until his death in 1889; see Griffin and Minchin, p. 237.
32. Sarianna Browning, sister to the poet, is buried in the Protestant Cemetery outside the *Porta Romana* of Florence, Italy: see "Miss Browning," *The Athenaeum*, 3940 (May 2, 1903), 564-5.

Textual Notes

Page 17
line 14   Page 11 in the handwritten manuscript ends with no punctuation; *all* begins p. 12 in lower case

Page 21
line 8   Mason often employs the lower case for the adjective *french*

11   Omitted after *"Browning* is the punctuation to close the quotation

Page 43
line 24   Duplicate *of*'s occur at the end of one manuscript line and the beginning of the next line

Page 49
line 11   Mason has neglected to italicize the title of Smollett's novel, *Roderick Random*

Page 69
line 29   *th--* appear as the final letters remaining because of a corner torn off p. 31 of Part Three in the manuscript

Page 70
line 6   The end of Part Three in the manuscript is almost a half page, torn off at that length, including eleven handwritten lines with three lined spaces remaining blank; at the bottom in blue pencil, seemingly in another hand, is written *"32"*

Page 107
lines 27-8   A line has been drawn in the manuscript from after *Paris* to in front of *replied* on the line below; *and the* is not marked out, but the intent is obviously to omit it, thus the editorial brackets

Page 113
line 18   After *them* the manuscript has a period which the editor has omitted. Mason obviously decided to add the final phrase and carelessly included a comma after the period

Page 115   The signature, location, and date are written in the same hand but are somewhat larger than the usual writing

Manuscript Alterations

The following terms and symbols will be helpful to the reader in understanding Mason's textual changes:

Inserted: refers to material which Mason has placed above his handwritten line with a caret to designate its placement in the sentence.

Marked out: indicates material which Mason has scored over either with a 〰〰〰 or a ⸻.

Superimposed on: denotes that Mason has written a new letter or word on top of the original without deleting the original.

XXXXX: designates illegibility in marked-out material; the number of X's is an attempt to reproduce the number of letters marked out.

Mason's hand is represented by italics in all the alterations.

In making corrections and deletions in much of Part Five, Mason has used a second type of lighter, almost gray, ink (see *A Note on the Text*). When making changes in this ink a single horizontal line has been employed to mark out deleted material. These changes have been noted in the textual alterations by a "(gray)" following the changes.

Page 7

line 15	Marked out are the words *through the career of a*; inserted is *upon occurances during my*
16	Marked out is *have been*; inserted is *am*

Page 8

line 5	Inserted between *of* and *dead* is *my*
14	Marked out is *curiosity felt*; inserted is *interest manifested*
15	Marked out between *Englishman* and the period is *I proceed to place on record much Browning history never yet printed*

Page 10

line 2	Marked out between *to* and *attempt* is *rectify*
3	Marked out between *fabrication* and *I* is *This duty I will perform to the best of my ability*
11	Marked out is *Woodyats*; inserted is *Dorsetshire*
12	Marked out between *bore* and *; all* is *to the days of their deaths*
15	Marked out between *though* and *singularly* is *a/* marked out between *diffident* and *and* is *man*

Page 11

line 8	Marked out between *Browning* and *had* is *on that date,*

9	Inserted before *a* is *at*
11	Marked out is *published*; inserted is *printed*

Page 12

line 3	Inserted between *demand* and *some* is *in the future*
14	Marked out between *while* and *engaged* is the insertion *he was*
15	Marked out between *his* and *early* is *his*; marked out above is the insertion *the*
23	Marked out is *influenced by circumstances happening, especially, annoying to himself,* ; inserted is *also*

Page 13

line 9	Marked out between *wise* and *to* is *not to interfere*
10	Marked out is *Robert Browning*; inserted is *the Poet*
12	Marked out is *the poet*; inserted is *he had*
17	Marked out is *Dommett*; inserted is *Alfred Domett*
23-4	Marked out is *of writing*; inserted is *that they were written*/marked out between *poet* and *struggling* is *was then*
25	Marked out between *neighbor,* and *his* is *and*

Page 14

line 1	Marked out between *tastes,* and *made* is *but he*/marked out is *no*; inserted is *little*
13	Marked out is *Dommett*; inserted is *Domett*
14	Marked out is *any great*; inserted is *much*
16-24	*to produce . . . two* appears on a neatly cut, eight-line portion of paper glued onto the top of the page nine in the original manuscript to coincide with its normal dimensions; it covers a portion of illegible manuscript

Page 15

line 3	Marked out between *Dorsetshire,* and *England* is *in*
4	Marked out is *three attainments*; inserted is *cultivated tastes*
6	Marked out between *boy's* and *rearing* is *training*
12	Marked out between *the* and *infant* is *child*
14	Marked out is *secretive*; inserted is *receptive*
16	Marked out after *boy* is *'s brain to secrete*; inserted is *to accumulate*
17	Marked out is *it's power as it developed*; inserted to replace *it's* is *his*, and inserted to replace *as it developed* is

to learn; all of which is marked out in favor of *its devel-opement and*

18   Marked out between *life* and *cultivated* is *he appreciated and*/marked out is *a*; inserted is *his*

24   Marked out between *from* and *family* is *the possession of*; replacing *possession* is *knowledge*, which is also marked out

24-5   Inserted betwen *by* and *personal* is *my own*/marked out between *observation* and the comma is *of my Uncle Robert's manner*

Page 16

line 2   Marked out is *uncle*; inserted is *my Uncle*

3   Marked out is *existence*; inserted is *life*

5   Inserted between *gratitude* and *to* is *never yet acknowl-edged,*

6   Marked out between *Dorsetshire* and *Reuben* are *culti-vated* and the inserted *uncle*; inserted is *learned*/marked out following *Browning.* is *never yet acknowledged*

9   Marked out between *London,* and *have* is *to a numerous family*

Page 17

line 6   Inserted between *reading* and *circumstances* is *of*

13   After *be* in the manuscript is an extended dash at the end of a line

14   Marked out is *of necessity largely*; inserted is *frequently*

15   The period after *assumption* is unusually dark and a capital *W* is superimposed on a lower case *w*

16   Between *courtesy* and *their* is an unusually short line

28   Marked out following *labor* is *from what I saw in my Uncle Robert Browning's home, I have every reason for stating that the Poet had never been expected to rub his own* XXXXX [*boots?*]

Page 18

line 3   Marked out is *related*; replacing it is *furnished*

5   Marked out between *of* and *kinsfolk* is the insertion *XXX*

13   Marked out after *Grandfather* is a comma

14   Marked out is *that*; inserted is *as*

Page 19

line 2   Inserted between *conclusion* and *the* is *that*

4   Marked out is *edest*; inserted is *eldest*

| 16 | Marked out is *shows*; inserted is *betrays* |
| 27 | Marked out is *rule*; inserted is *custom* |

Page 20

line 2 — Marked out between *name* and *forms* is *has become a part of the parent's religion and thus*; a line is drawn from the end of *name* to the front of *forms* on the line below

9 — Marked out is *a family of*; replacing it is *the*

18 — Inserted between *district* and *contained* is *of Marshwood*

20 — Inserted between *may* and *be* is *therefore*

Page 21

line 2 — Marked out between *forming* and *the* is *in a pleasant undulating country forming*

3 — Marked out between *Frome* and *River* is *valley*

14-15 — Marked out is *Brounynag*; inserted is *"Brounyng"*, *before*

Page 22

line 6 — Marked out is *Find*; inserted is *Fine*

12 — Marked out is *as*; inserted is *for*

19 — The *ing* on *trading* has been superimposed on an *e*

Page 23

line 16 — Inserted between *fighting* and *assisted* is *man,*

24 — Marked out is *Beaus*; inserted is *Brounyngs*

Page 24

line 15 — Marked out between *career,* and *it* is *for*

20 — Marked out between *was* and *a* is *produced by*

Page 25

line 1 — Marked out is *Aley*; inserted is *Alan*

3 — Marked out is *them of*; inserted is *de Rodburgh*

6 — Marked out is *receive*; inserted is *pay*/marked out between *offering* and *did* is *it*/marked out between *not* and *deter* is *to*

7 — Marked out on the end of *Mautraver* is *s*

10 — In *illegitimate* the second *i* has been superimposed on *a*

13-14 — Marked out between *he* and *in* is *in 1370*, which is inserted again after *court*

Page 26

line 20 — Between *was* and *friend*, marked out is *the*; inserted is *a*

Page 27

line 9 — Inserted between *or* and *a* is *the insertion of*

9-10 — Inserted between *plate* and *commemorating* is *in the chancel wall of Melbury Sampford Church,*

12 — Marked out between *the* and *clergy* is *church*; marked

out between *clergy* and the comma is *in the chancel wall of the Melbury Sampford Church*

Page 28

line 6   Marked out between *different* and *constituencies* is *constuencies*

14-15   Marked out between *and* and *the* is *then given*

17   Inserted between *a* and *family* is *county*

25   Marked out is *involved* [?]; inserted and marked out is *engaged*; inserted is *involved*

26   Marked out is *involved*; inserted is *connected*

Page 29

line 10   Inserted between *and* and *include* is *to*

20-1   Marked out between *the* and *marriage* is *subsequent*

Page 32

lines 13-14 Marked out between *by* and *Brownings* is *the two*; marked out between *Brownings* and *when* is *brothers*

24   Marked out is *real*; inserted is *Browning*

Page 33

lines 6-7   Marked out between *mention* and *made* is *is*/ marked out is *as*; inserted is *for*

7-8   Inserted before *place* is *real*

11   Marked out is *it proves*; inserted is *thus proving*

14   Marked out between *standard* and *book* is *of English*

17   Marked out is *residence*; inserted is *abode*

18   Marked out between *of* and *Grandfather* is *his*

Page 34

line 4   Marked out is *and which*; inserted is *for it*

5   Marked out after *biography.* is *requiring rectification*

13   Marked out after *Woodyats* is *was*; inserted before *Woodyats* is *is the*

17-18   Inserted between *men* and *residing* is *were*

27   Marked out is *resided*; inserted is *continued to reside*

Page 35

line 3   Inserted between *brought* and *from* is *with him*

6   Marked out between *state* and *to* is *of*

8   Marked out is *others*; inserted is *gentlefolk*

20   Marked out between *brought* and *across* is *by the XXXXXX*

21   Marked out is *English*; inserted is *British*/inserted between *channel* and *of* is *to English Ports,*

Page 39

line 16   Inserted between *cousin* and *Robert* is *the poet*

19   Inserted between *with* and *others* is *many*

21   Inserted between *were* and *well* is *then being*

Page 40

line 3   Marked out is *The*; inserted is *My*/marked out is *as*; inserted is *be considered when*

10   Inserted before *established* is *long*

13-14   Marked out is *his brother*; inserted is *grand uncle*

Page 41

line 13   Marked out between *in* and *writing* is *it*

Page 42

line 13   Inserted between *back,* and *occupied* is *then*

Page 43

line 3   Marked out is *declares*; inserted is *announces*

17   Marked out is *las*; inserted is *last*

31   Marked out is *abilities*; inserted is *energies*

Page 44

line 4   Marked out between *learning* and *possessed* is *and abilities*; inserted after *him* is *and his ability*

Page 45

line 13   The *es* in *especial* is superimposed on *s*

19   A *y* has been marked out at the end of *they* to form *the*; inserted after *the* is *Brothers*

Page 46

line 3   Marked out between *"Strafford"* and *as* is *for Robert Browning,*

6   Marked out between *Woodyats* and *Reuben* is *Rober*

11   Marked out between *name* and *Reuben* is *of*

20   Marked out between *one* and *brother* is *of*

Page 47

line 10   Inserted before *consideration* is *a*

Page 48

line 20   Marked out between *same* and *french* is *these same*

Page 49

line 3   Marked out is *life*; inserted is *lives*

Page 50

lines 3-4   Marked out is *it also*; inserted is *I have already*; the *ed* is superimposed on *s* at the end of *explain*

29   Marked out between *them* and *strained* is *even*; inserted after *strained* is *even*

Page 51

 line 2   A capital *R* has been superimposed on a lower case *r* in *Revolutionists*

   12   Inserted between *Browning* and *was* is *of Woodyats*; the *of* is marked out and *from* is placed before it

   16   Capital *D* and *V* have been superimposed on lower case letters in *Defence Volunteers*

   22   Lower case *v* superimposed on capital *V* in *volunteer*

   26   Inserted between *houses* and *situated* is *were*

Page 52

 lines 9-10 Marked out between *than* and *names* is *a*

  10-11 Marked out between *men* and *built* is *to inhale it*; inserted between *that* and *well* is *to inhale it*

   21   Inserted between *his* and *son* is *own*

   23   Marked out between *through* and *picturesque* is *lanes*

Page 53

 line 2   Inserted between *pointed* and *to* is *out*

   3   Marked out is *being*; inserted is *now*

Page 54

 lines 13-14 Marked out between *Chymist"*, and *there* is *to the afflicted*; inserted between *offered* and *in* is *to the bereaved*

Page 55

 line 13   Marked out is *the lad*; inserted is *him*

   15   Marked out is *which*; inserted is *that*

Page 56

 line 14   Marked out is *his uncle's*; inserted is *Reuben Browning's*

   15   The tail of the *g* on *Browning* is superimposed on *s*

   20   Inserted between *visit* and *residences* is *at*

   23   Capital *S* in *society* is superimposed on a partially erased lower case *s*

Page 57

 lines 4-5 Marked out is *begetting*; inserted is *thus attaining in their houses*

   5   Marked out between *intellectual* and *surrounding* is *atmosphere*

   9   Inserted between *stones,* and *becoming* is *these*

  15-16 Inserted between *be* and *realized* is *easily*

   17   *ha* seems to be superimposed over *wa* in *had/* marked out between *Browning,* and *but* is *who was in turn to become the father of the Poet*

	18	Marked out is *the*; inserted is *his*
	23	Marked out between *they* and *gladly* is *therefore*

Page 58

line 3	Marked out between *me,* and *to* is *to me*
10	Marked out between *father* and *always* is *afterwards.*
20	Marked out is *secretive*; inserted is *artistic*

Page 59

line 10	Marked out is *City forceful*; inserted is *arrogant City*
19	Marked out between *just* and *to* is *towards the Woodyats Robert Browning*
20	Marked out between *was* and *in* is *only*
22	Marked out between *careers;* and *it* is *with them*
23	Marked out is *regard*; inserted is *look upon*
24	Marked out is *they refused to consider*; inserted is *and to regard*
25	The *un* is inserted at the beginning of *unworthy*
26	Marked out is *when*; inserted is *because*
27	Inserted between *Buonaparte* and *designated* is *had*

Page 60

line 1	Marked out is *force*; inserted is *thrust*
13	Marked out is *so that*; inserted is *then*
22	Inserted between *young* and *he* is *family*
33	Marked out between *when* and *Robert* is *the brother*

Page 61

line 5	Marked out between *one,* and *regarded* is *only*
12	Marked out is *departure*; inserted is *sending*
13	Marked out between *found* and *subsequently* is *and*
17	Marked out is *became*; inserted is *being*
28-9	Marked out between *Browning;* and *reading* is *by*

Page 62

line 3	Marked out between *and* and *affection* is *his*
9-10	Inserted between *that* and *Church* is *the*
19	Marked out between *Browning* and *returned* is *the father of the Poet,*

Page 63

line 3	Marked out is *of*; inserted is *by*/ marked out is *teaching*; inserted is *instruction given*
4	Marked out is *by*; inserted is *from*/ marked out is *been given*; inserted is *imbibed*
12	Inserted between *given* and *a* is *in the West Indies*

Page 64

line 2   Marked out is *must have*; inserted is *had*

18   Marked out between *place* and *the* is *Robert Browning*

Page 65

line 14   Marked out between *The* and *love* is *remarkable*/marked out is *people*; inserted is *couple*

Page 66

line 15   Marked out is *rhy* and *rythmetrically*; inserted is *rhythmically*

16   Marked out between *dark* and *mysterious* is *way*/marked out is *a*; inserted is *his*

19   Marked out between *life* and *this* is *--at Camberwell*

Page 67

lines 2-3   Marked out between *nephew* and , *had* is *while residing at Camberwell*

Page 68

line 2   Marked out is *had*; inserted is *could avail themselves of*

12   Inserted between *parents* and *to* is *of Jane*

14   Marked out between *daughter* and *then* is *Jane*

15-16   Marked out between *disregard* and *doubling* is *m*

30-1   A dash is marked over the comma between *mother* and *her*

Page 69

line 9   Marked out is *when*; inserted is *for*

13   Marked out between *particulars* and , *that* is *related*

15   Marked out between *boy,* and *no* is *in*

20   Inserted between *near* and *Uncle* is *my*

27   Marked out between *many* and *traditions* is *garnered*; inserted after *traditions* is *garnered*

31   Marked out between *his* and *brain* is *secretive*

32   Inserted between *lost* and *determined* is *and*

Page 70

line 2   Marked out is *a poetic life*; inserted is *the*

3   Inserted between *father* and *reared* is *entirely*

Page 71

line 4   Marked out is *their valued*; inserted is *the former kindly*

5   Marked out between *pleasures,* and *only* is *for them*

11-12   Marked out between *Woodyats,* and *my* is *then*

15   Inserted between *Browning,* and *put* is *not long before his death*

Page 72

line 2 Marked out is *eldest*; inserted is *elder*

6 Marked out is *produced*; inserted is *occasioned*/marked out between *from* and *deference* is *a*

7 Marked out between *or* and *the* is *were influenced by*; inserted and marked out is *they were*

19 Marked out is *had rosy*; inserted is *exhibited clear*

Page 73

line 1 Marked out between *gave* and *a* is *to Uncle Reuben*

2 Marked out is *who*[?]; inserted is *he*

7 Marked out between *aroused* and *the* is *in him*

8-9 Marked out between *passenger* and *to* is *in 1827*; inserted between *shipped* and *as* is *in 1827 by his father*

16 Marked out is *ebulition*; inserted is *ebullition*

18 Marked out between *career,* and *family* is *a remarkable*

20 Capital *W* has been superimposed on lower case *w* in *Western*

Page 74

line 10 Marked out is *behavior to*; inserted is *estrangement from*

12 Marked out is *to be*; inserted is *if*

14 Marked out is *obtained*; inserted is *gained*

Page 75

line 1 Marked out is *his*; inserted is *the*/marked out is *of*; inserted is *in his*

9-10 Inserted between *there.* and *seemed* is *the massive tables and sideboards*

16-17 Marked out between *smile* and *approved* is *by the painter*; inserted between *given* and *that* is *by the painter*

23 Marked out between *for* and *in* is *when*

24 Marked out between *fear* and *that* is *they*

Page 76

line 18 Inserted between *I* and *remember* is *well*

Page 77

line 2 Inserted between *by* and *Robert* is *the poet*

6 Marked out between *and* and *her* is *two of*

9-10 Marked out is *education*; inserted above is *education*

10-11 Inserted between *and* and *daughters* is *remaining*

11-12 Inserted between *of* and *Thames* is *the*

Page 78

line 5 Marked out between *sister,* and *to* is *up*

7 Marked out is *pet*; inserted is *playful*

24 Marked out between *an* and *atmospheric* is *atmosperic*

Page 79

line 7 Marked out between *woods,* and *the* is *on*

9 Marked out between *knew,* and *at* is *when he*

Page 80

lines 13-14 Inserted between *particularly* and *adapted* is *well*

29 Marked out between *pre-occupied,* and *by* is *I learnt afterwards*

30 Marked out is *even civility*[?]; inserted is *much attention*

Page 81

line 2 Marked out between *to* and *visitors* is *a*; the *s* is an addition on *visitor*

18 Marked out is *acting*; inserted is *actor*

20 Marked out between *rapidly* and *and* is *by him*

23 Inserted between *days* and *many* is *there were*

25 Marked out after *stage* is *were debated*

Page 82

line 10 Marked out between *our* and *way* is *generous*

13-14 Inserted between *play* and *by* is *was found,*

14 Marked out between *audience* and *to* is *was found/* marked out is *the*; inserted is *it's*

14-15 Marked out between *plot* and *was* is *of the play to me/*inserted between *unsatisfactory* and the semicolon is *to us/*marked out is *on a climax*; inserted is *unfortunately*

20-1 Marked out is *sinister*; inserted is *suggestive*

22 Marked out is *sentimentally*; inserted is *romantically*

Page 83

line 1 Marked out is *then*; inserted is *the/*marked out is *manifested*; inserted is *exhibited*

9-17 *We . . . provider* is eight lines on a section of paper glued onto the bottom of Part Four, p. 12, in Mason's handwritten manuscript; marked out between *rehearsal,* and 'Young' is *of*; *of our tickets* is written in below the eighth line under *Reuben the provider*

17-20 *of admission . . . witnessed* is three lines glued onto the top of p. 13 with three blank lines at the top in Mason's handwritten manuscript; inserted between *Browning-Macready* and *were* is *quarrel*

Page 84

lines 13-14 *pictured . . . darkness,* is inserted above the following line *In . . . author,* thus accounting for the capital *I(n)*

Page 85
>   line 7   Inserted between the semicolon and *in* is *yet*
>   14   Marked out is *personal*; inserted is *my own*

Page 86
>   line 3   Marked out is *ever*; inserted is *always*/marked out is *some*; inserted is *other*
>   15   Marked out is *home life*; inserted is *family ties*
>   31   Marked out is *Such an*; inserted is *This*
>   32-3   Marked out between *family;* and *his* is *and*
>   35   Marked out is *when*; inserted is *in*

Page 87
>   line 25   Marked out between *an* and *interior* is *an*

Page 88
>   line 8   Inserted between *to* and *recognised* is *be*
>   9   Inserted between *told* and *that* is *me*
>   13-14   Inserted between *sometimes* and *on* is *join me*

Page 89
>   lines 16-17   Marked out between *remember* and *that* is *how*
>   21   Marked out is *strenuously*; inserted is *laboriously*
>   23   Inserted between *works* and *brought* is *had*
>   25   Inserted between *and* and *a* is *to*
>   27   Marked out is *disconted*; inserted is *discontented*

Page 90
>   line 1   Inserted before *he* is *that*
>   4   Marked out between *of* and *his* is *the*

Page 91
>   line 1   Capital *F* is superimposed on the partially erased lower case *f* in *Father*
>   2   Marked out is *to*; inserted is *came to*/marked out between *Street,* and *as* is *came*
>   6   Capital *P* is superimposed on lower case *p* in *Poet*
>   26   Marked out between *sister,* and *kinsfolk* is *or*

Page 92
>   line 17   Marked out between *in* and *an* is *the*
>   20   Marked out between *widow's* and *cap* is *pleated*/marked out is *ribbons*; inserted is *strings*
>   31-2   Inserted between *mistake!* and *A* is *according to the Book of Common Prayer*
>   34   Marked out between *stooped* and *and* is *his head*

Page 93
>   line 2   Marked out between *Robert "* and *suddenly* is *XX*

4	Marked out between *me,* and *hurriedly* is *he*
9	Inserted between *all* and *arrangements* is *the*
12	Marked out between *the* and *jesting* is *almost*
15	Marked out between *family,* and *constituted* is *constited*

Page 95

line 1	Marked out preceding *I* is *Having undertaken, as a duty to others, what I feel may prove a thankless task,*
11	Marked out between *I* and *was* is *am*

Page 96

lines 1-2	Inserted between *unprovided* and *brother* is *for*

Page 97

line 32	Marked out is *XXX*; inserted is *in truth*

Page 98

line 17	Marked out between *and* and *actually* is *that*
18	Marked out between *having,* and *through* is *and*
23	Inserted between *died,* and *was* is *she*

Page 99

line 9	Marked out is *compelled*; inserted is *impelled*

Page 100

line 25	Marked out between *he* and *bowed* is *XXX*

Page 101

line 1	Marked out between *his* and *bowings* is *greetings*
2	Marked out is *along*; inserted is *fronting*
7	Inserted between *Robert* and *a* is *to a lady,*
10	Marked out between *room* and *by* is *in W*
16	Marked out between *lonely,* and *neglected* is *and*
18	Marked out is *some*; inserted is *he felt that a*
19	Marked out is *mode of life was imperatively demanded*; inserted is *manner of living had become necessary;*
33	Inserted between *her,* and *was* is *it*

Page 102

line 13	Marked out is *horror*; inserted is *surprise*

Page 103

line 1	Marked out between *no* and *cause* is *doubt*
3	Marked out between *offended*; and *forgetting* is *unhappily her feeling of gentility too much shocked to allow her to perceive that by neglect she was responsible for her father's behavior:* This is all done in a different ink in the same hand, and is the first of the alterations which utilize a single horizontal line to mark out deletions (gray)
9	Marked out between *England* and the period is *, any*

divergence in the movement of that machine had never been imagined; the knowledge of her father's new acquaintance formed without her cognisance, came as a surprise, but when she learned that the acquaintance was a widow, she suffered an agitated shock, but; marked out after *when* is *she* and inserted is *Sarianna Browning*; a capital *W* is superimposed on a lower case *w* in *When* (gray)

13 Marked out is *Sarianna Browning*; inserted is *she* (gray)

16 Marked out *made*; and *felt* is *she* (gray)

20 Inserted between *disaster* and the semicolon is a check (√) in the same ink as the gray mark-outs; after the semicolon *really advocating that* is marked out and *and bring* is inserted (gray)

21 Marked out between *machine* and *back* is, *by some means, should be brought* (gray)

28 Marked out between *his* and *studious* is *simple*, (gray)

29 Inserted between *incredible;* and *that* is *the idea* (gray)

31 Marked out between *father's* and *unselfish* is *quiet*, (gray)/marked out is *ways through all the son's life,*; inserted is *habits* (gray)

32 Marked out is *feasible*; inserted is *possible*/ marked out is *possible was*; inserted is *appeared to be*

35 Marked out is *infatuation*; inserted is *affair* (gray)

Page 104

line 3 Marked out is *did not*; inserted is *failed to*

6-7 Marked out between *way* and *be* is *on his arrival there*,/ inserted between *might* and *prove* is *have*; the *d* on *proved* is an addition/inserted between *no* and *way* is *other* (gray)

8-9 Marked out is *could have persuaded*; inserted is *might have influenced* (gray)

10 Inserted between *return* and *to* is *with him*

12-13 Marked out between *Robert's"* and *dominating* is *had no such kindly thoughts, or felt no desire to meet his Kinsfolk, for his*; the *s* on *Robert* is an addition/marked out is *were*; inserted is *felt*

Page 105

line 3 Marked out between *had* and *at* is the insertion *had*

8-9 Marked out between *marrying* and *a* is *only*; marked out after *a* is *supposed*; inserted is *doubtful* (gray)

19 Marked out between *were* and *too* is *too incensed*, (gray)

29   Marked out is *which won*; inserted is *thereby gaining*

Page 106

line 2   Marked out is *the Poet, blinded to reason, by an overbearing temperament; to stop what he thought fit to conclude was a persecution;*; inserted is *Ignoring consequences the Poet*; the semicolon after *man* has been changed to a period (gray)

4   Marked out is *sweetheart*; inserted is *wife* (gray)/marked out is *most outrageous*; inserted is *greatest* (gray)

20   Marked out is *abominable*; inserted is *abusive* (gray)

23   Marked out is *the letter*; inserted is *it* (gray)

23-4   Marked out is *on considering*; inserted is *remembering* (gray)

24   Marked out between *manner,* and *concluded* is *justly* (gray)

Page 107

line 4   Inserted between *the* and *letter* is *Poet's Paris* (gray)

7-8   Inserted between *with* and *"You* is *the exclamation;* (gray)

15   Marked out between *the* and *letter* is *insulting* (gray)

17   Marked out is *at once confessed*; inserted is *expressed*

17-18   Marked out between *the* and *contents* is *letter and its*; inserted after *contents* is *of the letter but* (gray)

18   *ed* is superimposed on *ing* at the end of *add* (gray)

20-1   Marked out between *letter* and *, the* is *authenticity*; inserted between *admission* and *of* is *of the authenticity*; an *s* has been marked out at the end of *letter* (gray)

21-2   Marked out is *knowing all the*; inserted is *informed of all the*/inserted after *circumstances* is *promptly enquired;*: Mason retains *at once asked* in spite of the last insertion *promptly enquired* (gray)

27   Marked out between *Robert* and *still* is the inserted *was*

28   Marked out between *and* and *the* is *the intimidation practised by his children*; inserted is *the*/marked out between *without* and *giving* is *explaining or*/Mason does not capitalize *certainly* (gray)

29   Marked out is *which had induced him to alter*; inserted is *for the alteration of* (gray)

30   Marked out before *Such* is *Hearing*; capital *S* has been superimposed on lower case *s* (gray)/marked out between *only* and *one* is *left*; inserted between *refusal* and

| | *only* is *left* (gray)/marked out is *to*; inserted is *for* |
| 31 | Marked out is *follow, if resolved*; inserted is *take* (gray) |

Page 108

line 8	Marked out is *but that same outrageous*; inserted is *and the abusive*/marked out after *letter* is *of abuse* (gray)/inserted between *sent* and *to* is *by the son*; marked out is *the*; inserted is *his*
21	Marked out is *living in all*; inserted is *that*
29	Marked out between *for* and *being* is *we,* (gray)/marked out is *insulting*; inserted is *abusive* (gray)/marked out between *sent* and *from* is *to the plaintiff*

Page 110

line 4	Marked out is *Mueller*; inserted is *Müller*
16	Marked out between *own* and *secret* is *love infatuation*/ *marriage* is inserted between *courtship,* and *and* (gray)
21	Marked out between *father,* and *towards* is *into the position of a defaulter*
25	Marked out is *then came that*; inserted is *then followed the* (gray)
26	Marked out is *adoped*; inserted is *adopted*
27	Marked out is *the*; inserted is *family*/marked out is *suffered by kinsfolk*; inserted is *inflicted* (gray)
28	Marked out is *ordered*; inserted is *induced* (gray)

Page 111

line 8	Capital *P* in *Poet* has been superimposed on a lower case *p*/inserted between *who* and *for* is *had* (gray)
9	Marked out between *forgotten* and *assistance* is *the* (gray)/ marked out is *by them*; inserted is *to him* (gray)
10	Marked out between *when* and *he* is *by blundering* (gray)
12-13	Marked out between *engendered* and *which* is *in the family*
14	Marked out between *Poet,* and *Robert* is *Brow*

Page 112

line 2	Marked out between *pleasure* and *for* is *he never*/marked out is *desired to*; inserted is *he never*
3-4	Marked out is *to London*; inserted is *by his father* (gray)
4	Marked out is *by his father*; inserted is *to London* (gray)
6-7	Inserted between *destiny* and *allotted* is *he had*; inserted between *allotted* and *at* is *to him*
7	Marked out between *birth* and the semicolon is *as a poet*
10-11	Marked out is *I met*; inserted is *we met*

14   Marked out is *at*; inserted is *with*

30   Marked out between *wish* and *that* is *sincerely*

31   Marked out between *of* and *consideration* is *kindness or some/* marked out is *however small,*; inserted is *shewn* (gray)

Page 113

line 1   Marked out between *any* and *of* is *one* (gray)

4   Marked out is *of*; inserted is *that* (gray)/marked out between *ever* and *sought* is *having* (gray)

5   Marked out is *comfortably*; inserted in *prosperous/he* is superimposed on *his*

6   *ed* is added to the end of *return/* marked out between *London* and *; I* is *and was made a literary lion by society* (gray)

13   Marked out is *the*; inserted is *his*/marked out is *but meeting with only a cold response to her overture as a kinswoman and*; inserted is *but* (gray)

14   *s* on the end of *reception* has been marked out/marked out between *wanted* and *never* is *by a successful man*

15-19   *visit . . . . Anecdotes.* is written on a five-line piece of paper pasted on the top of p. 22 in the original manuscript

20-4   *Being . . . relations* is all inserted over the marked out: *When seeking for a cause to explain the Poet's perverse conduct, I remember his learned father's eccentric manner; to me it seems most charitable to explain the son's treatment of kinsfolk as due to inherited eccentricity, which developed under home education and parental indulgence into (any) a settled antipathy to (for) all relations,* (gray)

25   Marked out is *such antipathy*; inserted is *and*

30   Marked out following *disease.* is *which in its virulance destroyed materials which would have been of great service to previous Browning biographers*; the period after *disease* is superimposed on a comma (gray)

Page 115

line 8   Marked out is *produced*; inserted and then marked out is *developed*; inserted is *produced*

11-12   Marked out between *that* and *brain* is *development of*; inserted between *Woodyats* and *by* is *developed*

17   Inserted between *attain* and *one* is *the*

The following is a check list of Mason's irregular spellings and is included primarily as a means for the reader to ensure textual accuracy. In addition to misspellings, variants which are not current, primary English usage are included.

Because they are used recurrently throughout the manuscript, *Woodyats*, *developement*, *it's*, *learnt*, and *recognised* are noted only by their initial occurrence.

Page 5	line 4	[under *Part Two*] *Woodyats*, for Woodyates
Page 7	line 2	*developement*, for development
	15	*occurances*, for occurrences
Page 8	line 13	*it's*, for its
Page 10	line 7	*inuendoes*, for innuendoes
Page 16	line 24	*recognised*, for recognized
	27	*shewn*, for shown
Page 17	line 23	*Barratt*, for Barrett
Page 22	lines 16-17	*burthen*, for burden
	23	*artizan*, for artisan
Page 24	line 1	*Marswood*, for Marshwood
	3	*"lerned,"* for learned [in Leland quotation]
Page 25	line 3	*de Rodburgh* and
	11	*de Rodburg* are used interchangeably
Page 28	line 7	*summonded*, for summoned
Page 30	line 5	*turbulant*, for turbulent
Page 32	line 12	*Poets*, for Poet's
Page 33	line 4	*Dictonary*, for Dictionary
Page 35	line 4	*a*, for I
Page 37	lines 15-16	*destinguish*, for distinguish
Page 43	line 2	*"Ladie's,"* for "Ladies's"
Page 45	line 7	*pourtrayal*, for portrayal
Page 49	line 11	*Smollet*, for Smollett
Page 53	line 17	*pourtrayed*, for portrayed
Page 54	line 6	*Decads*, for Decades
	21	*paralels*, for parallels
Page 58	line 9	*recal*, for recall
	13	*develope*, for develop
Page 59	line 21	*begining*, for beginning
Page 60	line 15	*sensative*, for sensitive
Page 61	line 24	*covetted*, for coveted
Page 62	line 25	*abhorence*, for abhorrence

Page 64	line 26	*Geothe*, for Goethe
Page 65	line 3	*anotomical*, for anatomical
Page 68	line 32	*trowsers*, for trousers
Page 69	line 11	*ryhming*, for rhyming
Page 75	line 7	*sheherdess*, for shepherdess
Page 78	line 10	*Dovor*, for Dover
Page 82	line 7	*criticising*, for criticizing
Page 83	line 15	*shewn*, for shown
Page 87	line 10	*omniverous*, for omnivorous
Page 88	line 1	*recognises*, for recognizes
Page 90	line 22	*Roberts*, for Robert's
Page 91	lines 21-2	*chivalorously*, for chivalrously
Page 92	line 14	*recal*, for recall
Page 99	line 8	*criticised*, for criticized
Page 100	line 20	*monotous*, for monotonous
Page 107	22-3	*enquire*, for inquire
Page 109	24	*charactirised*, for characterized
Page 110	line 4	*characterised*, for characterized
	24	*sympathised*, for sympathized
Page 112	line 31	*shewn*, for shown
Page 113	line 20	*fathers*, for father's
Page 114	line 28	*Meditteraenan*, for Mediterranean

PENCIL MARKINGS

Throughout the handwritten text are pencil markings making additions, deletions, and corrections. They are in a less stable, apparently different hand than the ink manuscript. They consist of rewording, reconstructing, and omitting portions of the ink-written text. Often, sizeable sections—entire paragraphs and more—have been marked through with vertical pencil lines: these up-and-down lines vary from two or three lines through most paragraphs to as many as nine lines through the first paragraph of Part One. They include straight and curved vertical lines and diagonal slants in both directions and are often carelessly done making the extent of the intended deletion difficult to determine. Sometimes, within these vertical mark-outs are single horizontal lines deleting words, phrases, clauses, or sentences with insertions written in above the specific deletions. A number of pencil markings have been erased either purposely or because of the wear of time and handling: some of these erasures are readable while others are illegible. Because of the variety of the pencil deletions, the editor has chosen not to describe each deletion in detail, but rather has chosen to rely on the five shorthand terms listed below as typical. In order to furnish the reader with a notion of the variety and complexity involved in these pencil markings, however, a detailed description of the first three paragraphs has also been included below.

Beginning with page 7 of this edition (Part One, p. 1 of the original) there are two pencil checks (✓✓) in the lower right corner of each page in Part One; one check on each page of Part Two; one check on each page of Part Three except the last page with its lower right corner torn off (p. 70); Part Four has two checks on each page except page seven which has one check; Part Five has two checks on each page.

The following terms—with those listed at the beginning of Manuscript Alterations—will aid the reader in understanding the pencil markings:

above: refers to pencil material placed above the ink without a caret

below: refers to pencil material placed below the ink line

erased: refers to material erased either purposely or merely worn away by handling and age; such material is sometimes readable, sometimes not

marked out: refers to material marked out with horizontal lines drawn through it

V. marked out: refers to material vertically marked out

Unless otherwise stated, marked over material is written in black ink and has been retained in this edition. Material written in ink is set off by italics, while penciled material is included within quotation marks.

Page 3

V. marked out is the dedication

Page 5

V. marked out is the entire contents page

Page 7

The first three paragraphs of Part One (all on p. 1 of the original) have all been marked out by vertical lines: nine pencil lines extend vertically through the first paragraph, three of which extend into and mark out the second paragraph; one additional line is used entirely within paragraph two to mark it out; eleven pencil lines mark out original lines 1-2 of the third paragraph while one line extends diagonally through the entire third paragraph, two markings from lines 2-5, one through only lines 4-5, two through lines 5-8, and one through lines 6-8. The last line of p. 9 in the original, which consists of *Browning history*, is marked through only by the one line which extends through the entire paragraph.

Page 7

lines 17-18   Marked out is *when the many admirers of Browning should be made acquainted*; erased above *when . . . of* is "great interest will be felt"; inserted after *should* is "when the Public may"

20   A bracket is placed before *I am aware*; no end bracket is supplied

22   A bracket is placed before *I am the*; no end bracket is supplied

23   Erased after *history* [the end of p. 1 in the original] is "XXXXXXXXXXXXXXXXXXXX remains unquestioned by anything to date"

Page 8

line 1   What appears to be an inverted caret (∨) is placed before *Fortunately*

4-5   Marked out is *thus placing me in a position to do justice to the memory of my dead kinsfolk*

9   Above *world* is "reading"; above *in* is "and"

9-15   *in deference . . . Englishman.* is V. marked out

12   Above *mystery* is "supposed"

18   V. marked out is *she was* and *fine*

19   Above *specimen* is "remarkable"

Pages 8, 9-10

V. marked out are the entire paragraphs beginning *When in London . . . .*; *Having been absent . . . .*; *Unhappily, I only . . . .*

Page 8

line 21   Above *eyes bright* is "still"

23-4   Marked out is *just the same as*/above between *remember* and *seeing* is "it"; marked out is *seeing it*

Page 9

line 1   Marked out is *my*; above is "our"/added before *though* is "al"

7   Marked out is *to her at our meeting*

12-13   Marked out is *and concerning the Poet's life, as incorrect*; *with emotion*

15   marked out is *she*; above is "and"

23-6   Marked out is *Unhappily . . . indeed*; this very light mark out has probably been erased

30   V. marked out is *then*

Page 10

lines 1-2   Marked out is *possessed of the necessary information*;

above between *information,* and *it* is "that" [?]

8-9   A vertical line separates *RobertBrowning's*; after *kins-folk.* is "transferred to play"

12   Marked out is *were justifiably proud of their birth and the name they bore*

13   Above between *were* and *well* is "all"

23   Above *in* is the erased "I quote"

24   Above between *"Strafford"*; and *the* is "I quote"

25   Marked out is *This poem written by*; marked out is *I quote*; above *I* is "Poem"

Page 11

13   Above *guest,* and *had* is "and"; marked out is "then"

Pages 11-12

V. marked out is the entire paragraph which begins *Being a man*

Page 12

line 6   Above before *circumstances* is "there"; marked out is *in the family which*; inserted between *which* and *met* is "which"

7   Marked out is *destroying*; above is "+ removed"

7-8   Marked out is *he formerly had, to leave a*

16-24   V. marked out is *to get . . . papers.*

18   Above between *assisting* and *when* is a check (✓)

25   Before *I knew* is an X; marked out is *I knew Robert Browning*; above is "having known"

Page 13

line 1   After *I* is "should"/marked out is *find*; inserted after *find* is "have found it"

2   Marked out is *him*; above is "that he would have been"

3   Marked out is *leaving some account of his forefathers, or at the least,*

4   Inserted between *supplying* and *particulars* is "any" [?]

4-5   V. marked out is *when his learned father devoted all his leisure time to his son's education*

10   V. marked out between *After* and *death* is *the*; above is "his"; V. marked out is *of*; marked out is *the Poet*; marked out above after *Poet* is the pencil addition " 's death"

10-12   Marked out is *he had left among his papers, no particulars having reference to his kinsfolk; it is known that*; erased above *he had* is "Robert" [?]; marked out above between *known* and *that* is "and"

14   A diagonal line separates *kinsfolk,* and *if*

Pages 13-14
V. marked out are the entire paragraphs which begin *In a small* and *It would almost*

Page 13
line 16   Above *In a small volume* is "transposed"

Page 14
line 8   Two vertical lines separate *mysteriously* and *crooning*
9   Marked out is *at*; above is "in"
16   After *biography* is "(transferred)"
V. marked out is *If my record . . . Poet.*
23   Above between *This* and *part* is an illegible long word which seems to end in "XXXXence"
24   Inserted between *when* and *two* is "these"; "These" is superimposed on erased material: "Thus being read" [?]
25   V. marked out between *and* and *Grand* is *the*

Page 15
lines 3-4   Inserted between *London,* and *these* is the erased "their cultivated tastes"
5   V. marked out is *a*; above is "the"
9   V. marked out is *for*; above is "transferred"

Page 16
line 5   Above *the* is "learned"
6   Marked out is *learned*
15   In the upper left corner of p. 11 in the original [which begins *The first wife*] is the handwritten "Page 11"
17   V. marked out is *the*
Page 16, line 27-Page 17, line 7
V. marked out is *as shewn . . . related.*

Page 17
line 21   A pencil "d" is superimposed on the ink *s* in *has*
V. marked out is the entire paragraph which begins *In a love*

Page 18
lines 4-6   V. marked out is *I shall then give my own experience of kinsfolk gained by close association with generations of Brownings.*
In the lower right corner of p. 13 of the original is "* pedigree" and "erase page"

Page 19

On the top line of the first page of Part Two after *Part Two* is "to[?] page"; marked out is "page"

line 1   Marked out is *When I decided*; inserted before *endeavor* is "While"; above after *endeavor* is "g"

3   Inserted between *the* and *sons* is "eldest"

4-5   Marked out is *prove a safe guide; particularly the name given to the eldest son; Christian names*

8-9   Marked out is *added to and are*

10   Inserted between *a* and *son* is "the eldest"

10-25   V. marked out is *being bestowed . . . history.*

12-13   Inserted between *remains* and *unchanged* is "often"

Page 23

line 1   At the bottom of p. 4, Part Two, in the original is a diagonal line of about two inches extending from the *s* in *nobles* to below the *4* at the bottom center of the page

Page 27

line 12   Above after *clergy,* is a check

Page 31

line 3   After *"Robert"* is "* after pedigree"

6   V. marked out is *with*; marked out is *"Robert"*

6-7   Marked out is *demonstrate how that name became*; above between *how* and *that* is the erased "Robert"; above between *name* and *became* is "Robert"

12   V. marked out is *I* and *reproduce later*; marked out is *will*; inserted between *reproduce* and *later* is the V. marked out "this"

14-15   Marked out is *this book is not only a safe guide to me in following the Browning family career, but conclusively*; the *s* on the end of *proves* is V. marked out

16-17   Marked out is *the parents of the Browning boys, then being educated, must have been settled at Woodyates in Dorsetshire*; erased above between *the* and *Browning* is "these"[?]; "at" is superimposed on *in*

18   Marked out is *and then*; above is "the Parents of those boys"

19   Inserted between *as* and *other* is "is also shown by"

20   V. marked out is *to be mentioned subsequently*

20-1   Marked out is *will conclusively prove*

25-9   V. marked out is *The scenery . . . people;*; a caret is placed before *The scenery* and after *people;*

Page 32
  lines 4-5 Marked out is *he found near Woodyats*
    7-8 Marked out is *passed on to me*
    8-15 V. marked out is *the character . . . Dorsetshire.*
     14 Inserted before *Brownings* is "the"
     15 Above *to leave* is "they decided"
     15 After *Dorsetshire* is "for London g[?]"
     17 Marked out is *the Poet's*; above between *Poet's* and *family* is "his"
     20 V. marked out is *for*/ marked out is *and found, marked upon*
    22-3 Above *the words* is "showed"
     24 Marked out is *with*; above is "and"
    24-5 Marked out is *the Browning place of residence in existence on*; above *the* [*ancient*] is "in"

Page 32, line 25-Page 33, line 1
  Marked out is *the intending*; above is "a mile E from the Woodyats Inn"

Page 33
  lines 2-3 Marked out is *in Dorsetshire*; *this erroneous conclusion was*; above is "an error much"
     5 Marked out is *for*
     6 Marked out is *and*
     7 Inserted before *made* is "being"
    10-11 Below the last line of p. 14, Part Two, in the original (*to the . . . East,*) is "must have been an important place for residence"
  Marked out with a large X is the first line of p. 15, Part Two (*as . . . importance*) and the entire paragraph which begins *As this Topographical . . . .*
    13-14 Marked out is *was a work of great research, was*
     15 Marked out is *and*

Page 34
  V. marked out is the entire paragraph which begins *It was making*
    line 1 Marked out is *It was making* and *Dorsetshire*; above *a* is "using"; V. marked out is *the*; above is "as a"
    2-4 Marked out is *for her . . . for it*; above *also* is "has"
     5 Above *biography* is the erased "Published"; marked out is *-phy* on *biography*; above is -"phies"
    6-8 V. marked out is *The grandfather . . . road*; marked out is *The grandfather . . . road*

8   Marked out is *it*; inserted is "Woodyats"
11   Above *Dissolution* is "of monasteries"
13   V. marked out is *is the*/above *Woodyats* is "being really"
13-14   Above between *grandfather* and *and* is "B"/marked out
        is *and his ancestors*; above *ancestors* is "B"/above *and
        educated* is "were being educated"
16-18   V. marked out is *the very time . . . Woodyats*
22-6   V. marked out is *had ever been . . . dialect.*
27   Above before *The* is "that"

Page 34, line 27-Page 35, line 1
Above *Woodyats in 1783 as* is the erased "transferred to next XXX"

Page 35
lines 7-8   Marked out is *the two Browning brothers*; above is
            "Robert & Reuben Prowning"[*sic*]/an "X" is below
            before *the two*
8   V. marked out is *at*; above is "of"/the *e* on *the* has been
            V. marked out; above is "is" [to form "this"]
9-10   Marked out is *to seek employment in London*; after *London*
            is a large "for" superimposed on the erased "for pro-
            longed & disasters"
11   Marked out is *The*/lower case *p* on *prolonged* is marked
            out and above is capital "P"/ "s" has been added to
            war/marked out is *which had*
11-18   V. marked out is *which had raged . . . France*

Pages 35-6
V. marked out is the entire paragraph which begins *In 1785, two
years . . . .*

Page 36
line 6   Above between *stop* and *revolutions* is "a"
10   Above between *party,* and *of* is "and"
11   V. marked is *his*; above is "a"/marked out is *and*; above
            is "which"/marked out is *hope to*; inserted between *him*
            and *of* is "hopes"

Page 37
line 1   Inserted between *Robert,* and *thus* is "and"
6   Inserted between *used* and *in* is "by Bs"
7   Marked out is *by Brownings*
14-15   Added to *William* is "s"; marked out before *John* is *the*;
            added to *John* is "s"
15   Marked out before *Robert* is *the*; added to *Robert* is "s"
18   Marked out is *as will be found later*/marked out is *was*

Page 39
  lines 1-18   V. marked out is the entire paragraph which begins *In my eagerness*; an "X" also marks out the first eight lines
         5   Above between *now,* and *with* is a box (□)
         8   An initial bracket precedes *I* [it is never closed]
        12   Marked out between *him* and *Wife* is *a*; above is "his"/ inserted after *and* is "then"
     12-13   Marked out is *Robert, to become the father of the Poet*
        13   Marked out is *that*; above is "the"/*time* has been marked out by a single line which has been erased;
     13-14   Marked out is *when the Woodyates Robert Browning*; above *the* is "is"; inserted after *Woodyats* is "the elder"
        14   V. marked out is *then on*
     16-17   Marked out is *Robert Browning*; above is "thus"
        17   Marked out is *been* and *to*; above is "the RB from Dorsetshire his son and XXX XXX XXX XXX" [4 or 5 short words have been erased after "and"]
Pages 39-40
          V. marked out is the entire paragraph which begins *The books in my* . . . .
Page 39
  line 22   V. marked out is *my*; erased above is a box
       24   Above added to *the* before *family* is "ir"
Page 40
  line 2   After *gentlemen.* is some erased material which includes "my Grandfather as a p_____"
       3   Between *date,* and *to* is "is"
    13-14   After the inserted *grand uncle* is "Rueben" [*sic*]
Page 42
  line 11   Above between *of* and *fine* is "the"
    12-13   *forceful . . . years* forms the last line of p. 3 in the original; below *the family* is "260"
       19   Marked out is *to be*
       20   Marked out is *brought when a*; above is "the"; inserted between *child* and *from* is "brought"
Page 43
  line 15   Marked out is *of this book*
       17   An opening quotation mark is added before *war* [it is not closed]; a capital "W" is superimposed on the lower case ink *w* in *war*; an "o" is added before the *f* in *for* and the *or* in *for* is marked out

23-4   V. marked out is *the year in which the Independence of of the United States of America was acknowledged.*

26   Above *Such* is a box

Page 44

line 4   Inserted before *possessed* is "he"/marked out is *by him and his ability*

5   Marked out is *required*; above is "needed"

8   Marked out is *a*; above is "his"

9   Marked out is *his*; above is "little"

9-10   Marked out is *Robert, then a child, to become in after years, the father of the Poet.*

16   Above between *manner* and *indicating* is "which"; the *g* in *indicating* is V. marked out and "es" has been superimposed on the remaining *in* [forming "indicates"]

Page 45

line 6   Marked out at the end of *quaintness* is *ness*; marked out after *quaintness* is *of*

8   Marked out is *display of*

9   Marked out is *so*

14   Marked out is *the Browning*

19   Above *Browning* is "the Poet"

19-20   Marked out is *after the Brothers left Woodyats and arrived in London.*

25   V. marked out is *the*; marked out is *which was*

Page 46

lines 5-13   V. marked out is *I like to . . . Great Britain.*

5-9   Marked out is *I like to . . . 1724,*

V. marked out is the entire paragraph which begins *The three books . . . .*

line 15   Before *on* is an asterisk; V. marked through is *ir* on the end of *their*; after *Woodyates* is an asterisk

17   A box surrounds *to*/marked out is *me*

30   Marked out is *There*/marked out is *by Browning biographers*

Page 46, line 30-Page 47, line 1

A pencil line has been drawn from after *exhibited*, above *has been exhibited* and down between *imagination* and *around* on the line below

Page 47

line 1   Marked out is *around*; above is "regarding"/above between *the* and *wife* is "1st"

2-3   Marked out is *Grandmother of the Poet.*

4-6   V. marked out is *Guided by . . . wife*

4-5   Marked out is *from my*

5   Underlined is *of*; an "s" has been added to *conversation*; marked out is *both*

6   Superimposed on *e* in *the* is "is" [forming "this"]; after *wife* is a short diagonal line [perhaps a comma]

6-7   Marked out is *and influenced by tradition, current in the family, I have*

8   Marked out is *conclusion*; above is "belief"/marked out is *by*; above is "to"

9-11   V. marked out is *this conclusion . . . London*

11   Marked out is *by French refugees*

13   Before *Towards* is a circle with a dot in it (☉); erased above *end* is "beginning"; V. marked out is *18* in *18th*; above is "17"

16   Marked out is *making their*; above *escape* is "ing"

17   Marked out is *available*

18   Erased above *for* is "available"

22-3   Erased above *Havre,* is "and"[?]; marked out is *much used to embark refugees eager to reach England;*

23   Marked out is *if*; above is "refugees"

Page 48

line 2   Marked out after *road* is *to*; above is "and"

3   Marked out is *these french refugees, it is known;* above *these* is "them"

4-7   Marked out is *and among them . . . during*

6-7   Above *unsupported by the direct evidence* is erased "Statements made to me by my Parents and the"

7   Above *frequent* is "I had"

10   Marked out before *children* is *the*; above is "both"; "at" is superimposed on the *e* in *the* before *first*; erased above *first* is "lady"

12   Marked out is *with*; above is "in"

13   Marked out is *of them*

14   Marked out is *quite foreign*

15   Marked out is *with both*; above is "in"

17   Marked out is *Robert Browning*; above *Poet* is "P"

17-19   Marked out is *whom I met at his father's house and in the house of grandmother Browning*; inserted after *of* is "our"

19-20   Marked out is *markedly displayed*; erased above is an illegibility

21-2   Erased above *knew* is "best"; above *could* is "best"

Pages 48-9

V. marked out is the entire paragraph which begins *Again, if further support* . . . .

Page 49

V. marked out are the entire paragraphs beginning *The Browning* . . . ., *If the Brownings* . . . ., and *Having traced* . . . .

lines 7-8   Marked out is *on this journey of about 100 miles through a most picturesque part*

25-6   Marked out is *mode of life*; above is "of the Brothers after"; marked out is *and describe their*/a line is drawn from before *after*, around *occupations*, and under *and* and *pursuits* on the line below in the original

27   Marked out is *to myself*

27-8   Marked out is *first, if only to offer, what is termed, a guarantee of good faith*; above *first* is "here"; after *a* is added "s" and "a" [to form "as a"]

Page 50

lines 1-3   Marked out is *This somewhat remarkable and placed me in the position to hear and*; above between *This* and *somewhat* is "a"; erased above *remarkable* is "unusual"; above after *remarkable* is "a"; erased above *placed me* is "which enabled placed"; a vertical line separates *hear* and *and*; erased above *and* is "to here [*sic*] which"

3   Marked out is *use*; erased above is "describe circumstances"; marked out is *traditions* and then erased is the mark-out line

4   Marked out is *the* and *which I have used*

V. marked out is the entire paragraph which begins *I have been* . . . .

13-14   Marked out is *be conscientiously related.*

V. marked out is the entire paragraph which begins *The stage coach* . . . .

15-16   Marked out is *The stage coach or stage waggon conveying the Brownings to*; before *Brownings* a line has been added to the top of the lower case *t* in *the* to form a capital; above *to* is "reach"

16-17   Marked out is *to reach the City*; above after *City* is "the Brownings"

18   Marked out is *south of the*; after *Thames* is a large asterisk

19-21   Marked out is *The Brownings had . . . that*

19-20   Erased above after *reside* is "a suburb south of the River Thames and less than three miles from London"; the semicolon after *Camberwell* has a box around it

21   Inserted after *they* is the erased "The Brownings"

22   Above *be* is "have"; added to *be* is "en"; after *undesirable.* is erased "Page 18 par 2 page 13 par 2"; this erasure has been written over an earlier, illegible erasure

23   Marked out is *one of the brothers*; erased above is "the eldest"

24   Marked out is *soon*

25   Inserted after *time* is "that"; erased above *was* is "that"; marked out is *being*

26   Marked out is *the Continent of Europe*

27-8   Marked out is *The fighting taking place, becoming disastrous to the allied Powers*; inserted after *Powers* is "and"

28-9   Marked out is *of money required by them*; above the *ed* in *strained* is "ing"; erased above *even* is "even"

Page 51

line 1   An "X" is superimposed on the semicolon; marked out is *when*

1-9   V. marked out is the remainder of the paragraph from *the French King . . . notes.*

10   Above before *Throughout* is an "X"

11-12   Marked out is *before cash payments were renewed*

12   Marked out is *from Woodyats*

16   Before *became* is inserted "and"

18-19   V. marked out is *and wondering . . . soldiers.*

V. marked out is the entire paragraph which begins *This Woodyats Robert . . . .*

22   The lower case *v* in *volunteer* is altered into a capital "V"

25   Before *In 1785* is a large asterisk

25-6   Marked out is *the neighborhood of Camberwell, as a place for residence, was very attractive, the*; erased above *for* is "of"

26   Above after *the* is an asterisk; erased above *houses* is "there"; marked out is *were*

26-7   Above *situated in well* is "in Camberwell were"

Page 52

line 2 After *flowers.* is a box and "they therefore selected this attractive neighborhood for their future residence"

V. marked out is the entire paragraph which begins *Many names given . . . .*

7   Marked out is *comprised*

13-15 Marked out is *It is not . . . Camberwell*

15   Above and after *Camberwell* is "and in that neighborhood"

16   Marked out is *and developed*; inserted before *instructed* is "and"

17   Marked out is *he*

19   Marked out is *and*/above *of* is "the"

24   Marked out is *then*

Page 53

line 1 Marked out is *When*; capital "I" is superimposed on lower case *i* in *in*

6   Marked out is *ruminate*; after *ruminate* is "meditge" and a circle with a dot in it

7   Above *Leaving* is a circle with a dot in it

7-8   Marked out is *the quiet life, which for over thirty years, he had passed in Dorsetshire*; above *the quiet life* is "Dorsetshire"

9-13 Marked out is *and performing . . . itself*; erased above the semicolon is a box with a dot in it

14-15 Marked out is *assumed the importance and what I must term*; above is "developed"

16-18 Marked out is *easily to be . . . seen*

19   Marked out is *pencil*; above is "brush"

24   Above after *maintenance* is "for"

Page 54

line 1 Inserted between *he* and *married* is "whom"; above *Woodyats, how long* is "I am not aware"

3   Marked out is *I am not aware* and *near me as I write*

8   Marked out is *given*

11   Above *afforded* is "may have"

11-12 Erased above *residing* is "while"[?]

18   Marked out is *and attention*

22   Marked out is *employed*/ marked out is *divert and*

24   Inserted between *give,* and *made* is "here" and the

erased "were in the Browning books"

25   Marked out is *Browning books*; above the marked out *one* is "the 1st" superimposed on the erased "the first"

Page 55

line 1   Erased over *second* is "other"

1-2   Marked out is *when they are compared*; above is "in 1793"

4   Marked out is *evidences*; above is "shows"

5   Marked out is *shows*

6   Marked out before *Bank* is "the"

6-7   Marked out is *men of business*

14-16   V. marked out is *fortunately* and *averted consequences that might have prevented the name Browning from becoming famous in literature*; marked out is *occurred which*

17   Added to *lad* is " 's"; marked out is *Robert's*

18-20   Marked out is *at the Bank of England, every week becoming more perplexing to him in consequence*

20-2   V. marked out is *of the effect . . . Europe*

22   Marked out is *found no time or opportunity to indulge*; erased above *opportunity* is "no"; inserted after *indulge* is "had relinquished as puerile"

23-5   Marked out is *Robert Browning . . . citizen*; crossed out is *his*; marked out is *mind*; above is "thoughts being"

26   Marked out is *London*

28   Marked out is *Browning*

30   Marked out is *of Woodyats while*; above is "still"

32   Marked out is *had used great judgement in*; erased above *in* is "which"; the *ing* on *humouring* has been marked out and "ed" is erased above

Page 56

lines 1-2   Marked out before *woods* is *in the*

3   Marked out is *had*; above is "and"; marked out is *the boy*; above is "him"

4   "y" has been added to *an*; marked out is *advanced*; above is "but a practical"; marked out is *and*; inserted after *and* is "but had excused"; marked out is *excused*; marked out is the *is* in *his*; "t" has been placed before the remaining *h* and "e" after the *h* [to form "the"]

5   Inserted before *arising* is "as"

6   Marked out is *official*/above *Uncle* is "his"

7-10   Marked out is *and had . . . remarried*

9-10   Erased above *that* is "the"; erased above *Woodyats re-married* is "when his father"; erased above after *re-married* is "and"

10   Inserted before *in* is "apparently"

11   Erased above *and* is "for he"

11-12   Marked out is *and, though the new house was at no great distance from Camberwell he*

13   Erased above *decided* is "had"/below *decided to stop his son's studies* [part of the last line of p. 17 in the original] is "the guidance of Reuben Browning"; after "Browning" is the ink *17*; after *17* is a penciled box

13-14   Marked out is *being continued under Reuben Browning's guidance.*

14   Erased after *guidance* is a box with a circle in it with a dot in the circle; erased above is "only teaching"

Pages 56-7

V. marked out are the entire next four paragraphs which begin *The retired quiet life . . . .; The Woodyats Brownings . . . .; Visiting a theatre . . . .;* and *Leading such a retired . . . .*

Page 57

line 15   Marked out is *Leading such a retired mode of life*; erased above after is " □ of"

17   Marked out is *but*; above is "until"

18   Marked out is *was*; above is "had been"

20-1   Marked out is *After the removal of the Woodyats Robert Browning to Peckham*; erased before *After* is the inserted "but"; erased above before *of* is "to"; erased above *the* [*Woodyates*] is "his"; above *it* is a box with a dot in it; erased is a line which marked out *it soon*; a vertical line separates *that* and the marked out *his*; above is "the"

23   Marked out is *they*/inserted before *gladly* is "who"/inserted after *with* is "their

24   Erased above after *Camberwell* is "but the"

Page 58

line 1   Erased above *lad's education* is "imminent change in"; marked out is *therefore was*; erased above is being; erased above *continued in* is "averted for a time XXX in"; superimposed on the erasure is "for awhile"

2   After *formerly.* is a circle with a dot in it ⊙

3-17   V. marked out is the entire paragraph which begins *It is a pleasure . . . .*

9	A pencil "l" has been added to *recal*
18	Inserted between *be* and *understood* is "easily"
19	Marked out is *developed at Camberwell*; erased above is "had"; above after is "had fixed"; after *in the* is "lads"
20	Marked out is *Robert Browning*
21	After *poetry* is a circle with a dot in it

Page 58

Erased are the vertical lines which mark out the entire paragraph which begins *It can be understood . . . .*

Pages 58-59

V. marked out are the entire paragraphs which begin *As proof of . . . .* and *In the year 1800 . . . .*

Page 59

line 9	Erased after *Margaret* is an "X"
10	Marked out after Woodyats is *Robert Browning*; *his arrogant City*
19	Before *It* is a circle with a dot in it; marked out is *just*; above is "fair"; mark out line through *this* has been erased; erased above *against* is "the" [?]
20	Marked out is *cultivated*; above is "artisting"; a pencil line is drawn under *was*; above is "[erasure] quite"
22	Above before *it* is "for"
23	Marked out is *all*
24	After *vagabonds*, is an "X"
24-9	V. marked out is *and to regard . . . City man*
30	Marked out is *country's commerce, now that*; inserted after *that* is "X disdaining art in any form the City Aristocrat when"; erased after "when" is "his"; the entire phrase is written over an erasure

Page 60

line 1	Marked out is *had*/marked out is *his father*
3	Inserted between *checking* and *literary* is "his"
4	Marked out is *his son* and the *ing* on *making*; superimposed at the end of *making* is an "e" [to form "make"]/above *a* is "him"
7	Marked out is the *g* at the end of *belonging*; superimposed on the *in* is "ed"
13	Marked out is *even ridiculed a literary training*; *then*
15	A pencil "i" has been superimposed on the *a* in *sensative*
16	Above *was shipped* is "as a young"

32   Erased above after *brothers* is "had"; marked out is *a time had*; above is "had awhile"

Page 61

lines 1-3   Marked out is *and through that position was associated with the leading financiers and wealthy citizens of London*

4   Marked out is *as*

5-6   Marked out is *by those occupying substantial residences*

10   Marked out is *I sometimes think that it was the*; above is a circle with a dot and "this"

11-12   Marked out is *at Camberwell, which hastened the sending of*; above is "may have had some weight in"

12   "s" has been added to *Browning*; above *to* is "being"

13   Marked out is *as will be found subsequently*; inserted after *subsequently* is "but"

16   Above *Jane Browning* is "my Mother"

17   Above between *marriage,* and *when* is "being"

17-18   Marked out is *being a great favorite with*; above is "a frequent visitor at"

18   Inserted after *Reuben* is "house"; erased after "house" is "where she"

19-21   Marked out is *while assisting her . . . Jane Browning*

22   Marked out is *when my Mother*; inserted after is "she"/after *of* is "her"

23-5   V. marked out is *though passed without the many excitements covetted now by girls filling a similar position in society*

V. marked out is the entire paragraph which begins *It is only fair* . . . .

33   Marked out is *the*; above is "her"

Page 62

lines 1-2   Marked out is *the Woodyats*/marked out is *Browning*; V. marked out is *which*; erased above is "it"

3   Marked out is *and affection for his Niece*

6   Marked out is *yet*

12   Inserted above between *his* and *daughter* is "2nd"

18   Before *Robert* is "Young"

26   Marked out is *prospects*; above is "interests"/marked out is *on*; above is "in"

27   Inserted after *witness* is "the"

31   Marked out is *a*; above is "the least"/marked out is *abuses*; above is "cruelties"

Page 63
lines 3-4   Marked out is *by the early instruction given by Reuben Browning, from him he had imbibed*; inserted after *imbibed* is "and"
5-8   Marked out is *his refined instincts . . . home.*

Page 64
line 1   Marked out is *to produce the reflection*
5   Inserted between *him* and *command* is "the"
6-11   Marked out is *to a refined artistic . . . England.*
12   A pencil mark underlines *The good*; marked out is *of London*
12-13   Marked out is *Woodyats Robert Browning, his*; above is "his Father's"; erased above after *intimacy* is "of XXX XXXX"
14-15   Marked out is *who, after the battle of Waterloo, was a man of great influence, when he*; above is "and"; above *founded* is an illegible scribble
24   Erased is a line marking out *This*; above is "yet" superimposed on an erasure

Page 65
line 13   After *absence.* is an inverted caret and "After his marriage"
14-19   Crossed out is the entire paragraph which begins *The love felt by . . . 1812.*
17   Marked out is *combined to bring forward*; above is "brought"
19   After *1812.* is an "X"
20-1   V. marked out is *The representatives of two generations of Brownings, born at Woodyats*; superimposed on an erasure above is "RB + his Sister [?]"; a line is drawn from in front of *The* under *The representatives of two* and down to divide *infant* from *Browning* on the line below/ marked out is *at*; above is an "X" and "of"
21-2   Marked out is *Browning at Camberwell*
22   Erased is a pencil line marking out *planned*
22-3   Marked out is *he should be reared and educated to become a poet!*
23   Above *The same system* is "It was resolved"

Page 65, line 24-Page 66, line 1
Marked out is *it was resolved*

Page 66
    line 3   Marked out is *when first brought to Camberwell*
    10-11   Marked out is *for the infant son*
    14   Marked out is *a*
    19-22   V. marked out is the entire paragraph which begins *This beginning of a poet's . . . .*

Page 67
    line 2   V. marked out is *employed*
    6-26   V. marked out is *whether from a dread . . . South.*

Pages 67-8
    V. marked out are the entire paragraphs which begin *Facilities for reaching. . . .; One unexpected development. . . .;* and *Aunt Reuben's son . . . .*

Page 68
    line 25   V. marked out is *paternal and maternal*
    27   Inserted between *their* and *nephew* is "new"

Page 68, line 28-Page 69, line 3
    V. marked out is *as he grew . . . City.*

Page 69
    line 4   Above *When* is "After"
    6   Marked out is *the*; above is "a"; above between *local* and *school* is "day"
    10   Inserted after *repeating* is "his"
    15   Marked out is *as a boy*
    18   Marked out is the *d* at the end of *justified*; "y" is superimposed on *ie* [to form "justify"]
    24   Above *ever* is "had"
    29   Inserted after *given* is "by his Father"; V. marked out is *own*
    29-30   Marked out is *by his own*
    30   Marked out is *made the*; a "d" is added to *resolve*
    31   Inserted between *his* and *brain* is "own"
    33   Marked out is *own*

Page 70
    line 3   Marked out is *reared*

Page 71
    lines 1-2   Marked out is *of Woodyats*
    3   Marked out is *the familiar*
    3-6   V. marked out is *of Surrey, without the former kindly teacher, though associated with many pleasures, only retained a mournful interest*

6-7   Marked out is *being situated*
7-8   Marked out is *Islington, I was*
8   Inserted after *child* is "was"

Page 71, line 14-Page 72, line 8
Erased are vertical lines marking out the paragraph which begins
When at Colebrook Row . . . .

Page 72
line 1   Marked out is the second *his*; above is "the"
17   V. marked out is the *ne* on the end of *none* [leaving "no"]
18   V. marked out is *the*/inserted after *tall* is "with"
19   Marked out is *robust and exhibited*

Page 73
line 2   Inserted after *years* is "he"
5   Marked out is *The*; above is "Thomas"
6   Marked out is *Thomas, named after his grandfather*
7   Marked out is *he*; erased above is "and"; marked out is *ed* on *aroused*; above is "ing"
8   Marked out is *and*; above is "he"; erased before *was* is an insertion
9-18   V. marked out is *When a lad he . . . career*

Page 74
line 1   Marked out is *in a fit of temper*; above is "lately" [?]
3-13   V. marked out is *Knowing at the time . . . fame*
8-9   Marked out is *of race*
11   Marked out is *in*; before is "to"
13   Marked out is *after this disregard of opportunity, Uncle Thomas*; above is "and"
14   Marked out is *in Melbourne*
15-16   Marked out is *a strange*; above is "his"
16   Marked out is *in something incomprehensible to me*
18-27   V. marked out is the entire paragraph which begins *Grandfather Browning in his* . . . .

Page 75
line 3   Marked out is *tolerated*; above is "kindly treated"
14   Above before *whenever* is "and"
16   Marked out is *though their*

Pages 75-6
V. Marked out is *very red lips . . . house!*

Page 76
V. marked out are the entire paragraphs which begin *How*

changed the customs . . . . and *The Colebrook Row garden* . . . .

lines 30-1   Marked out is *I think, a romantic feeling or an instinct created in the family by association with localities*; erased after *family* is the inserted "created"

32   Inserted after *with* is "happy"; below after *Camberwell* is an "X"

32-3   Marked out is *by the Woodyats Browning brothers, on first coming to London; that influenced its members*; above after *members* is a circle with a dot

Page 77

line 3   Above after *Surrey* is an "X" and "which led the family"; marked out is *situated*

19   Inserted before *Uncle* is "my"

Page 77, line 22-Page 78, line 6

V. marked out is *one of my sisters . . . death.*

Page 78

line 7   Marked out is *playful naming from*; above is "puzzled remark on"

9   Marked out is *his*; above is "whose"

12   Marked out is *of the house*

15   Marked out is *inconsistent*; above is "inconcievable" [*sic*]

16   Marked out is *admirers*; above is "readers"

17   Marked out is *writings not one of them has suggested*; above is "Poem no attempt has been made for"

18   After *Cottage.* is "were [*sic*] so many of them were written"; marked out is "them"; above is "his works"

Page 79

line 4   Inserted after *that* is "a"

5   Marked out is *Robert*/above after *favor*, is "which"/ superimposed on *ing* in *opening* is "ed"

6   After *meadows* is a pencil comma

13   Marked out is *or*; above is "and"

Page 80

lines 2-3   Marked out is *when writing*; above after is "and"

4   "ir" has been added to *the*

7   Above *living* is "with him"

27   Erased is the mark-out line through *absorbed in her own*

27-8   Marked out is *importance or considering*; inserted after is "with"

30   Marked out is *much*; above is "any"

Page 80, line 31-Page 81, line 2
    V. marked out is *Uncle Robert's family . . . dampness.*

Page 81
    line 3   Marked out is *The Poet's*; above is "Young Robert's"/
                  inserted after *from* is "his"/marked out is *gave*/
                  erased above after *rise* is "even"/marked out is *at this*
    4   V. marked out is *to* after *that*
    5   Marked out is *credit for*
    6   Marked out is *Robert Browning's*; inserted is "the
                  Poet's"
    6-7   Marked out is *we really had some justification for our
                  belief*; before *all* is a check
    8   Marked out is *a man*; inserted before *very* is "was"
    10   Marked out is *Uncle Robert's*; above is "his"
    11-12   Marked out is *hence that belief I often heard expressed in
                  the*
    12-13   V. marked is *expressed in the family that Uncle Robert
                  assisted in the production of the early Browning poems.*
    15   Above after *irritation* is "for"
    17   Erased before *The* is "when"; V. marked out is *London*
    18   Above after *manager* is "in London"
    20-3   V. marked out is *at a time when . . . days*
    22   V. marked out is *to*; inserted is "from"/above after
                  those is "now"
    23   Marked out is *in these days*; erased above *days* is "and"
    24   Marked out is *on*; above is "as to"

Page 82
    line 4   Marked out is *not by our Cousin the author of the play, but*
    7-8   Marked out is *fully resolved that in criticising the new
                  play, we would be generous towards it's faults and*
    8   Above after *would* is an "X"; after *and* is an "X"
    9   Marked out is *for the sake of the family; unhappily*
    10   A line is drawn from after *audience* under *in the audience* to
                  before *soon* on the line below in the original; marked out
                  is *were not of our way of thinking and*; erased above *and* is
                  "many"
    14   Marked out is *in the audience*
    15   Marked out is *was certainly*; marked out is *to us;
                  unfortunately*
    22   Marked out is *by the author*

Page 83

line 1   Inserted before *the* is "and When"; marked out is *by/* above *of* is "their"

1-2   Marked out is *at this manifestation, the author's Cousins*; inserted is "we"

3-4   Marked out is *themselves or*; inserted is "ourselves and"; the "and" is superimposed over an erased "or"/marked out is *they*; above is "we"/erased above after *were* is "as"

5   Inserted after *or* is "we" [?]/after *with* is a circle with a dot; above is "or"

7   "s" has been added to the end of *writer*

8   Marked out is *towards*

9   Marked out is *We were not particularly concerned at the non-success*; after is an "X"

10   Before *had* is an "X"

11   After *during* is a circle with a dot/marked out is *it's*; above is "the"

10-19   V. marked out is *had we known . . . time.*

20-1   Marked out is *One ebullition of the Robert Browning temper was witnessed by me most unexpectedly*

29   Marked out is *savagely*

Page 84

line 1   Marked out is *for he*

2   Marked out is *he savagely*

5   V. marked out is *a*; inserted is "the"

8   Erased above after *rider* is "had"

14   Marked out is *I saw in fancy*; above is "I recollected"

22   Marked out is *to my awakened imagination*

23   Marked out is *on that dark night long ago*

24   Marked out is *horse*

27-8   Marked out is *I can trace how*

28-9   Marked out is *at the time of writing*

Page 85

line 1   Marked out is *still*

2-3   Marked out is *kinsfolk are*; erased above after *ignored* is "his kinsfolk"

3-4   Marked out is *one mode of mentioning a kinswoman I particularly regret.*; erased above is "one instance of mention"

6   Marked out is *and, it will be remembered*

14-15	Marked out is *I can state from my own knowledge, that*
16	V. marked out is *more*
16-17	V. marked out is *likely to . . . kinship!*
21	Above after *"York"* is "is"
22	Marked out is *was Uncle Reuben's Saddle horse*

Page 86

lines 1-2	Marked out is *who not only placed the animal at his nephew's disposal, but was*
3	Erased above *always* is "always"; V. marked out is *other*; after *kindness.* is "to his nephew"
5	Marked out is *of him*
5-6	Marked out is *at the time they were written*
8	Marked out is *or help towards*
9	Marked out is *mere*; above is "proper"
9-10	Marked out is *by those whom he objected to*
10	Marked out is *consider his kinsfolk; he absorbed his father's*
10-16	V. marked out is *consider his kinsfolk . . . domesticity.*
15-16	Marked out is *or a knowledge of the meaning of the word domesticity.*
30	Marked out is *after*; above is "at"
31	Erased above before *This* is "This"
32-3	Inserted between *family;* and *his* is "and"

Pages 86-7

V. marked out is *This expressed intention . . . "Browning"*

Page 87

line 18	Marked out is *I can state on the best of evidence*
19	Marked out is *for*

Page 88

line 17	Marked out is *we then journeyed together, as was the custom*; above is "which"
18	Inserted after *ago,* is "meant"
19	Marked out is *we had to*; inserted is "and"; inserted after *hold* is "ing"

Page 89

lines 1-2	Marked out is *ourselves from*; marked out is *in*
3	Marked out is *we were*/ marked out is *ed* at the end of *subjected*
4	V. marked out is *I*/erased is a line through the *ed* on *used* and *to think*/ marked out is *even then, that such*
5	Marked out is *ill* and the *ed* on *ill-accorded*; above is "ill" and "ing"

6-8	Marked out is *standing at my side, for I knew that the Robert Browning establishment*; above is "whose"
8-9	Marked out is *with my Uncle's*; above is "his"
9-15	Marked out is *long since taking . . . parties.*
11	Marked out is *that*; erased above is "somehow" [?]; inserted after *Robert* is "was"
12	Marked out is *very*
13-14	Marked out is *upon pleasant times he was enjoying with newly made fine friends, but deploring*
16-19	V. marked out is *Uncle Robert . . . persevering*
20	Marked out is *endeavors to remove the cause of my suffering.*
21	Marked out is *laboriously*
22	Marked out is *the writing of*; above is "his"
24	A horizontal line is drawn immediately above *no*; above is "him no"
26	Marked out is *unknown to*; above is "unshared by"/marked out is *at a time*
26-7	Marked out is *felt discontented with his position and*

Page 90

lines 4-8	V. marked out is *towards the middle . . . others.*
9	Marked out is *Whatever faults*; added to *Young Robert* is " 's"; erased above after "Young Robert's" is "faults were due to his"
9-10	Marked out is *exhibited, resulting mainly from his home training*; superimposed on the *ing* in *resulting* is "ed"
10	Marked out is *was assuredly*
11-12	Marked out is *morals, the whole family knew, his writings substantiate this fact, that*
13	Marked out is *and*
15	Above the semicolon after *innocence* is "and"/marked out is *the*; above is "his"
17	Inserted after *must* is "also"
19	Marked out is *sent to New Zealand*
20-1	Marked out is *at the time of writing.*
23	Marked out is *both the lovers, assisted by the*; above is "the aid of"

Page 91

line 2	Erased above before *as* is "to Wimpole Street"
7	Marked out is *impelled*; above is "compelled"
10-11	Marked out is *perfectly secured*

11	Marked out is *as admitted*
13	Marked out is *of*; above is "from"
14	Marked out is *exhibiting*
16-17	Superimposed on the *'s* of *poet's* is "ic"/marked out is *for the mysterious, by the selfish*; inserted is "for the"/ marked out is *to some natures*
17	Marked out is *derived from*; above is "of"; marked out between *or* and *the* is *from*
18	Marked out is *in*; inserted is "from"; marked out is *arising from*; above is "involved in a"
19	Marked out is *in Wimpole Street*; above is "to her home"
20	Marked out is *a*; above is "the"; above after *characteristic,* is "of"
22	Inserted after *sacred* is "ly"
27	Marked out is *were*; above *all* is "were"
27-8	Marked out is *the affection they felt for him or his sweetheart*

Page 92

line 2	V. marked out is *middle aged invalid who had accepted his love*
6	Marked out is *this fancy*
7	Inserted after *confirmed* is "the idea"
7-8	Marked out is *I remember hearing at the time that*
8	Inserted after *"Robert"* is "it was thought"
10-11	Marked out is *who had been*
12	Marked out is the *t* on *dreamt*; above is "ed"
13	Marked out is *a*; above is "their"
14	Marked out is *one courteous and*; above is "a"
16	Marked out is *in calm state*
25	Marked out is *as*

Page 93

line 3	Marked out is *to the old lady*
7	Marked out is *I thought afterwards*
11	Marked out is *had*; inserted is "may have"
18-24	Marked out is the entire paragraph which begins *I remember, after. . . .* Below this final paragraph of Part Four is "gy was it ever repaid"; in the lower right corner of p. 23 in the original is the diagonally written "8300"

Page 95

V. marked out is the entire first paragraph which begins *I now have to touch* . . . .

Page 96

line 1	Marked out after *and* is *an*; above is "the"
13	Marked out is *connected with*; inserted is "for"
19-20	Marked out is *surprise my*; erased above *Whatever . . . treatment* is a long illegible pencil entry
20	Inserted after "*Robert*" is "neither"
21	Marked out is *showed it very little*; inserted is "nor"; erased after *had* is the inserted "all"
22-3	Marked out is *never alluded to his*
24	Marked out is *the elders of the family*; above is "them"

Page 97

line 2	Inserted after *Aunts* is "they"; it is superimposed on an erasure
3-13	V. marked out is the entire paragraph which begins *Having always been* . . . .
18-19	A vertical line extends through *shaking* and through *Terrace* on the line below
22	Marked out is *this great change in his hopes*
23	After *philosopher* is a caret
24	Marked out is the *ing* on *expressing*; above is "ed"
33	Marked out is the *ity* on *humanity*; above is "nature"

Page 97, line 33-Page 98, line 2

V. marked out is *she quite lost . . . you*"

| 34 | Marked out is *I heard*/above after *say* is "ing" |

Page 98

V. marked out is the entire paragraph which begins *I remember one* . . . .

line 16	Marked out is *I confess*; above after *never* is "had"; marked out is *much*
17	Marked out is *actually*
17-19	V. marked out is *expressed her . . . Sarianna.*
19	Marked out is *one*; erased above is "when one of my"
20	Marked out after *of* is *the*
22	Marked out is *patiently*
25	Above after *death* is "and"; erased above after *Sarianna* is "and"; erased after *Browning* is the inserted "the Poet"

Page 99

lines 3-4   Before *until* is an "X"; marked out is *until existence became to him simply mechanical*

5   Inserted after *performed* is "but"

9-10   Inserted after *seek* is "for sympathy"; marked out is *for sympathy*

17-18   Marked out is *property*; inserted after *never* is "I believe"

18   Marked out is *as far as I am aware*

20   Erased after *ladies* is the inserted "Grandmother and the widow of the Aust"

24   Inserted after *his* is "own"

Page 100

line 1   V. marked out is *a*; added to *strip* is "s"

2   Added to *garden* is "s"

10   Marked out is *other*; inserted is "Lady" which is super-imposed on an erasure; inserted after *widow* is "of an Austrian Capt" which is superimposed on an erasure

11   Marked out is *one*

23-4   A line is drawn from after *expression,* to in front of *to ripen* on the line below

25   Inserted before *iron* is "the"

30   Marked out is *simple minded*

Page 101

line 2   Marked out is *fronting the road*

9-10   Marked out is *that*; above is "Young Roberts"/marked out is *a stranger, begun*; above is "made" which is superimposed on an erasure/marked out is *by* "Young Robert"

10-11   A line is drawn from in front of *in* curving under *in Wimpole Street* and curving up after *Street*

13   Marked out is *both the ladies*; after is "to them all"

23-4   Marked out is *to both their sweethearts*

Page 102

line 2   Marked out is *and resolute management*

3   Inserted after *over* is "the"

4-5   Marked out is *from Wimpole Street*; crossed out is *his*

5-6   Marked out is *old father, in his eagerness to follow up the success attending his anonymous letter*; erased above *father* is "man"

7-9   V. marked out is *in the house . . . courtship.*

8-9	Marked out is *that occupied . . . courtship.*
8	Inserted after *by* is "to" [?] and the erased "that of"
10-13	V. marked out is *As grandmother Browning . . . bow*
13	Marked out is *to the old lady's surprise the*; above is "and a"
14	Erased above *when* is an illegibility; marked out is *she*; above is "the old lady"
16-17	Pencil parentheses are around *at first*
17	After *was* is inserted "at first"
19	Marked out is *when*; above is "he"; marked out is the *g* on *passing* and superimposed on the *in* is "ed"; marked out is *the next door*; above is "her neighbors"
19-20	Marked out is *with head turned*; erased above is an illegibility
21	Marked out is *the astounded old lady*; above before is "unnoticed"; inserted is "she"
24	A vertical line separates *"grin"*, and *so*; another vertical line separates *smile* and , *through*; marked out is *the*
25	After *without* is a check
32	Erased above after *Browning* is "after XXXX"
33-35	Marked out is *made . . . makings*; above is "wrote to her Brother the Poet comfortably settled in Italy begging him to at once take action to avert disaster, this letter intended to divert disaster proved more disastrous than any ~~previous~~ than any previous event in the family for"; erased after "for" is "XXX XX betrayed"

Page 102, line 35-Page 103, line 3

Marked out is *his daughter, having no cause to doubt her father's sanity, felt that her self-importance had been ignored, her dignity offended*

Page 103

lines 3-21	V. marked out is *forgetting that her . . . order.*
4	Marked out is *realize that by*; above is "see"; marked out is the *ing* on *discouraging*; above is "ment"
4-5	Marked out is *if not slighting*
5	Marked out is *simple*; erased above is "artist's"; marked out is *she*
8	Marked out is *simply*; above is "merely"
10	Above after *machine* is "which worked for more than 40 years"
11	Below after *smile* is an "X"
11-12	Underlined is *between iron pickets*

15	Marked out is *his*
16	Marked out after *of* is *the*; above is "his"
20	Erased above *bread-winning* is "and bring the"
21	Erased above after *machine* is "shamed"
22	Erased above *The letter* is "This le"
23	Marked out is *his*; above is "him"
24-5	Marked out is *the time*
22-32	V. marked out is *The letter sent . . . thought*;
25	Marked out is *of*
30	Marked out is *father*; above after is "had"/marked out is *himself*
31	Marked out is *his father's unselfish*
31-2	Marked out is *forbade the thought*
33	Marked out is *his father's simple nature*; erased above is "the"

Page 104

line 1	Marked out is *completely*
2	Marked out is *at New Cross*
3-19	V. marked out is the entire paragraph which begins *Filial affection failed . . . .*
12-14	Marked out is *dominating nature prompted him to take upon himself in Italy, the management of his father's love affair at New Cross.*; above marked out is "his impetuous"
15	Marked out is *the poet*; above is "he"
18	Marked out is *and*; above after *after* is "wards"; marked out is *their meeting*
20	Marked out is *We never learnt what really*; erased is the inserted "whatever"
22	Marked out is *simple minded*; inserted is "their"

Page 105

line 4	Marked out is *being*; inserted is "having been"
5	Inserted after *she* is "had"
7-8	Marked out is *past doubts were revived and magnified*
12	Marked out is *to marry the Austrian Captain's widow*
12-14	V. marked out is *as grandmother Browning had formerly said "poor Robert could not call his soul, his own"; the breadwinner*
14-16	Marked out is *departed from Paris instructed by his children to stop all further communication with his sweetheart*
17	Marked out is *her*; above is "the lady"
18	After *father.* is "but in his haste forgetting to see"

19-20 Marked out is *Robert and Sarianna Browning were too anxious to prevent their father re-marrying, to perceive*

Page 106

line 2 Marked out is *simple*; above is "foolish"

3 Erased before *wrote* is the inserted "the Poet"

19 Inserted after *exceed* is "ed"

21 Above after *1850*, is "gr" [?]

Page 107

line 2 Above *son-in-law* is "Sutor"

4 Erased above after *letter* is "to the Bank of england"

7 Marked out is *by the simple old man*; erased above is "him"; erased after *with* is "the remark"

10 Erased above after *was* is "being"

22 Erased above after *circumstances* is "and"

27 Erased above *visit to Paris* is "to XXXX children in"

28 Marked out is *and the*

Page 108

line 12 Above after *publication;* is "which"

21 Marked out is *that*

27 After *an* is a check

Page 109

lines 1-2 Pencil quotation marks have been placed around *designing woman*

11-12 Marked out is *known and respected*

24 V. marked out is *he*; inserted is "but"; inserted after *the* is "the old mans"

24-5 Marked out is *sent by his client*

Page 110

line 11 Marked out is *is*; above is "was"

18-19 Marked out is *otherwise, regardless of results and forbade the marriage*

19-20 Marked out is *the Poet*

22 Erased above after *defaulter;* is "for"

29-30 Marked out is *his feelings receiving small consideration from his children, his regard for punctuality and*

Page 111

line 5 V. marked out is the entire paragraph which begins *After the evidence* . . . .

9 Erased above after *assistance* is "they had"

10-11 Marked out is *he caused*; erased above is "unreas"; above "from" is superimposed on the erased "for this"

11	Marked out is *of his father*; above is "of"
13	Marked out is *reticence*
15	Inserted after *has* is "in my silence"
16	Erased after *Uncle Robert's* is an inserted illegibility
16-17	Marked out is *as I have endeavored to show*
19-22	V. marked out is *Though he had been . . . body.*
22-5	Marked out is *From relations who . . . "own",*
29	Erased above after *Being* is "by a pension from the Bank of England"
30-1	Marked out is *free from his children's interference, simple minded but learned*

Page 112

lines 1-2	Marked out is *philosophy turning his exile into a pleasure*
2-5	Marked out is *he never returned . . . Camberwell;*
9	Marked out is *in her ways*
9-10	Marked out before *simple minded* is *as*/marked out is *we*
11	Above after *met* is "by us"
18	V. marked out is *us*; above is "the"/above after *people* is "amongst us"
23	Inserted after *be* is "again"
25-8	V. marked out is *she must be . . . mourners.* The period has been marked through and after is "only given to men"
29	V. marked out is *undertaken as a duty*
29-30	Marked out is *my family*/marked out is *wish*; above is "gladly"/marked out is *I was able*
31	Marked out is *conscientiously to*/above after *record* is "ed"/marked out is *any act of*; above is "some small"

Page 113

line 2	Marked out is *all of*; above is "all"
5	Marked out is *the Poet*
5-10	Marked out is *in Italy or after . . . visit*
10	Above before *my* is "His Aunt"; erased after *Mother* is the inserted "his Fathers sister"
14	Above *made aware* are some illegible erasures/erased above after *her* is "Nephew"/marked out is *wanted*; above is "welcome never repeated her visit"
15	Marked out is *troubled him with another*; above is "paid"
16	Marked out is *also called, but*
16-17	Marked out is *a feeling of*; above is "their"

23   Above after *his* is "Reuben"/above before *parental* is "the"

Page 114

line 3   Marked out is *blooded*

6-7   V. marked out is *the want of something which makes poetry speak to throbbing hearts of all generations?*

8-19   Crossed out is the entire paragraph which begins *In the early days* . . . .

APPENDIX I

Newspaper Accounts of *Von Müller* v. *Browning*

The following newspaper accounts of the trial for breach-of-promise of marriage involving Robert Browning Senior appeared in "Law Report," *The* (London) *Times*, Friday, July 2, 1852, p. 6, and "Law Report," *The* (London) *Morning Chronicle*, Friday, July 2, 1852, pp. 7-8. Mason discusses this case in Part Five.

The Times.

COURT OF QUEEN'S BENCH, Thursday, July 1.

(Sittings at Nisi Prius at Guildhall,
before Lord Campbell and a Special Jury.)

Von Müller v. *Browning*

Sir A. Cockburn and another learned gentleman were counsel for the plaintiff; and Mr. Willes for the defendant.

Sir A. Cockburn stated that this was an action to recover compensation in damages for a breach of promise of marriage. These cases had more or less romance in them, but he was sorry to say that in this he could not present any such attraction. The plaintiff was a lady of mature age, being 45 years old, and the defendant was 20 years older; but although there was no romance, there was peculiar interest in it on account of the peculiar circumstances of the case. The plaintiff, Mrs. Von Müller, was the widow of an officer in the Austrian service. She was an English lady, whose maiden name was Haynes. In early life she had married a Mr. Meredith. Her first marriage was a very unfortunate one; her husband proved to be a spendthrift and a libertine; he got into debt, fell into licentious habits, ruined his family, went into the Spanish service, and ultimately died in that kingdom. Mrs. Meredith, upon her husband's leaving, took refuge with her father and mother, and remained for several years without receiving any tidings of her husband. Rumours arrived from Spain that he had perished there. She had a son and daughter. She met with Captain Von Müller, who was very much struck with her, paid her great attention, and proposed marriage to her; she accepted him conditionally that she should not marry until she got evidence of her husband's death. In the year 1836 she received conclusive evidence of Meredith's death, and then she married Captain Von Müller.

170

Mr. Willes said he did not mean to cast the smallest imputation on the plaintiff—his client was incapable of it.

Sir A. Cockburn—The defendant might be incapable of doing so in court, but he had done it again and again in the most cold-blooded manner. The action was brought not only for the purpose of recovering compensation for the breach of promise, but for the wanton and malicious manner in which he had acted in endeavouring to defame her character. Her second marriage was a happy one, but again this lady was doomed to misfortune; for having had another child, she was a second time left a widow. She then again went to live with her father and mother at New Cross. The defendant, who had been for nearly 50 years in the Bank of England, resided near their residence; he was struck with her appearance. He used to pass the house waving his hand and looking with great earnestness. There was some talk about her going abroad. This, it would seem, was too painful for him, and he sent her an anonymous letter to this effect:—"I hope you will forgive the question, as you are the last person I would give offence to. May I ask, is it true that you are going to quit England? I do not ask from motives of idle curiosity. Need I mention my name? December, 1850." Some amusement was afforded by this letter; but one lady who was in the house had no doubt from whom the letter had come. In a short time the defendant met her in the street, and accosted her, asked leave to accompany her home, and declared his intentions. The plaintiff shortly afterwards went to reside at Upton, and the defendant then commenced a correspondence with her. At first the letters began with "My dear Mrs. Von Müller," but they soon grew warmer. The learned counsel then read upwards of 50 letters which were written by the defendant to the plaintiff; most of them commenced with "My dearest, dearest, dearest, dearest, dearest, dearest, much-loved Minny"; they were couched in terms of greatest warmth, and professed the most intense love of the writer for the lady whom he was addressing. Sometimes there was introduced a considerable essay upon theological subjects, then they would refer in terms of doubt of the propriety of marrying her, in consequence of the statement the plaintiff had made to him regarding the history of her former life, and particularly as to her second marriage, charging her with having been guilty of crime or gross error; but the letters following these would express the greatest regret, and would contain the most abject apologies, even upon his knee, for having written such letters, and assuring her that the hateful subject should never be mentioned again, and that the whole should be confined to his own breast. All these letters proved the defendant to be a man of education and considerable literary attainments. The defendant had returned two or three of the plaintiff's letters, which were evidently written by a very sensible woman. At last the defendant went to his son at Paris, and on the 1st of November a letter was received from the defendant's son, stating that his father had informed him of the manner in which she had annoyed him, and of the persecution he had undergone for some time. The plaintiff wrote a letter in answer, expressing her extreme surprise. Upon this the defendant wrote to her, beginning his letter with "Mrs. Von Müller," and in that letter he gave as a reason for breaking off the match her misconduct from the time she was a girl, "Has not your whole career, from your running away from school to your settling at New Cross, been one continued series of everything but respectable? I believe that when you married your second husband you knew that your first husband was alive." The learned counsel then charged the defendant with having been guilty of the most cruel cold-blooded cowardice in the conduct to the woman to whom he had professed so much attachment. The defendant concluded the last letter by stating that he should write to her brother, her son-in-law, and her doctor, who had been a most intimate friend of hers, stating the circumstances to which he had alluded. Those circumstances he knew to be a deliberate, villainous lie. The three persons the defendant had named immediately went to him, and then he said he should reserve his defence until an action should be brought against him. Under such villainy he now called upon the jury to give large damages.

The following evidence was then adduced:—

Samuel Sutor.—I am a shipowner. I married the plaintiff's daughter. I first knew her about 1846. She then lived at New Cross with her father and sisters. Her father died in 1850. I afterwards went to reside at that house. In December the plaintiff received an anonymous letter; she was going to put it in the fire, I stopped her, saying, it was a document that ought not to be destroyed. The defendant introduced himself to me in the Bank of England some time after the receipt of that letter. I had frequently seen a gentleman pass the front of the house in the month of December or January. He used to wave his hand at the windows of the house for, perhaps, the 16th part of a mile, until he waved himself out of sight; this was after the receipt of the anonymous letter. I had my suspicions as to whom was meant. I afterwards found this person was the defendant. I afterwards went to Brighton, and the plaintiff went to stay at my house at Upton. I knew by the letters that the plaintiff and defendant were corresponding. I carried two letters to him at the Bank. He said, "You are Mr. Sutor, I know you by your portrait." That was in

May. There was a portrait of me at my house at Upton. I returned to town in May. In November last I went with Mr. Hales and Mr. Collinson to the defendant at his house at New Cross. I told him I was very sorry I could not call upon him earlier, but I had just arrived from America. I had waited upon him in reference to Mrs. Von Müller. I referred to his letter of the 6th of November, and I handed it to him, and asked him if it was in his handwriting. He said, "Yes." I read to him that part which alluded to myself, Mr. Hales, and Mr. Collinson, and asked him for an explanation. He said he should reserve his answer for his self-defence. I asked him if he knew the contents of his son's letter. He replied, he did not, but that it was his son's letter. I then alluded to the anonymous letter Mrs. Von Müller had received. He said it was his writing. I then showed him several packages of letters, which he admitted to be in his handwriting. I asked, as he was not then under the influence of his son, whether it was his intention to carry out his original views with Mrs. Von Müller. His reply was "What do you mean?— marry Mrs. Von Müller?—Certainly not." I then said I had no other course to pursue than to send him a letter from a solicitor. I know several branches of his family.

Cross examined.—He said Mrs. Von Müller had threatened him with an action, and he reserved his answer. The defendant has grown up children. The plaintiff has a family. I married her daughter. She has a son and daughter by Mr. Meredith and a son by Captain Von Müller; he is about 14 or 15. I took no great interest in the matter.

Re-examined.—The plaintiff is 47 or 48 years of age.

Mrs. Sutor.—I am the daughter of the plaintiff. I was brought up by my grandfather. He died in 1850. My mother told me she was corresponding with the defendant. I knew his sisters who had resided next door to my grandfather. One of them made me a present on my marriage. I had seen the defendant kiss his hand to the window. My mother introduced me to Mr. Browning at Mr. Collinson's in May. My mother went to live at Mrs. Hart's who was a friend of hers. The defendant visited my mother at her house. He appeared to be paying her attention.

Mr. Alfred Collinson.—I am a surgeon, and resided at New Cross. I know the plaintiff very well, and have done so for six years. She resided with her father. I have known the defendant. I attended his first wife, who died in 1849. I should think he was from 60 to 65 years of age, strong and active. I accompanied Mr. Sutor and Mr. Hales to call on the defendant. I have known the defendant to call upon the plaintiff at my house. I was aware there was a very busy correspondence going on. I have seen them walking together on very amicable pleasant terms. I heard some of the extracts of the letters read—some of the theological parts.

By Lord Campbell.—The amorous parts were not read. It is just possible that some of those parts were read to me.

Re-examined.—The plaintiff was proud of the defendant's intellectual acquirements. He lived as a man of 500£, or 600£, a year would. He lived in a quiet gentlemanly way.

Cross-examined.—I did not visit him as a friend.

By Lord Campbell.—When she read the letters it was with strong expressions of esteem, not at all with levity. She was much pleased with his regard for religion.

Mrs. Collinson.—I have known the plaintiff some years. She communicated to me the circumstances that had taken place between her and the defendant. The defendant has frequently come to my house with messages for the plaintiff. The breaking off the match has affected her very much. Her energy is gone. She has suffered a very great deal. Our intimacy still continues.

Mr. Hart.—My wife and the plaintiff are very old friends. My wife is very ill. I have known the plaintiff from her childhood. I have seen her with the defendant.

Mrs. Sophia Carter.—In September, 1851, Mr. and Mrs. Hart came to live with me. The plaintiff came to visit me about the 23d of September. The defendant came to see her immediately, and continued to come frequently. They were alone together. The defendant came to me early this year. He told me of the action. He said she had made a statement to him which was very much against her; that no person was ever loved as he had loved her at one time.

The official return of Mr. Meredith's death was put in; he died on the 17th of March, 1836, in Spain. The certificate of the marriage of the plaintiff with her second husband on the 19th of May, 1836, was put in.

Mr. Willes then addressed the jury for the defendant. He designated the action as an idle and trumpery case. There was one case in the books something similar to it, and that was the great case of "Bardell v. Pickwick." The letters were those of a besotted old man; they were the encores of dotage. His client was a poor old dotard in love. The learned counsel went through the letters with the acumen of a clever special pleader, and called upon the jury to give the smallest amount of damages.

Lord Campbell then summed up.—It seemed to him that this was a case where the damages should not be so large as some that came before the Court, nor by any means so small as to mark any opinion of theirs that the plaintiff had misconducted herself. He did not discover that this lady had held out any lure to this old gentleman; his folly was his own folly. He was smitten with her charms, became attached to her, and asked her to marry him, which she had consented to do. He was a clerk in the Bank, living in a very creditable manner, and was evidently a man of great intellectual powers and of considerable attainments. The plaintiff had been disappointed in her expectations, and was entitled to damages. He agreed with Sir A. Cockburn that if this old gentleman, thinking better of the matter, had come to the opinion that at his advanced period of life, and with his son and daughter, it would be more prudent and expedient not to enter into a fresh matrimonial contract—if he had made a representation upon this subject to the lady—he might have been blamed to a certain degree, but very little to that which it seemed to him he was now to answer. But how had he conducted himself? He must say in a most cowardly manner. He had written the letter of November, wherein he made the imputation against the plaintiff. It appeared to him a very gross case. Exemplary damages the law did not recognize; damages should only be a compensation for injury sustained.

The Jury wished to know what salary the defendant received.

A clerk in the Bank stated that it was about 320£ a year.

The Jury then retired, and in a short time returned into court and gave a verdict for the plaintiff—Damages, 800£.

The Morning Chronicle.
COURT OF QUEEN'S BENCH
[Sittings in London before Lord Campbell
and a Special Jury.]
Thursday, July 1

Von Müller v. *Browning*

Sir A. E. Cockburn, with whom was Mr. T. Chambers, stated that this was an action for a breach of promise of marriage, which the plaintiff had been compelled to bring, nor merely on account of the manner in which it had been broken. In truth, not only had her feelings been wounded, and her just and reasonable hopes disappointed, but the defendant, in the meanest and most scandalous manner, had feigned reasons for the breach of his contract. There was little romance about the case. The defendant was a clerk in the Bank of England, of about the age of 65. The plaintiff was a widow lady of the age of 45, the widow of an officer in the Austrian service. She was an English lady, whose maiden name was Haynes. In early life she had married a Mr. Meredith. Her first marriage was a very unfortunate one, for her husband proved himself a spendthrift and a libertine, who, by his licentious habits, ruined alike himself and his family. This first husband went into the Spanish service, and ultimately died in Spain while in service in the Legion there. Left by that husband without provision, she took refuge with her father and mother. For some years she remained without receiving any information of her husband. But though he sent her no information, rumours of his conduct reached this country, and finally it was said that he was dead. In these circumstances she met with Captain Von Müller, who admired her very much, paid her great attentions, and proposed marriage. She had led a very unhappy life with Meredith; she was then in a state of dependency; she admired and esteemed the man who sought her hand, and it might well be conceived that she was glad to accept an offer which promised her that happiness she had failed to win in her first marriage. She accepted his offer conditionally. If the news of Meredith's death was confirmed she agreed to marry. The news was confirmed in the beginning of the year 1836, and then she married Captain Von Müller. He mentioned these things, because in a letter of the defendant's which put an end to his promise, he had wantonly, falsely, and grievously misrepresented her conduct.

Mr. Willes, who appeared for the defendant, said that he did not mean to cast the slightest imputation on the plaintiff—his client was incapable of it.

Sir A. Cockburn said that the defendant might be incapable of doing this in court at this moment, but he had done it before in writing, and in the most cold-blooded manner. The lady had, as he said, married again. She had another child, and she was very happy in her marriage, but her husband died, and she was again an inmate of her father's house at New Cross. The plaintiff had been living with her father and mother, and the defendant, who resided near them, had seen her and had admired, and had become attached to her. The defendant was considerably advanced in life, the lady was not a very young woman, but she was many years younger than he. Still, however, though no longer a young man, he was hearty, active, and full of spirits, and might reasonably be deemed a younger man in life than his years would denote. He introduced himself to the lady first by writing an anonymous letter, and then by avowing himself the author of it. The jury must recollect this fact, for it would be this day set up as a defence that the lady was entrapping him, and that she was taking advantage of his folly, and turning it to her purposes. The fact was the other way. The defendant introduced himself, pressed his suit with ardour, was unceasing in his letter-writing, and sought to give the plaintiff a high idea of him, not only on account of his literary acquirements and his general knowledge, but also on account of his theological inquiries and his religious sentiments. All these letters were couched in language of the warmest affection and the sincerest respect. The learned counsel read a great number of letters, in which the efforts at display on all these points of erudition were considerable, and in which the expressions of affection were of the very tenderest nature. Having gone through these letters, he said he now came to the breach of the promise which in these very affectionate terms had been made to the plaintiff. He had told the jury of the painful circumstances of her first husband's misconduct. She had in the most frank, and honourable, and confiding manner told the defendant all that history. After being told it, though he was at first disposed to blame her for her hasty acceptance of the offer of Captain Von Müller, he afterwards withdrew his suggestions of blame, and declared that his respect for her was as great as his affection. The defendant had a son who was married; this son was going abroad; the defendant went with him to Paris, and there, no doubt under the influence of the son, he broke off the match. But, instead of doing it in a frank, honorable, and manly manner, acknowledging that his own wishes had led him into an engagement which, though his feelings and his honour required him to fulfill it, his family demanded its breach, and that he threw himself on her generosity to pardon the sacrifice he was making to his family's wishes; instead of doing this, he indicted a most scandalous, mean, and cowardly letter, full of falsehoods, in which he insinuated that he was the victim of her arts, and that her whole course of life had been anything but respectable, and said—"I believe that when you married your second husband you knew that your first husband was alive." To this scandalous and false imputation of misconduct he added the threat that he would lay the whole matter before the plaintiff's son-in-law and two other gentlemen who were intimate with her family. The plaintiff's answer to this threat was to put his letter into their hands, and to abide by their advice as to the conduct she should pursue towards the man who had thus wronged her. She wrote him a very beautiful and ladylike answer (the learned counsel read it), and then submitted to their advice; and she now appeared to claim from the jury the compensation to which she was entitled for conduct as mean, false, base, and cowardly as could be perpetrated towards any woman.

Mr. Samuel Suter: I am a shipowner at Stratford. I married the plaintiff's daughter. I have known the plaintiff about five years. She was then residing at Hatcham-terrace, New-cross, with her father and sisters. Her father died, I think, in 1859. I went to Hatcham-terrace in December. I went to have the advantage of Mr. Collinson's assistance. Plaintiff was there at that time, my wife was with me. Plaintiff received an anonymous letter, that was in December. It was shown to me. She was going to throw it in the fire. I said that is a document, which ought not to be destroyed. I occupied a room on the second floor front. That gave me a view of the opposite side of the road. Defendant introduced himself to me in the Bank of England about May or June, 1851. I had seen a gentleman pass the front of the house in the months of December and January. I did not know him. I afterwards found it was the defendant. He used to begin on the opposite side of the road and wave his hand towards the window. I could not make out which window it was. He used to do so for the distance of the 16th part of a mile. He continued waving till he waved himself up to the house. After the anonymous letter another came acknowledging the anonymous letter. I afterwards went to Brighton. The house in Hatcham-terrace was afterwards given up. I then arranged with plaintiff, my mother-in-law, to come and stay at my house. After my return from Brighton I carried two letters to the defendant at the Bank. That was when he had introduced himself. Defendant recognized me by my portrait. I was at Marseilles, in March and April. I returned to town in the early part of May; while I was absent plaintiff had charge of my house. I had an interview with the defendant on the 26th of November last. I went to him with Mr. Hales and Dr. Collinson. He had made use of my name in a letter. I saw him at his house. I had just arrived from America. I told him I had waited on him with reference to Mrs. Von Müller. I then referred to his letter of the 6th of November from Paris. I had the letter with me, and handed it to him. I asked him if it was in his handwriting? He said, "Yes." I then read him that part which alluded to Mr. Hales, Mr. Collinson, and myself, and asked him for an explanation. He said he should reserve his answer for his self-defence. I then asked him if he knew the contents of his son's letter? He said "No," but that the letter was in the handwriting of the son. I then alluded to the anonymous letter. I showed him the other letters which had been put in my hand, and said I had no other course to pursue than to put the letter into the hands of my attorneys.

Cross-examined: The plaintiff had threatened the defendant with an action, and he said that it was upon that he should reserve himself, for his self-defence. The defendant was a widower. I did not know his family. I have heard that his daughter was keeping his house for him.

Re-examined: Plaintiff is about 47 or 48.

Mrs. Suter: I am the wife of the last witness. I was brought up by my grandfather. In the beginning of 1851 I went with my husband to New Cross, then to Brighton, and thence to Marseilles. I remember my mother receiving an anonymous letter. She was going to throw it in the fire. My husband prevented her from doing so. I knew defendant before that letter. I had seen him bow to the house and kiss his hand.

Cross-examined: I had not seen the defendant, to speak to him, before I returned from Marseilles. I know his daughter by sight. The defendant's son is a married man, with a family.

Mr. Collinson: I am a surgeon, residing in Cromwell-terrace, Harrow-road. I resided at New-cross for ten years. I knew the plaintiff. She resided with her father and mother. I also knew the step-mother of the defendant, who resided next door. The defendant is about sixty or sixty-five yars of age. He is an active, healthy man. I don't know whether he has much power of conversation. I believe he has considerable attainments. I went on 26th November last, with Mr. Suter and Mr. Hales, to call on the defendant. I have seen the defendant call on the plaintiff while she has been staying at my house. I was aware that there was a busy correspondence going on—a great many postman's knocks at my door. I have seen them walking together. I have heard extracts from the letters.

Cross-examined: I mean the theological parts, on the doctrine of election and Strauss' opinion about the Christian religion.

Re-examined: The lady was proud of the defendant's intellectual attainments, and that was the reason she read these extracts. He lived at the rate of about £500 or £600 a year, in a quiet gentlemanly style.

Again cross-examined: I never visited him as a friend, but only as a medical man; attending first on his wife in 1849, and then, after her death, on himself.

By the Chief Justice: Plaintiff spoke in a tone of great admiration of his acquirements and his religious sentiments. She spoke of his letters with pleasure, but never with levity.

Mrs. Collinson: I have known the plaintiff five or six years. She communicated to me the circumstances that took place between herself and Mr. Browning. I have seen them together, and met them in the street; they were walking arm in arm, and appeared quite friendly. Since this affair was broken off, she has suffered a great deal. Mr. Collinson has been attending her. She has been in my house.

Mr. Hart: I have known the plaintiff from her childhood. I have known the defendant since his acquaintance with the plaintiff began. He has called at my house with a note for her.

Mrs. Sophia Carter: I remember in 1851 a Mr. and Mrs. Hart coming to lodge in my house. Plaintiff came to visit Mrs. Hart. Mr. Browning came there to see her. My husband was very ill at the time. Defendant came frequently.

The official return of the death of the first husband, Thomas Meredith, was put in. He died on the 17th of March, 1836.

The plaintiff was married at St. Pancras on the 19th of May, 1836, to Mr. Von Müller.

Mr. Lofty, the plaintiff's attorney: I knew plaintiff before her marriage with Captain Von Müller.

Mr. Willes then addressed the jury for the defendant, and contended that the damages here ought to be of the smallest possible amount. There was no pretence to talk of wounded feelings and blighted hopes, and the cause was a very dull cause, because the action was a trumpery action. He was sure he was not exaggerating, or using an improper expression, when he said that the plaintiff was infatuating this old man, and that the defendant was only rescued from the folly of his dotage by the legitimate and proper influence exercised over him by his son at Paris. There the old man had, in the natural confidence of his heart, told to his son, and then he had been brought back to a reasonable and proper line of conduct. The learned counsel referred to a great many passages in the letters to prove that his client was a dotard over whom the plaintiff had the power to exercise an influence which required to be put an end to. There must probably be a verdict for the plaintiff, but he trusted that the jury would look on the case as one requiring the smallest possible amount of damages.

Lord Campbell in the course of his charge to the jury said that this was a form of action in which the damages might vary very much. It seemed to him that the damages here ought not to be so large as in some cases, where the tenderest feelings of the heart had been cruelly crushed, nor so small as not to mark the opinion of the jury that the plaintiff had been guilty of no misconduct.

The jury at first said that the damages ought to be a year's salary of the defendant, on which a question arose what that salary really was; and at the suggestion of Mr. Willes, and by the consent of Sir A. Cockburn, a clerk in the Bank was called, who said he did not think it was more than £300 to £310 a year. On cross-examination he said that the defendant had been there nearly fifty years, but he did not believe his salary to be above what he had stated. He did not know whether the defendant had any property besides his salary.

The jury retired to consider the case, and returned a verdict for the plaintiff—damages, £800.

APPENDIX II

Newspaper Articles Based on Mason's Manuscript

The following are newspaper articles based on Mason's manuscript and written by his great-grandson, John R. Scarlett, for the *Sydney*, Australia, *Morning Herald*; they are taken from photostatic copies in the Armstrong Browning Library. The article entitled " 'Young Robert' " is dated November 27, 1937, and is found on p. 7, column 7, of the *Morning Herald*, while "Lawsuit of the Long Ago" is from p. 13, column 7, of the June 25, 1938, *Herald.*

"YOUNG ROBERT"
Browning's Bad Temper.
AUSTRALIAN RECORD.
By John R. Scarlett

A young man, filled with vitality, quick to take offence, short-tempered, and immensely fond of praise, is a description of Robert Browning, which I found in a collection of notes and manuscripts in the bookcase.

In faded ink, the name-page reads: "The Poet Robert Browning, and His Kinsfolk, by his Cousin, Cyrus Mason."

Cyrus Mason, who lived in Sandringham, Victoria, was my great-grandfather, and, as a first cousin of the poet, he was the last of his generation conversant with that race of Brownings who came to London from Dorsetshire about 1785.

When he was in London, in 1900, Cyrus Mason visited his aunt, Sarah Browning, the last survivor of the Dorsetshire Robert Browning's children. Although aged 85, the old lady retained an almost youthful charm. She spoke of the poet's death, and his funeral, which she had attended, at Westminster Abbey, a recollection which caused her eyes to flash, as she condemned published accounts of Browning's family history as "monstrous fabrication." This was not unnatural, for the poet's forebears, although familiar with their interesting ancestry, left no record of family history behind them, and when Robert Browning's death occurred it was found that he had ordered his friends to destroy the letters which he had written to them.

In a small book, a few of Browning's letters to Alfred Dommett, a friend living in New Zealand, have been preserved. They were written at a critical stage of the young man's life, when he was struggling against adverse circumstances. Although Dommett was an intimate friend, Browning made no mention of his people, whom he seemed to regard with unnatural antagonism. From the day when his eccentric Aunt Margaret was seen, crooning strange prophecies over his cot in the house at Camberwell, to the years when the world began to acknowledge his work, everyone looked upon "young Robert" as a superior being, and believed implicitly in the future for him.

The House at New Cross.

Shortly after Browning published "Sordello," my great-grandfather's parents moved to New Cross, Surrey, where the poet's family also lived. The Browning house, on the south side of the Dover Road, was about three-quarters of a mile from Deptford. It was an ideal setting for young Browning to weave his thoughts into those verses which were to become his first successes. From his mother's rose garden, a little path led to a wicket gate, opening on to the broad Surrey meadows, and Dulwich Woods.

All these surroundings of the poet my great-grandfather knew, at the time when Browning was describing them in letters addressed to a Miss Elizabeth Barrett of Wimpole Street, London. The story of that romance, which has been dramatised on Stage and screen, is well known. Little wonder that Browning's impassioned descriptions of Surrey fields and hedgerows made Elizabeth Barrett resolve to leave her invalid couch and to enjoy the beauties of Regent's Park.

Browning was conveniently placed, for each member of the New Cross household was constantly self-absorbed. His father's leisure was devoted to reading, or to wandering through the fields with his prized sketchbook; his mother's first thought was her garden, and his sister, Sarianna, was always busy with her work at the chapel she attended.

The family heard Macready, a leading actor-manager in London, had asked Browning to write a play which would be produced at the Drury Lane Theatre. The news was received with mixed feelings, and there were grave debates on the propriety of the young man's entrance to affairs connected with the stage.

Accompanied by another Robert Browning, my great-grandfather attended the first performance of "The Blot on the 'Scutcheon." The production was poor, however, and the play did not succeed. One scene, intended by the author to be romantic, caused much merriment. On a rope ladder, attached with reckless insecurity to the heroine's window, swung the lover, murmuring a gentle serenade. He had reached the end of a line when the word "Drop" was hissed with quiet urgency. The stage-hands' failure to comply immediately with his request added to the confusion.

Browning's disappointment at the reception given to his play was not shared by his people, when they heard later of his violent outbursts of temper at the rehearsals.

A Midnight Encounter.

An illustration of the poet's ungovernable temper, apparently inherited from his grandfather, is shown by a dramatic incident which occurred on the New Cross Road in the early hours of the morning.

Cyrus Mason had attended a theatre in the city, and was walking home along the road beside the Greenwich Railway. It had been raining heavily, but the storm had passed, and the moon made the shadows of the trees lie in black pools on the roadway. He had reached a turn in the road, when he heard the beat of a horse's hoofs. The next moment a horseman, riding at a vicious gallop toward London, swept upon him. Leaping to one side, as the animal brushed his cloak, the young man shouted in astonishment:

"Are you mad!"

Unable to stop at once, the rider pulled his horse on to its haunches, wheeled about, and rode at his accuser with uplifted whip. Mason stood still, and then recognised horse and rider. The horse was "York," which belonged to Reuben Browning, the poet's uncle, and its angry rider was Robert Browning himself. Seeing that it was his cousin who stood before him he lowered his whip, and turning again, he galloped off.

When Browning's love-letters to Elizabeth Barrett were published, the family's opinion was confirmed that "young Robert's" upbringing had so implanted in him notions of his own superiority that he regarded personal assistance as fitting tribute to his genius.

A remark made by him on one occasion in my great-grandfather's presence is typical of the lofty attitude he adopted when he was with his people. The two young men were talking with the poet's grandmother in the drawing-room of the house at New Cross, when the old lady asked her grandson:

"Robert, why don't you write something we ordinary folk can understand?"

Browning did not reply at once. He rose, and walked to the windows, where he stood looking out, hands clasped behind his back. Then, without turning his head, he answered petulantly:

"I must tell you that what I do write is not intended to be understood by this generation."

This unexpected reply so surprised his grandmother that she flushed and shook her cap strings indignantly. Her grandson left the room hurriedly, leaving a member of a first and third generation looking at each other in astonishment.

Browning's farewell to that same old lady was for him unusually flattering. As she sat in her chair one morning the door was thrown open, and Browning ran to her side, his face alight with excitement. Taking his startled grandmother's hands in his own, he exclaimed:

"A monstrous mistake! According to the Book of Common Prayer, a man is forbidden to marry his grandmother—the pity of it!" He then kissed her impressively, and walked briskly from the room.

It was undoubtedly the completion of arrangements for his elopement with Elizabeth Barrett that caused his excitement. Probably the gallant kiss given to the oldest member of the family, constituted to his mind a poet's farewell of mother, father, sister, friends, and native land!

LAWSUIT OF THE LONG AGO.

The Browning Family.

A Quaint Romance.

By John R. Scarlett.

When Robert Browning fled to Europe with Elizabeth Moulton Barrett, without having once presented her to his family, he caused his people much grief. But it was not the last occasion on which he was to prove a source of unhappiness for them, for, although it is not generally known, a single thoughtless action, typical of his reckless nature, led, indirectly, to the banishment of his father from England.

In personal appearance, Robert Browning the elder, the father of the poet, bore a strong resemblance to the pictures of John Wesley. He was a loveable, eccentric old man, and, above all, was immensely proud of his reputation for punctuality. Only once did he arrive late at his desk at the Bank of England. He had been caught in a noisy crowd of Londoners who had gathered to see 14 men hanged!

The Captain's Widow.

At the death of his wife in 1849, the poet's father become [sic] completely dominated by his daughter, Sarianna. His modest expenditure was criticised, his little peculiarities ridiculed, and his love of study treated almost with contempt. It was no wonder that the old man's affectionate nature prompted him, at the age of 68, to seek sympathy elsewhere. He found that sympathy in the smiles of a Mrs. Von Müller, the widow of an Austrian army Captain, who lived next door to his mother in Hatcham Terrace, New Cross.

His old mother always looked for her son's return from the city, and acknowledged his bow as a part of the day's proceedings. A day came, however, when, through absent-mindedness or miscalculation, the filial bow was made too soon—before the house of the captain's widow. Mrs. Von Müller often sat at her window, and recognising the elderly passer-by, she graciously answered the salutation, which became a regular occurrence.

So prettily did she respond that the elderly Browning, unaccustomed to affection for so long, soon bowed himself into her presence, and made his introductions. He lost no time in assuring her of his love, and like his enterprising son, the poet, he wrote many impassioned letters. He, too, felt it wisest to keep his romance a secret, and when he heard that Mrs. Von Müller was thinking of visiting Europe, he sent her, in December, 1850, an impetuous letter, without signing his name, and avowing his "undying affection." It was a test of reciprocity, and it succeeded.

"Poor Robert."

His aged mother's surprise may be imagined, when she saw her son come into view one day, not striding along as usual, but bowing low, and backing along the pavement, hat in hand, and his face creased in a happy smile. When he passed her house, without looking in her direction, she called quickly to her daughter, and told that "poor Robert" had "lost his senses." No sane man, she said, would "grin" in such a fashion, without turning once to his mother's window. Robert was obviously mad. His daughter must be told. It was Sarianna's duty to look after him, and if she failed in her duty the police must be summoned immediately!

Sarianna Browning, the poet's sister, was deeply offended when she found that her father intended to marry again. She considered that her importance was being ignored, and that her brother should be informed. Robert Browning, the poet, on receiving his sister's letter in Italy, was incredulous. He was convinced that his father was being victimised, and in his reply he ordered his sister to bring their father to Paris, where he would decide what should be done.

His forceful children soon made their father promise to forget Mrs. von [sic] Müller. This was relatively easy, for without thought of subterfuge the old man confided innocently that he had once doubted whether

her first husband was dead when she married Captain von Müller. To his children this was proof of their father's credulity. They did not know that the lady had received many passionate letters, and that her acceptance of his proposal was based on real affection.

Blind to these facts, the poet wrote from Paris to Mrs. Von Müller probably the most insulting letter a woman could receive. He questioned her "respectability," and threatened public exposure if she continued her "persecutions."

Mrs. Von Müller, when she received the letter, wrote at once to the elder Browning, expressing her grief and "supreme surprise." Her letter was not answered, and she would have been content to take no further action, but her son-in-law, a Mr. Sutor, was present when the poet's letter arrived. He went straight to Threadneedle Street. The old man confessed his complete ignorance of the letter, but added: "I recognise my son's handwriting."

This was enough for Sutor, who asked bluntly:

"Now that you are not under your son's influence, is it your intention to carry out your original views, and marry Mrs. Von Müller?"

"Certainly not," was the reply.

The answer left Sutor no alternative. His wife's mother had been unjustly insulted in writing, and he immediately instructed his lawyer to bring an action for breach of promise.

"From the Old Lady."

The trial began in 1851, before Lord Campbell, and was reported in the "Morning Chronicle" and "The Times." In open Court 50 of the elder Browning's love-letters were read aloud, to the amusement of his friends in Threadneedle Street and St. Swithin's Lane, who, satisfied that the gossip about the plaintiff was true, and not knowing of the poet's letter, thought it was a huge joke. One letter had begged for a glove as a token. When a cousin of the poet arrived at his office at Rothschild's he found a collection of old gloves, shoes, handkerchiefs, and caps, with a card explaining that the gifts were from "The Old Lady of Threadneedle Street."

Counsel for the defence described the letters as those of "a poor old dotard in love," to be unheeded by intelligent men. He would ask the Court to award the plaintiff, whose respectability was unquestioned, "the smallest amount of damages."

Lord Campbell held that the elder Browning was "a man of great intellectual powers and considerable literary attainments." The letter from his son to the plaintiff was a "very gross case."

The jury returned a verdict in Mrs. Von Müller's favour, and the poet's father was ordered to pay damages of £800.

The extraordinary fact was that both parties were genuinely fond of each other. The poet not only humiliated his family; he put his father into the position of a defaulter, for the old man was unable to pay the damages and costs, and he had to leave England.

He never returned, but remained in Paris until his death, 15 years later. He became a familiar figure, as he peered among the books and treasures of the curiosity shops, or sat with his sketch-book in the parks. At the age of 84 died, happy in the knowledge that he had seen his wayward son's destiny fulfilled.

APPENDIX III
GENEALOGY

Robert Browning m Elizabeth Pethebridge
(of Woodyates, Pentridge,
Dorsetshire; 1695?-1746)

Thomas (of Woodyates Inn; 1721-1794) — (twins) — Robert (1721-1746) m ???

Reuben (1722-?)

Elizabeth (1719-?) m Thomas Harper

m Jane Morris

Elizabeth (1750-1757)

Thomas (1753-1755)

Reuben (1756-1827) m Widow Mason, with son John 2nd m (1794) Jane Smith (1771-1848)

Christian Rose (1757-1813)

William (1759-1781)

Richard (died in infancy)

Thomas Pethebridge m ??? Robert (1780-1866) m Mary Freeman Mary Louisa m J. J. Baddeley E. Baddeley (female) Vincent Baddeley

Robert (of Dorsetshire; 1749-1833) m Margaret Tittle (1754-1789)

Margaret (1783-1858)

William (b. 1784-died in infancy)

Robert (Father of Poet; 1782-1866) m Sarah Anna Wiedemann (1772-1849)

Sarianna (1814-1903)

Clara (d. 1818)

Robert (Poet; 1812-1889) m Elizabeth Barrett (1806-1861)

Robert Wiedemann Barrett (1849-1912) m

William   Christiana   Jane Eliza   Reuben   Mary   Louisa   Thomas   Jemima   Sarah
Shergold   (1799-1825) (1800-1880) (favorite uncle;   (1805-1864)   (1807-1887)   (1809-1878)   (1811-1880)   (1814-1902)
(1797-1874)   1803-1879)

Jane Eliza
m
John Mason

Reuben
m
Margaret Lewis

• Cyrus Mason
(1828/9-1915)
(4th of 9 children)
m
Mrs. John Conway Montague
(widow with 2 children)

Elizabeth
m
Cornelius Deacon

Laura Mason   Other children

Vyvyan m ?

Richard McDonnell
m

Elaine m W. F. Baly

Barbara Constance   Laura Madelaine

Alfred Scarlett
m

John R. Scarlett

Locket portrait of Jane Browning, the poet's aunt and Mason's mother. Courtesy of Elaine Baly.

AFTERWORD

How seriously to take Cyrus I am not sure, yet as the poet's cousin and near neighbor he was in a position to observe, and if we allow for a certain bias, his observations are worth noting.

Maisie Ward's *Browning*, I, 10

My account drawn from traditions which I have heard related by our kinsfolk, coupled with circumstances that I have personally observed, will I trust furnish the admirers of Browning's writings with interesting matter for reflection; the intrinsic value of his poetry will remain unquestioned by anything which I am able to relate.

Cyrus Mason, p. 7

"The Poet Robert Browning and his Kinsfolk" provides a most interesting family portrait to reflect on, and certainly first reflections should focus on its author, Cyrus Mason. Biographical facts known about him are few: he was born in London into the large family of Jane Eliza Browning and John Mason, emigrated to Australia where he secured a government appointment with the railways, married and reared his own large family, and died in 1915 at the age of eighty-six in Melbourne. Though his maternal grandfather, Robert Browning of Woodyates, occupied an important post in the Bank of England and earned a substantial salary, Cyrus's immediate family seems to have been less well set, vocationally, financially, and socially. John Maynard even regards them as "poor relations" in their following first the grandfather and later his widow in several moves about London and its environs.[1]

----

1. *Browning's Youth*, p. 363. Several disparate bits of information together seem to corroborate such an impression. John Mason, stepson to the Reuben of Woodyates who held a minor position in the Bank of England, grew up in a household which was less financially and socially successful and more interested—by Mason's own testimony—in the arts and liberal education. The Dorsetshire Robert gave to Jane Eliza £100 when she married John Mason—a consideration which he does not seem to have conferred upon any of his other children and which was presumably made

While John Mason's vocation is not known, it is perhaps
revealing that, in contrast to the family tradition of setting up
relatives in banking careers, all of his sons except the eldest left
England to pursue careers: Cyrus and Philip went to Australia
and Arthur to New York. Even Reuben, the eldest, seems to have
left London for Bristol.[2] The overall pattern here, however, is the
familiar Browning ideal of moderate, if only relative, middle-
class success as each generation sought to advance the clan in
accordance with the Victorian ideal of progress. And in most
respects Cyrus Mason seems firmly rooted in the Victorian middle class, one generation removed from the rural counties, which
proliferated in and around London in the early nineteenth
century.[3]

In accordance with middle-class standards of his day, Mason
probably received at least a moderate grammar school education.[4]
Like most of the London Brownings, however, Cousin Cyrus
had to rely on the self-help method for any substantial education
he wished to achieve. Certainly he developed the family proclivity
for art and used it to help expand his education by offering
painting lessons in exchange for French lessons when he lived in
Paris as a young man.[5] But Cyrus Mason did not have the advan-
tages of Robert Senior's library and guidance, and, most impor-
tantly, his support and encouragement. Nor, of course, did Cyrus
possess Robert Browning's genius. The result is that while

because of the young couple's need (the "gift" has been recorded in this Robert's
will: see Furnivall's "Ancestors," p. 39). Also, Mason's own recollections of his
grandfather's residence with its "massive tables and sideboards," the "nearly life
size" oil portraits of his grandparents mounted in their "massive frames," and the
"well furnished rooms . . . no veneering there" seem to represent significant childhood impressions of a rather grand place (see p. 75). Similarly, Cousin Cyrus
remembers that Robert Senior's household "was maintained in some style with my
Uncle's salary" (p. 89); yet this Robert's salary was significantly less (probably about
£320) than his father's (£561).

2. Furnivall's "Ancestors," p. 44.

3. Richard D. Altick, *Victorian People and Ideas* (New York: Norton, 1973), pp.
27-33, gives a brief, very general picture of such a Victorian middle class.

4. Altick, *Victorian People and Ideas*, pp. 246-58, briefly discusses middle-class
education of the period.

5. See Introduction above; esp. Letter, Mrs. Scarlett to Mrs. Armstrong, August
29, 1955, Baylor, n. 4. Baly, "Talking of the Brownings," pp. 7-8, notes that many
members of the London Brownings were "gifted artist[s]."

Mason likely acquired at least an average middle-class education through formal schooling and self-help, he certainly achieved neither the breadth nor the depth of the education of his more gifted cousin.

"The Poet Robert Browning and his Kinsfolk" itself does not reveal much remarkable about Mason's education and background. While its language is not learned it is assuredly that of a literate, intelligent adult. Similarly, Mason's own allusions and references throughout the holograph reveal little of significance: Smollett's *Roderick Random*, Hogarth, Burns, Goethe, and Teniers comprise his artistic references, while he alludes to the political figures of Gambetta and Charles Gavan Duffy and to the religious personage of John Wesley.[6] Written when he was about seventy-nine years old, the manuscript does include much aberrant punctuation, a few misspelled words, and a generally poor prose style characterized by frequent awkward, rambling constructions and numerous sentence fragments and run-on sentences. But it is not the work of an unintelligent or uneducated man, especially when one considers Mason's age and the fact that he was not a writer either by vocation or as a primary avocation. What emerges about his background here is a picture of Cyrus Mason as a moderately educated, reasonably intelligent man with at least limited knowledge of some popular representatives of the arts.

Mason's own interest in and aptitude for art are more clearly documented. He has been remembered as "a clever amateur painter" who was associated with various Australians in the founding of the Buonarotti Club, a middle-class "coterie" for the encouragement of the arts.[7] His descendants still retain some of his watercolors and relate that these have been "admired by many."[8] Though he maintained a lifelong interest in and had some aptitude for painting, Cyrus Mason did not possess artistic

6. Perhaps indicative of Mason's provincial, middle-class success is the fact that he seems as a subordinate to have known Duffy, later Prime Minister of Victoria, at least well enough to ask his help in trying to secure employment for his Uncle Thomas Browning (p. 74).

7. Luxton, "The Buonarotti Club," p. 3.

8. See Introduction: esp. Letter, Mrs. Scarlett to Mrs. Armstrong, November 20, 1957, Baylor.

genius. In this regard he is much more typically a Browning than the poet himself. For a number of the London Brownings— particularly Robert Senior, William Shergold, and Reuben— demonstrated talents in various of the arts, but they, too, lacked the genius of a Robert Browning.

Mason also differed from Browning in the matter of personal vision, or ambition. In contrast with the poet, Mason probably suffered home disadvantages both financially and sympatheti- cally. But Cyrus still seems to have readily adopted the safe family pattern of middle-class professional or semiprofessional employ- ment while maintaining his interest in the arts through a provin- cial club. Perhaps his position as a lithographic draughtsman in some ways helped to assuage his artistic inclinations. This much is certain: lacking Browning's superior talents, self-education, and vision, Cyrus Mason chose the conventional method of middle-class advancement through emigration—a mode open to and probably even urged upon Browning himself.[9]

In this migration to success Mason unconsciously followed the pattern of his strong-willed, materially ambitious Grandfather Robert. Indeed, except for his artistic interests Cyrus seems to have had much in common with the Woodyates Robert. Though the grandson is almost certainly mistaken in his insistence on an aristocractic heritage, the main thrust of his reason for his grand- father's removal to London and service to the Tory cause in hopes of "recovering former family importance" (p. 36) is probably accurate: the Woodyates Robert was a most ambitious man who sought to elevate and establish—not recover—family importance in London. His narrow insistence on conservative politics, con- servative religion, practical education, and conventional careers for his family are part of his larger concern for that most exalted Victorian virtue, respectability. But Grandfather Robert's re- spectability was not the common Evangelical middle-class re- spectability of the nineteenth-century masses; he was reaching for the kind of elevated respectability that would allow him to look down on his common middle-class roots. Perhaps the clear-

---

9. Alfred Domett, the poet's friend, followed such a pattern after studying law by emigrating to New Zealand.

est example of his social climbing may be seen in this Robert's purchase of a coat of arms in an attempt to help secure the newly achieved family rung on the social and economic scale. Similarly, his grandson Cyrus emerges from "The Poet Robert Browning and his Kinsfolk" as the successful—though thoroughly middle-class—government appointee, founder of the Buonarotti Club, and cousin to the poet Robert Browning trying to maintain this kind of respectability through anecdotes such as his Uncle's shaving his whiskers to avoid resemblance with a man of questionable character (pp. 16-17) and his looking back for a suitably respectable lineage among the Dorsetshire gentry!

Also like his Grandfather Robert, Cyrus Mason appears to have been a provincial, somewhat narrow man. His mention of middle-class antipathy for the theatre (p. 81) and of Robert Senior's "ungenteel" taste in art (p. 87) betrays, one feels, something of Cousin Cyrus's own narrowness as well as a touch of snobbery. In fact, Robert Senior's "eccentric" behavior throughout Mason's work is treated with condescension and occasional puritanical distaste. Such narrow insistence on undeviating middle-class mores Mason builds into another Victorian concern—family pride. The poet is constantly chastised for not sharing this virtue because he did not thrust his fellow kinsmen into the limelight in his letters and, presumably, through obsequious public acknowledgments of familial gratitude. In this vein Cyrus has at his worst expressed such foolish and wrong-headed comments as his feeling "disappointment, almost regret, that [the Browning-Domett letters] were preserved, for there is no reference made in them to the kindly assistance being rendered by kinsfolk at the very time that they were written" (p. 13). For, unfortunately, "The Poet Robert Browning and his Kinsfolk" contains a number of statements that are either foolish or wrong—and in some cases both. Some of these are essentially innocent—such as Mason's wrong dating of Robert of Dorsetshire's removal to London and one of the remarkably stretched reasons he advances for the change.[10] Other errors serve Mason's various purposes: to declare that Brownings "always have been

---

10. See Part One, n. 19, and pp. 35-6.

pronounced Tories" (p. 36) is to help substantiate, albeit in a small way, their Dorsetshire pedigree and their London respectability; to have Uncle Reuben provide the poet's honeymoon money (p. 93) is to have the family render aid—particularly financially—right up to the poet's elopement; and to have Robert and Sarianna drift apart (p. 115) is to emphasize the lack of "natural affection" in the poet and his immediate family.

Mason's biases, his penchant for telling a good anecdote, his familiarity with published biographical material, his heavy reliance on family tradition, and his faulty memory (probably contributed to by all of the above, his advanced age, and the many years which had intervened between the primary incidents and impressions and their being recorded) all work together to contribute inaccurate "facts" and fanciful stories to the holograph. One example of the complex forces at work in Mason as he wrote occurs in his explanation for the beginning of the Von Müller episode (pp. 99ff.): his memory of Robert Senior's walking by and waving both to his stepmother and to the Widow Von Müller is invalidated by Jane Smith Browning's having died three years before the courtship began. In this instance of both factual error and fanciful story, Cyrus Mason seems to have read the newspaper accounts of the trial that record Robert Senior's waving to the Widow, remembered the proximity of Robert Senior's and Jane Smith's residences before her death, and combined the two to create a good story that he could compare with Young Robert's courtship and that emphasized his opinion regarding Robert Senior's absent-mindedness and Sarianna's and the poet's heartlessness.

While this obviously incorrect anecdote renders Cyrus Mason's other stories somewhat suspect, his typical fault is exaggeration, not prevarication. Most of these exaggerations, however, seem calculated to support one or another of Mason's themes: to exaggerate the importance of Christian names (pp. 19-20) is to help establish the Brownings of Dorsetshire as gentry; to exaggerate "former family importance" (p. 36) is to further substantiate the claims to gentry; and to exaggerate the Browning "friendship" with the Rothschilds (p. 72) is to solidify the family's social status in London. Mason exaggerates the peculiarities of Robert Senior and Aunt Margaret in order to base the poet's lack of familial affection on "inherited eccentricity" (p. 14). He inflates the importance of the Woodyates Reuben's education of Robert Senior so that "the literary world" will owe "a debt of gratitude" to the family who trained such a great poet (p. 16). Cousin Cyrus can even exaggerate both sides of one issue to suit his fancy: Young Robert's home training and teaching created a great poet (p. 14) while the same home education was responsible for his faults, chiefly his disregard for kinsfolk (pp. 113-14).

Such exaggerations are most troublesome to the student of Browning who turns to Cyrus Mason for information. But, it must be remembered, they are usually exaggerations, not complete falsehoods; most, in fact, seemed aimed at the truth but overshoot their mark. For example, the Christian names William, John, and Robert seem to have served Mason well in tracing *a* Browning family from among the gentry of Dorsetshire; unfortunately, it seems not to be the poet's family. Further, the "former family importance" of Woodyates Brownings may be found in "the solid and educated middle class," though not among the gentry.[11] While the Brownings were certainly not intimates of the Rothschilds, Robert Senior did, as a subordinate, have business dealings with them, and Reuben and William Shergold did work for them in responsible positions. Certainly Robert Senior (and probably Aunt Margaret, too) was not an adherent to the strait-laced respectability so valued by his father, the Woodyates Robert; and certainly this lack of loyalty to paternal ideals was reflected in the poet—not only as liberality but also as something of a family rift. Also, the elder Reuben probably did influence his nephew, though no one can "teach" genius as he might "teach" mathematics. Cyrus's usual fault, it seems, lies not in making his claims, but in claiming too much.

Maisie Ward has concluded that Cyrus Mason's "observations are worth noting" if his bias is taken into account, while John Maynard surmises that his work is an account "which no student of the poet can completely ignore and no student should completely trust."[12] For in spite of the fact that Mason's tracing of the

---

11. Chesterton's *Browning*, p. 3.
12. *Browning*, I, 10; *Browning's Youth*, p. 363.

early Browning ancestry is probably incorrect, and his charges against the poet for lack of familial affection seem dubious; in spite of his factual errors, fanciful stories, and calculated exaggerations; Cyrus's "history" is nevertheless valuable. He affords his readers intimate glimpses into the London Brownings' households; his general family portrait and the individual pictures of family members are presented from a unique perspective; and his emphasis on the young poet's early environment is well taken. Indeed sometimes, as in the case of Reuben of Woodyates, Cyrus even offers unique material regarding the poet's family and childhood environment. Though he offers little that is actually "new," Cousin Cyrus does present different emphases and different perspectives. For instance, his emphasis on the education of Brownings before the poet—while exaggerated and in contrast with the widely held view of the Woodyates Robert as barbaric— seems basically correct.

In spite of the ill-advised hunting expedition among the Dorsetshire gentry, the primary picture of the Browning clan in "The Poet Robert Browning and his Kinsfolk" is of a conventional, rather puritanical, and somewhat successful middle-class family. Similarly, Cyrus Mason's unconscious self-portrait is of a thoroughly common middle-class Victorian man who happened to be the cousin of a famous poet. Just how unusual Browning's immediate family—the household of Robert Senior—was is much easier to evaluate in light of the perspective of Cousin Cyrus Mason, much more typically a Browning than the poet himself.

Cyrus Mason in 1908 primarily concerned himself with two difficult, very hazy areas of Browning biography: the poet's distant ancestry and his immediate family environment as a youth. The question of Browning's ancestry will possibly never be "proven" one way or the other, for the evidence is inconclusive and the question seems rather moot to the twentieth-century biographer. The problem of Browning's early family life and environment waited almost seventy years before John Maynard began its in-depth exploration—and even then Maynard cautiously employed Cyrus's work as one of his tools. In an effort to render this tool more readily usable, I have divided my further evaluation of Mason and his manuscript into the three areas which I think the material dictates: Mason's theory about Browning ancestry; his treatment of various family members and groups; and the attitudes which prompted Mason to present the material as he has.

In the sections on Ancestry, and particularly on Family, I have frequently summarized and attempted to systematize Mason's treatment of the material in order to clarify what he has done and to help organize my own evaluation of his work. Such selective ordering and summarization of Mason's discussions of clan members is important because Cousin Cyrus's most significant contributions fall in the family area and because a systematic look at his approach toward family members and groups reveals much about his attitude in writing the manuscript. The Attitude segment will, I think, help guide the reader in a cautious, perhaps even wary, examination of what Mason has done and why he has done it.

Any appreciation of the value of "The Poet Robert Browning and his Kinsfolk" should begin with the realization that its author is neither scholar nor biographer. Rather, Cyrus Mason, prompted by what he considered inaccurate demeaning of Browning ancestry by biographers and improper neglect of kinsfolk by Robert Browning himself, wrote his version of the family history as an aged Australian nostalgically reminiscing over personal memories and family traditions.

I

ANCESTRY

I feel impelled to rectify statements which have been published respecting the Poet's forefathers.

Cyrus Mason, p. 7

Cyrus Mason wrote "The Poet Robert Browning and his
Kinsfolk" so that "a correct history" of the Browning family
would "clear away a mystery surrounding it's origin" (p. 8).
Either directly or obliquely, Mason attempts to counter three
major heresies published in regard to the ancestry of the Browning family. He rather subtly—never directly calling attention to it
as he does to the other two theories—seeks to parry the idea of a
Creole heritage of black blood derived from his paternal grandmother, Margaret Tittle. The idea of Browning black blood
seems to have originated, in print at least, with F. J. Furnivall
(who cites an anonymous source):

> An old friend, who has often sat in the house of the poet's father, and
> knew the family well, says that they were all very dark, and he
> believes in their dark blood.[1]

---

1. Furnivall's "Ancestors," p. 31, n. 2; see also the text above the note in which
Furnivall asserts:
   In colour, the poet's father was so dark that when as a youth, he went out to his
   Creole mother's sugar-plantation in St Kits's, the beadle of the Church orderd
   him to come away from the white folk among whom he was sitting, and take his
   place among the colourd people.

Again without naming his sources, Furnivall asserts that this "dash of the tar-brush" in Margaret Tittle Browning "was understood by some" of her husband's second family after her death, "and the eyes and colour of Robert IV. [the poet's father] confirmd it." Furnivall includes in his paper a lengthy discussion of the word "Creole": its original reference to " 'persons born in the colony, of parents born out of the colony' " is carried through to its broader contemporary definition as "a person born in the West Indies or Louisiana, so that there are both Creole whites and Creole negroes." Since Margaret Tittle, wife of the Woodyates Robert, was born in the West Indies to English parents, she is almost invariably referred to as "Creole." Upon this fuzzy word and several unidentified sources Furnivall has built his "dark blood" theory.

    Mason's only reference to another origin is that there has been "much play of imagination around the nationality of the wife of the Woodyats Robert Browning, Grandmother of the Poet."[2] His circuitous response to a black Creole Margaret Tittle is his avowal that she derived from French origins. Wrongly assuming that the poet's grandparents married in Dorsetshire,[3] Mason concludes that Miss Tittle was among the numbers of upperclass Frenchmen seeking safety in England prior to the outbreak of the French Revolution. According to Mason, many landed at Poole Harbor, and some—including Margaret Tittle—remained in Dorsetshire instead of immigrating to London. The French mannerisms of her children and the easy adaptation by her son, Robert Senior, to Paris in later life furnish additional "support" for Mason's claim. In the middle of his discussion of Margaret Tittle, one of Mason's phrases stands out as possibly a response to Furnivall: ". . . the *almost* black, wavy, *not curly*, hair of both Robert and Margaret Browning the children of the first wife" (p. 48; italics mine). While Mason's discussion of Margaret Tittle concurs that her two children had "dark complexions" (p. 48), he

---

  2. For Mason's discussion of Margaret Tittle Browning, see pp. 46-8.
  3. According to Mrs. Orr, I, 5, Robert of Woodyates married Margaret Tittle in 1778, nine years after his removal to London: see Part One, n. 19, and Part Three, n. 13.

later asserts that the children of the Woodyates Robert "exhibited clear pink and white complexions" (p. 72).

Mason's avowal of a French Margaret Tittle reveals the poet's cousin at his imaginative and speculative worst. Armed only with his sense of duty "to attempt the rectification of 'monstrous fabrication' " (p. 10), Cousin Cyrus creates his own plausible, but obviously incorrect, theory. That Margaret was born in St. Kitt's there can be little doubt: the poet himself writes to Elizabeth of his grandmother's having been born in the West Indies (*RBEBK*, II, 1005); Sharp, Orr, Chesterton, Griffin and Minchin, and Sir Vincent Baddeley, also a Browning relative, all confidently place her birth in the West Indies as well.[4] In contrast with both Furnivall's and Mason's descriptions of the dark complexions of the children, Mrs. Orr comments on Robert Senior's "clear, ruddy complexion" (I, 10), while Maisie Ward's *Browning* concludes that the mother's "portrait is almost aggressively Aryan" (I, 5). Mrs. Orr also contradicts Furnivall's assertion that Robert Senior's eyes were evidence of the "touch of the tar brush" by noting that he "had light blue eyes" (I, 10).

Jeannette Marks, however, in her book on the Barretts refers to Furnivall's theory and regards black blood as a possible explanation for the strange treatment of Margaret Tittle's father, John, by his family.[5] She also hints that Margaret may not have been the daughter of John Tittle's wife, also Margaret. Neither Marks nor Furnivall, however, offers the least firm support for such assumptions; indeed, their speculations are apparently as groundless as Mason's French idea. Griffin and Minchin are careful to point out that "Margaret Tittle was a Creole only in the sense that she was born in the West Indies"; their footnote to this statement obviously attempts rectification of Furnivall's discussion of the word: "This is the proper connotation of the word Creole, often mistakenly supposed to imply an admixture of black blood" (p. 299). Furnivall, Mason, and even Marks all have their personal axes to grind, and one must conclude that there exists no evidence for either French or African blood in Browning's grandmother.

---

4. See Sharp's *Life*, p. 1; Mrs. Orr, I, 5; Chesterton's *Browning*, p. 4; Griffin and Minchin, pp. 2, 299; and Baddeley's "Ancestry," p. 2. See also Part Three, n. 20.
  5. *The Family of the Barrett*, pp. 6, 105, 148-53.

In response to "the assumption, made by biographers, that Jewish blood flowed in the Poet's veins," Mason offers his defense against the second heresy by citing the "Christian names" of the Dorsetshire Robert's children as "recorded in Church of England registers" (p. 72). "I can positively assert," Mason writes, "that they possessed none of the characteristics of Hebrew personality, all being tall, singularly robust and exhibited clear pink and white complexions" (p. 72). Cyrus feels that perhaps one factor behind the Jewish theory is to be found in the friendship between the Rothschilds and the Brownings: Uncles William and Reuben both served the Rothschild firm throughout their adult lives (pp. 72-3). Also, the first sentence of Furnivall's "Ancestors" similarly asserts that "there is no ground for supposing the presence of any Jewish blood in the poet's veins" (p. 26)—an assertion concurred in by Sharp's *Life* (p. 16), Mrs. Orr (I, 2), and Chesterton's *Browning* (p. 8).

Thus, the idea of Jewish blood in the Browning family line had been discounted by every major biographer of the poet before Mason composed his history in 1908. Mason, therefore, offers only minimal defense against an idea already generally disregarded. Similarly, one feels, Mason expended little effort trying to counter a black blood theory strongly discounted by Mrs. Orr, mildly discounted by Chesterton (p. 4), and probably a bit too outlandish for most readers to take seriously. Perhaps, also, Mason the Australian does not name this heresy in the hopes of letting sleeping sheep lie.

It is the third heresy, therefore, which most upsets Mason and to which he devotes most of his writing energies: this final and most difficult mystery regarding past Brownings concerns their station, or rank, as a Dorsetshire family. Cousin Cyrus seems here to be responding to another Furnivall theory as propounded in his articles "Robert Browning's Ancestors" (1890) and "Browning's Footman Ancestor" (*The Academy*, 62 [April 12, 1902], 394). In the earlier article—almost certainly the one which so upset Aunt Sarah (p. 9)—Furnivall claims: "The earliest ancestor I have been able to find for the poet is Robert Browning (I.) who must have been born before 1700, and who was ultimately head-butler to Sir John Bankes of Corfe Castle" (p. 26); Furnivall records as his source a "Statement of the late Robert Browning, the tenant of Morley's Hotel, who died 18 July 1866." The later article is actually a letter to *The Academy* chiding the *Dictionary of National Biography* for ignoring Furnivall's earlier piece and tracing the poet's lineage no deeper than the great-grandfather who owned Woodyates Inn. Sneering at this Thomas Browning as a "village publican," grandfather Robert as the purchaser "for a couple of guineas" of that "charm coat-of-arms" later flaunted in Venice, and Robert Senior as ridiculous in his "scrape with Cockburn's discarded mistress,"[6] Furnivall contends that his fancy is taken by the earliest Robert,

> the first ancestor, the footman and butler to Sir John Bankes . . . one of those 'faithful servants' whom Mr. Arthur J. Munby pictures and praises so highly . . . a class to which almost every family in the realm has owed, and owes, so much of its comfort and content—a class which has given us Charles Lamb, and no doubt many another honoured name.

Cyrus Mason—successful railway employee, amateur painter, founder and president of the Buonarotti Club, and cousin to one of England's most distinguished poets—quite naturally takes exception with "the thought of [his] family being given in print, an origin so different to that which pride in [his] descent had for years delighted [his] contemplation" (p. 9). His opening section describes the Browning family as members of "the educated class" (p. 8), a "well born race" (p. 9), "proud of their birth and the name they bore" (p. 10), sharing "a very pronounced pride in their race" (p. 16) and "not belonging to the laboring class" (p. 17). He proudly exhibits the preceding generation by parading through his early pages the talents and accomplishments—particularly in learning and literature—of uncles Robert, William, and Reuben (pp. 10-12). He then lays out his plan for discovering his early Dorsetshire progenitors: he intends not to use materials previously "employed by the Poet's biographers," but to "trace through English County histories and Church

---

6. I.e., the widow Von Müller.

records, the 'Brunings'—'Brounyngs'—and 'Brownings' " (p.
17), relying particularly upon the names William, John, and
Robert on the assumption "that the Brownings, bearing those
three Christian names, continuously, were the ancestors of the
Poet Robert Browning" (p. 20). John Hutchins's *The History and
Antiquities of the County of Dorsetshire* (1774) comprises Mason's
primary source of information regarding the early Brownings in
his Part Two. Despite Cyrus's statement to the contrary, Hutchins's *History* is—with Sir Richard Colt Hoare's *History of Wiltshire*, another source cited by Mason (pp. 32-3)—one of Furnivall's noted sources in his "Ancestors" article. Beginning with a
William Browning who was granted the manor of Beaushin
during the reign of Edward III (1327-1377), Mason, through
Hutchins, traces various William-John-Robert Brunings-Broun-
yngs-Brownings down to a Sir William Browning from whom
the Browning Dorsetshire holdings passed into the hands of the
Strangeways family in the monarchy of Henry VIII (1509-
1547).[7]

Mason, having established a line of squirely Brownings dating
from c. 1330 to c. 1525, proceeds to the nineteenth century to
blame " 'Carey's Road Map of England' " (1826) and Samuel
Lewis's " 'The Topographical Dictionary' " (1835) for confusing would-be biographers by listing only Woodyates Inn, or
Woodyates West. The Browning place of residence, he asserts,
was the former Woodyates East which had been absorbed by
Gussich St. Andrews, Gussich All Saints, and Gussich St.
Michael—"all of them churches belonging to the ancient manor
of Woodyates" (p. 33). So jumbled are these Woodyates that
Mason himself has confused East Woodyates with West Wood-
yates and further muddled his argument (see Part Two, n. 28).
His contention, however, that this early Browning place of resi-
dence has been lost to later topographers does seem justified:
Hutchins's distinction between the ancient manor of West-
Woodyates (II, 221) and the inn of East-Woodyates (II, 158) has

---

7. With the possible exception of the Robert Bruning who served Melcombe
Regis in Parliaments called by Henry VI, Mason has, it seems, done an adequate
(though sometimes confusing) job of tracing a single family of Brownings with
substantial holdings in Dorsetshire.

not been noted by either Carey or Lewis. Such a distinction has been rendered moot, however, by the fact that the eighteenth-century Brownings were undoubtedly associated with the inn at Woodyates. According to the Reverend Anthony J. Lane of Pentridge, Thomas Browning, the poet's great-grandfather, "seems certainly to have been landlord of Woodyates Inn."[8]

Despite Cyrus's statement that the inn background was the cause of Aunt Sarah's wounded pride (p. 34), he seems most intent to dissociate the family from the taint of a labor heritage and to prove that they were learned and of a literary bent. Or, as Cyrus himself puts it, the Woodyates Brownings were "educated" and "occupied no subordinate position in society" (p. 31). Much of his Part Three deals with books brought from Woodyates by the Browning brothers which he cites in order to prove that they were being educated, that they did read and study (he seems especially intent to demonstrate that they were interested in poetry), and perhaps that one of the Dorsetshire brothers was even "associated with educational pursuits" (p. 46; see also p. 32). Cousin Cyrus moves from books to personal knowledge as a guide to prove that the Brownings in Dorsetshire were "well educated" and "belonged to a superior class of society" (p. 39). Having known four generations of Brownings—Robert and Reuben of Woodyates, their children (e.g., Robert Senior, Jane Eliza Browning Mason), their grandchildren (e.g., the poet, Cyrus himself), and their great-grandchildren (e.g., Pen, Constance Mason Macdonnell)—Mason feels qualified and justified in picturing the personalities, characteristics, and stations of various Brownings to support his assertions.[9]

The early Browning name—Bruning—Mason attributes to French origins in an effort to link his predecessors with a Norman French past (p. 21). Browning himself told Moncure Con-

---

8. "The Brownings at Woodyates and Pentridge," *Dorset: The County Magazine*, Winter 1972, pp. 50-9. Furnivall, of course, concurs with this in both his "Ancestors" (pp. 26, 44) and his "Browning's Footman Ancestor" (p. 394); Sharp's *Life*, p. 14, also agrees. Baddeley's "Ancestry," however, maintains that the first Robert, "who died at Woodyates in the parish of Pentridge in 1746, occupied a house which was *afterwards* a coaching inn" (p. 4; italics mine).

9. Mason's treatment of the family will be dealt with later in the Afterword.

way that he thought the origin was "DeBruni."[10] Sharp derives
the "Bruning" name from Teutonic sources (p. 15); Mrs. Orr
places the origins in Anglo-Saxon stock (I, 2). Another Browning
kinsman, Sir Vincent Baddeley, feels that the source was
"Brun," a Saxon name of a local chieftain; he further asserts that
the "forerunners of the modern Brownings were pure Saxons of
Wessex."[11] Sharp most wisely adds to his discussion of the derivation that the "origin is too remote to be of practical concern."
Indeed, he might have added that the plausible possibilities are
too numerous and the family line too unsure to be anything more
than conjectural.

Cyrus Mason does not conclusively prove—as he would wish—
that his Browning ancestors founded knightly or squirely families in Dorsetshire. He does demonstrate that *a* Bruning-
Brounyng-Browning family did achieve such a status in that
county in the fourteenth and fifteenth centuries, but an unequiv-
ocal direct connection between that family and the poet's seems
impossible to make with the evidence available. As Mrs. Orr
points out, Browning family tradition asserts that they descended
from "a decayed branch, of an Anglo-Saxon stock settled . . . in
the south, and probably also southwest, of England. A line of
Brownings owned the manors of Melbury-Sampford and Melbury-
Osmond, in northwest Dorsetshire; their last representative
disappeared—or was believed to do so—in the time of Henry
VII. . . ."[12] It is suggestive, as she hints, that Brownings of
elevated status have been recorded "within twenty miles of Pentridge, where the first distinct traces of the poet's family appear."
Suggestive, but by no means conclusive. In fact, testimony to the
contrary exists. The Brownings associated with Melbury Sampford have been claimed by Oscar Browning as ancestors; he
particularly calls attention to the marriage of John Browning and
Alianora Fitznichol in 1399, a marriage also noted by Mason in

10. Sharp's *Life*, p. 15; a lengthy, rather pedantic discussion of the possible sources
for the derivation of the name Browning—with no particular reference to the poet or
his family—has been compiled by C. H. Browning in "Browning: Origin of the
Surname," *American Historical Register*, III (February 1896), 650-9.
11. Baddeley's "Ancestry," p. 2.
12. Mrs. Orr, I, 2-3.

his attempt to identify the Brownings buried in the Melbury church (pp. 24-5).[13] "But there is no evidence to show that the family of Robert Browning was in any way connected with that branch, and I am reluctantly brought to the conclusion that there is probably no connection between the poet and myself, except the connection of friendship . . . ," Oscar Browning decides. Furnivall, as one might guess, similarly states that "no connection is known to exist" between the poet's family and the holders of Melbury Sampford and Melbury Osmond.[14] Sir Vincent Baddeley, a distant relation of the poet and likewise a descendant of Woodyates Brownings, agrees that the ancestry can be traced "no further back than his great-great-grandfather Robert," the earliest known Woodyates Browning.[15]

For Cyrus Mason to associate his family with such distinguished Brownings of the past is understandable. According to Mrs. Orr (I, 116), Uncle William—whom Cyrus cites as "a great student of genealogy" (p. 10)—used to tell the poet and his sister "stories of their probable ancestors, Micaiah Browning, who distinguished himself at the siege of Derry, and that commander of the ship *Holy Ghost* who conveyed Henry V. to France before the battle of Agincourt, and received the coat-of-arms, with its emblematic waves, in reward for his service." Indeed, Sharp writes that "Browning *believed*, but always conscientiously maintained there was *no proof* in support of the assumption, that he was a descendant" of Micaiah Browning and the Captain Browning who sailed with Henry V (p. 17; italics mine). The poet also told Oscar Browning that he "believed himself to be descended" from the two legendary Brownings.[16] His Cousin Cyrus, also nephew to William Browning, must have heard the same stories as a youth; much later, as an elderly man settled in Australia, he was naturally aroused by statements which he knew to be contrary to family tradition and thus took up Hutchins in search of a distin-

---

13. For Oscar Browning's discussion of his ancestry and possible kinship with the poet's family, see *Memories*, pp. 4-6.

14. Furnivall's "Ancestors," p. 35.

15. Baddeley's "Ancestry," p. 2; for Baddeley's relationship to the poet, see the Genealogy, Appendix III.

16. *Memories*, p. 6.

guished Browning family in Dorsetshire, preferably one with a military heritage. It is unfortunate for Cyrus (or perhaps fortunate, if the outcome were not pleasing) that the Pentridge records go back no further than 1704, and, therefore, no definite connection can be made between those squirely sixteenth-century Brownings and the eighteenth-century Brownings of Wood-yates.

Mason's anger at having the family traced to a "footman ancestor," however, appears to be justified.[17] Thirty years after Mason's composition of "The Poet Robert Browning and his Kinsfolk," another Browning descendant, Sir Vincent Baddeley, was similarly angered and also set out to refute Furnivall by writing "The Ancestry of Robert Browning." In a 1955 letter to the Director of the Armstrong Browning Library, Baddeley writes that he was prompted to publish his article "in order to dispose of the extraordinary myth which Dr. Furnivall invented about 'the footman ancestor.' "[18] Furnivall, according to Baddeley, made "a deliberate attempt to foist some derogatory source upon a respectable if undistinguished family."[19] Baddeley also briefly mentions the Jewish and black blood theories, noting the lack of foundation for either, before proceeding—as Cyrus had done three decades earlier—to Furnivall's "more serious" allegation. That the only known Sir John Banks of Corfe Castle died in 1644 (102 years prior to this Browning footman-butler's death) and that Corfe Castle was destroyed in the Civil War and thus "was an uninhabited ruin at the time of the supposed chief butler-ship" should completely demolish Furnivall's theory, reasons Sir Vincent. But if that is not enough, Baddeley cites both the verbal and the written statements of Thomas Wise that "Furnivall had to publish a repudiation of his footman story very soon after its publication," though no copy of the repudiation is known to be

---

17. Naturally no concrete proof exists that Mason read and was responding to Furnivall; however, his distaste for the inn, his antipathy for labor roots, his mention of Jewish blood, his hints at refuting black blood, and his use of two sources cited by Furnivall in the "Ancestors" article (Hutchins and Hoare) all point to Furnivall's "Ancestors" as the logical chief offender.

18. Baddeley to Mrs. Armstrong, September 29, 1955, Baylor.

19. "Ancestry," p. 3; his entire article, which is the source for the remainder of the paragraph, includes pp. 1-6.

extant. The footman-butler story was revived, however, in Furnivall's 1902 letter to *The Academy* in response to Edmund Gosse's life of Browning in the *Dictionary of National Biography*. Furnivall went so far as to establish a marble tablet dedicated to Browning's footman-butler ancestor in the Pentridge church, a monument which has since been altered at the instigation of Baddeley.

Something, albeit brief, must be said of this fascinating man, Frederick J. Furnivall. He was in many ways and in most instances an able, incisive scholar. His work with such figures as Shakespeare and Browning—probably his two favorite subjects—resulted in notable contributions; he participated in founding societies to propagate the reading and study of Shakespeare, Shelley, and Browning. He was an able researcher and an avid publisher. What, then, could prompt this scholarly, energetic cofounder of the Browning Society to "foist" two such controversial "myths" about the ancestry of Robert Browning as the black blood and footman-butler theories? Furnivall's aggressiveness, love of controversy, and lack of decorum in dealing with controversy are well-documented facts.[20] Also, he was, as he himself states in "Ancestors," "a radical and democrat" who would "of course rejoice that the descendant of a Dorsetshire footman has been buried with solemn pomp in Westminister Abbey (31 Dec., 1889), and that I preside over the Society which I helpt to found in his honour (July 1881)" (p. 36). His vituperative letter to *The Academy* closes with the rather pugnacious questions: "Can any reader of this letter give me instances of persons of note, besides Charles Lamb and Robert Browning, who were descended from household servants? Will anyone subscribe to put up a brass to the footman founder of the Browning family in Pentridge Church?"[21] It seems that, as Baddeley has written, "One of Doctor Furnivall's pet theories was that men of genius were descended either from Jews or from some mean origin."[22]

20. E.g., see Charles Michael Hancher, "The London Browning Society, 1881-1892" (Ph.D. diss., Yale, 1968), pp. 1-10, 234-8; and William S. Peterson, "Furnivallos Furioso," *Interrogating the Oracle* (Athens, Ohio: University of Ohio Press, 1969), pp. 31-50.

21. "Browning's Footman Ancestor," p. 394.

22. "Ancestry," p. 3.

Little wonder then that Furnivall, the year after Browning's death, read to the Browning Society a paper in which he fosters two possible "mean origins" for the poet.[23] That he should republish the allegation after an earlier withdrawal "was entirely characteristic of Doctor Furnivall" according to his friend Thomas Wise.[24] The revival of the footman-butler story may have been promoted in part by Furnivall's longstanding quarrel with Sir Edmund Gosse, who was chosen to write the *DNB* piece on Browning (which Furnivall thought he should have written) and who altogether ignored Furnivall's earlier work.[25] Furnivall had correctly traced Browning's ancestry back to the first Robert who died in Pentridge in 1740, correctly associated the family with Woodyates, and correctly dissociated the Browning line from Jewish origin; most likely, however, he has incorrectly suggested for the family line a black heritage and incorrectly identified the first Robert as footman-become-butler to Sir John Banks.

Whatever his occupation, the poet's great-great-grandfather "was clearly a respected citizen of Woodyates"; Maynard wisely surmises that the Browning family tradition of at least "relative, if not extraordinary success, and of increasing comfort and security" was more important than any "mythical pasts" that might be invoked.[26] Maynard traces such increasing relative success through the five generations culminating with the poet: the great-great-grandfather was "a substantial citizen" of Woodyates, though "certainly not part of the gentry" (p. 355); his son Thomas, proprietor of the Woodyates Inn so objectionable to Mr. Barrett, occupied a "prominent position in his hamlet, second only to the local gentry," and was accorded the distinction of being labeled "Mr." Browning in parish records (p. 356); Thomas's son, the Dorsetshire Robert, was first to claim the signature "Robert Browning, Esquire," an appellation also used by his son and grandson, "an acknowledgment of their new status

23. The paper was read before the Browning Society on February 28, 1890, and subsequently published as "Robert Browning's Ancestors."
24. Quoted in Baddeley's "Ancestry," p. 5.
25. For more on the Furnivall-Gosse feud—and some interesting comments allegedly made by Browning about Furnivall—see Hancher, "The London Browning Society," pp. 60-2; Peterson, *Interrogating the Oracle*, pp. 178-81.
26. *Browning's Youth*, p. 20.

as gentlemen among the middle classes" (p. 21). Thus, the significant aspect of the poet's family background is, as G. K. Chesterton has pointed out, that "his whole family would appear to have belonged to the solid and educated middle class."[27] And, except for his fruitless fishing expedition into the history of Brownings in Dorsetshire, Mason seems most intent on establishing just such middle class respectability for his ancestors by arguing the Browning antipathy for labor and the education brought by Dorsetshire Brownings to London. Indeed, Cyrus once seems to clearly identify himself and his kinsfolk with the solid middle class: "During it's [*A Blot in the 'Scutcheon*'s] rehearsal, at a time when all business connected with a Theatre was regarded by *middle class* families, with very different feelings to those entertained by a similar class in these days there were many serious discussions on the propriety of 'Young Robert's' entering upon affairs connected with the stage" (p. 81; italics mine). Further, he tacitly assigns the poet's family to such a middle-class status in his reference to Robert Senior's and Mrs. Von Müller's occupying "the same social position" (p. 110). Even Mason's reference to the Woodyates Robert's transformation "from a courteous country gentleman, into a full blooded citizen" after the move to London must be understood in a nineteenth-century urban context rather than an eighteenth-century genteel one: this Robert was certainly no "country gentleman" in the sense of Jane Austen's gentry, but he did leave a substantial provincial home to become a respected bank officer referred to as early as 1771 as "Robert Browning of the Bank of England Gentleman" and in 1784 as "Robert Browning of the Bank of England in the City of London Esquire."[28]

John Maynard has succinctly summed up what seems of most importance in regard to Browning's ancestry:

27. *Browning*, p. 3; Chesterton, whose biography of the poet was published in 1903, makes some most pertinent—though at times heavily Victorian—statements regarding Browning's background (see his first chapter, especially pp. 1-15).

28. "Release" of October 21, 1771; a Bond of 1784 for one hundred and twenty pounds: MS, Armstrong Browning Library, Baylor University. It is interesting to notice that nowhere in his history does Cyrus Mason lay claim to or even refer to the Browning coat of arms purchased by his grandfather, Robert of Woodyates, and used by the poet and his son (e.g., see Mrs. Orr, I, 4).

Neither truly a part of the traditional ruling classes of gentry or aristocracy, nor, like the great majority of English people, entirely rooted in a local region and in the routine of manual labor, they indicate that Browning's real roots were not in a particular region or a special past but in the middle class that created places like Camberwell and that was to play such a significant, even dominating, role in nineteenth-century England.[29]

Having removed to the city and established themselves as respectable citizens of Camberwell, Robert and Reuben of Dorsetshire founded a family of London Brownings grounded in middle-class suburban prosperity.

---

29. *Browning's Youth*, p. 20.

II

FAMILY

> We do not want to know about a man like Browning,
> whether he had a right to a shield used in the Wars of the
> Roses, or whether the tenth grandfather of his Creole
> grandmother had been white or black: we want to know
> something about his family, which is quite a different thing.
>
> G. K. Chesterton, *Robert Browning*, p. 5

Cyrus Mason, grandson of Robert of Dorsetshire and step-grandson of Reuben of Dorsetshire, enjoys the unique posture among Browning biographers of having known all members of the London Browning clan. In his family history Cousin Cyrus emphasizes several characteristics as general among the Brownings in addition to the individualized sketches of family members. The Brownings, for instance, all exhibited "robust health brought from Dorsetshire"—"no instance of bodily or mental deficiency" among this clan![1] The Brownings also took great pride in their "birth" (p. 10) and were all well-educated; but perhaps their strongest family trait, according to Mason, was "the old Browning forceful manner."[2] Indeed, their "forceful manner" sometimes manifested itself as ill temper in men so

---

1. P. 16. Mrs. Orr, I, 27-31, describes the poet's health as not so good, and one must wonder if Mason had read Orr and is thus trying to rectify what he considered another wrong to his family. Some more recent assessments of Browning as unhealthy have been offered in Richard Altick's "The Private Life of Robert Browning," *Yale Review*, 41 (December 1951), 247-62; and Miller's *Portrait*, pp. 3, 13-4.

2. P. 53; Mason refers to the Browning "forceful manner" throughout his manuscript, but he particularly associates this characteristic with Robert of Wood-yates (e.g., p. 60 contains two such references to his grandfather).

diverse as Grandfather Robert of Woodyates (pp. 71-2), his son
Thomas (p. 73), and the third generation Robert, the poet (p. 83).
Mason even speaks of his own "naturally high spirits" as a child
(p. 75)—an early hint of his own inherited forceful nature.
Mason's personal knowledge of past Brownings, as well as the
bonuses of family gossip and traditions, enables Cousin Cyrus to
render sketches of family members which, if not always unique in
themselves, are at least drawn from a unique vantage point. His
verbal portraits of Robert and Reuben, the Woodyates brothers,
provide excellent examples: in comparison with other Browning
biographers, Mason's picture of this Robert offers a broadened
and deepened perspective, while the sketch of this Reuben furnishes an almost completely unique portrait.

Though his rendering of the poet's grandfather does portray
the tyrannical father drawn by other biographers, Mason also
offers more. Robert of Woodyates has most often been remembered for sending his eldest son, Robert Senior, to the West
Indies in order to assume control of the maternal inheritance of a
sugar plantation. Robert Senior found the slave system there
unacceptable and abandoned his inheritance to return to England.[3] Upon his son's unexpected return, the enraged Robert of
Woodyates presented Robert Senior with a bill for the expenses of
rearing him and refused further support, thus discouraging his
son's artistic inclinations and forcing him to take a position with
the Bank of England. Mason embellishes this picture of paternal
unkindness by offering different motivations for both father and
son, and by adding a similar instance of the father's tyranny over
another son. According to Cyrus, the Woodyates Robert disapproved of the "high class education" his son was receiving from
his Uncle Reuben, feared his son's artistic inclinations would
lead to no good end, and "resolved to thrust him into trade" by
shipping him to the West Indies.[4] Though Mason does present a

---

3. The most famous telling of this story occurs in the poet's own words to
Elizabeth (Letter 523, *RBEBK*, II, 1003 ff.); other accounts may be found in Mrs.
Orr, I, 7-8; Chesterton's *Browning*, pp. 10-11; Griffin and Minchin, p. 3; Ward, I,
8-9; and Irvine and Honan, p. 2.
4. Mason's discussion of this episode and the circumstances surrounding it occu-
pies much of Part Three (see particularly pp. 55-64).

half-hearted defense of the elder Browning as a man of his age in his distrust of the arts and in his pride as a man of commerce, Cyrus clearly portrays the Woodyates Robert as dogmatically practical and unalterably opposed to the influence of his brother over his son—an influence that emphasized not only a liberal education but also included an inclination towards Methodism and attendance at Chapel meetings.[5] The son's return from the West Indies Mason attributes not so much to slavery as to Robert Senior's "love of literary work" and his inability to satisfy the "yearning for study" ingrained in him by his Uncle Reuben.

Having read Mason's account, Maynard, in *Browning's Youth*, concludes that Robert Senior "no doubt rejected St. Kitt's as much for its provinciality and isolation as for its immorality" (p. 36). Though previous biographers have followed the poet's emphasis on his father's disgust with slavery, perhaps Mrs. Orr's early record of Robert Senior's frustration at being prohibited from teaching a negro boy to read best captures both the immorality and the insularity so objectionable to the sensitive, artistic nature of Uncle Reuben's star pupil.[6] At any rate, one may conclude that the colonial life of St. Kitt's must have been totally alien to the artistic interests and aspirations of Robert Senior. He thus returned to London with hopes of continuing his education and pursuing his artistic inclinations—hopes he was never allowed to fulfill.

Thomas Browning, the Woodyates Robert's youngest son by his second marriage (and thus half brother to Robert Senior), also fell victim to paternal wrath. Thomas, according to Mason (pp. 73-5), aroused the elder Robert's "irascible temper" and "was shipped in 1827 by his father" to Tasmania—"then only known as a fitting place for criminals." Though Mason offers no reason for the sudden banishment (other than the tempers of both men), Elaine Baly, great-great-granddaughter of Robert of Woodyates, has explained that Thomas "was put to work in the bank, in the House of Rothschild, but did not like it and went to Australia."[7]

5. Maynard's *Browning's Youth*, p. 357, points out that what Mason refers to as Methodism may well "have been a Dissenter church, even Congregationalism."
6. Mrs. Orr, I, 18.
7. Baly to the editor, February 3, 1976.

Mason does relate, however, that Thomas's pride and ungovernable temper continually interfered with his colonial career. Nephew Cyrus interestingly contrasts the eldest and the youngest sons of the tyrannical patriarch: "Uncle Robert happily had the courage to return from the West Indies, Uncle Thomas, influenced by pride, refused all offers to enable him to return to England, he died after fifty years of separation from the family and is buried in the Melbourne Cemetery." Like his older half brother, Thomas also was all but omitted from his father's will.[8] Had they been treated with more tolerance and sympathy by their father, Cyrus muses, both sons would have had more successful careers in London: one as poet and artist; the other as a respected citizen and student of commerce.

The Woodyates Robert was not a barbarian though—at least not according to his grandson Cyrus. Mrs. Orr, however, had sketched him as a "provincial type" of Englishman whose literary tastes were limited to the Bible and *Tom Jones*, "both of which he is said to have read through once a year" (I, 5). Similarly, Griffin and Minchin (probably relying on Mrs. Orr) have noted that his reading was said to be "mainly confined" to the Bible and *Tom Jones* (p. 7); Chesterton's *Browning* pictures the Woodyates Robert as "apparently a father of a somewhat primitive, not to say barbaric type" (p. 10). Cyrus, however, portrays a well-educated Woodyates Robert who with Reuben brought numerous books with him on his removal to the city.[9] Robert of Woodyates, for example, owned a copy of *The Young Gentlemen and Ladies' Monitor* (n. d.) which included a section entitled "A Collection of Select Pieces from our Best Modern Writers"; to Mason this "suggests to its owner . . . being a man with a taste for good literature." "To show that the Woodyates Browning studied literature, particularly poetry," Cyrus describes how this Robert's name has been stamped into *Scots Poems wrote by The Ingenious before 1600* (Edinburgh, 1761), a collection written in the Scottish dialect: "good proof that the Poet's grandfather must have been a

---

8. Thomas was to be left fifty pounds upon the death of his mother, but was not to share in the division of his father's property; the will has been published in Furnivall's "Ancestors," pp. 39-40.

9. Mason's discussion of these books is found in Part Three, pp. 39-46, 54-5.

devoted student of poetry." Later, in connection with the death of Robert's first wife, Margaret Tittle, Cyrus envisions the comfort which must have been afforded by grandfather's copy of a third book, William Spurstow's *The Spiritual Chymist or Six Decads of Divine Meditations.*

Mason's calculated effort to present two "well educated" Dorsetshire brothers moving with their books to the city is, of course, a part of his plan to furnish evidence of their elevated county status. One wonders, however, if Cyrus had read Mrs. Orr's statement (published in 1891) and is here attempting to counter yet another family slight, this time specifically aimed at his maternal grandfather. Whatever the motive, the grandson is probably correct in picturing the Woodyates Browning as reading more than the Bible and *Tom Jones*, though one who makes a point of reading through these two works yearly seems above charges of primitivism. John Maynard lists nine extant books known to have belonged to this Robert (including the three mentioned by Mason): they include Thomas Brookes's *Precious Remedies Against Satan's Devices* (London, 1656), Samuel Smith's *Noah's Dove, or, Tydings of Peace to the Godly* (London, 1619), and William Martin's *Historie of Twentie Kings*—a volume owned and autographed by five generations of Brownings.[10] Most, obviously, are of a spiritual orientation and contribute to a more detailed portrait of Robert of Woodyates as a rather religious man.[11] Maynard even sees in him a possible "conduit for the sober, almost rabbinical, scholarly streak that came out so strongly in his son and grandson" (p. 23). Firmly grounded in the Church of England and well read in a narrow puritanical vein of religious literature of the seventeenth century, the Woodyates Robert would seem to have been more than merely a practical bank official when he objected to Robert Senior's artistic leanings

---

10. *Browning's Youth*, Appendix A, p. 358; see Part Three, n. 8, above regarding Martin's *Historie.*

11. This image has been corroborated by Elaine Baly, the Woodyates Robert's great-great-granddaughter, in a conversation on May 7, 1976. Family tradition accords to this Robert—and several other Brownings as well—an extensive library of religious books.

and exposure to Methodism; he probably also objected as a sternly religious man.[12]

The composite picture offered by Orr, Chesterton, and Griffin and Minchin of a somewhat mechanically talented but uneducated, barbaric bank clerk is probably misleading: Mason's emphasis on an "educated" Grandfather Robert seems closer to the truth. Maisie Ward agrees that "Mason is on surer ground when showing that his grandfather was an educated man."[13] John Maynard records that this Robert "was given an education good enough to qualify him for an appointment at London in the Bank of England, a choice, semiprofessional position"; indeed that "Education to him was clearly a good thing."[14] Griffin and Minchin even emphasize that he "certainly gave all three of his sons an excellent education."[15]

Mrs. Orr's characterization of the Woodyates Robert as provincial is, nevertheless, probably accurate. In addition to his narrow, puritanical, middle-class Church of England theology, this Robert's disapproval of "high class education" and "cultivated learning" has been recorded by his grandson Cyrus (p. 59). The Dorsetshire Robert seems to have approved of what one may

---

12. Mason, p. 61, attributes "the tendency to Methodism" fostered by Uncle Reuben as having "hastened the sending of young Robert Browning [Senior] to the West Indies." The elder Robert all but excluded Robert Senior and Margaret—both students of Uncle Reuben—from any paternal bequest on the pretext of their having a maternal inheritance from his first wife; but he also specifically limited his bequest to Jane Eliza Browning Mason, a favorite of her Uncle Reuben's and wife of his stepson and pupil, John Mason (see Furnivall's "Ancestors," pp. 39-40, for a copy of the will and its codicils).

13. *Browning*, I, 4.

14. *Browning's Youth*, pp. 20-1, 24.

15. P. 7. By "educated" Mason certainly does not mean a classical, aristocratic schooling culminating with a degree from Oxford or Cambridge. What he does seem to refer to is the type of learning Browning himself acquired through limited formal training, liberal reading, and genuine intellectual curiosity. William Shergold, for example, has been characterized by Maynard as "a prodigious amateur scholar and regular poker into the odd corners of history," the results of which were the several historical novels and respected history noted below; Reuben he has classified as "a man of broad culture and learning," a financial authority "well enough esteemed by the 1850's for Gladstone himself to appeal to him concerning the advisability of a new government annuity" (*Browning's Youth*, pp. 114-16). Robert Senior, of course, has long been known for his erudition and love of books (see *Browning's Youth*, p. 24, regarding this Robert's education).

term a practical education—one designed to produce a "genuine City man" involved in a monetarily rewarding middle-class occupation.[16] Maynard qualifies the type of education the patriarch approved of, noting that it was a "good thing, as long as it served the ultimate end of advancing his son toward the colonial squire's role planned for him."[17] Advanced liberal education and passionate interest and absorption in painting and literature were anathema to the Woodyates Robert as both a conservatively religious and a practical, provincial, middle-class social climber. It is perhaps indicative of both his restricted interest in learning and his practical materialism that the Dorsetshire Robert's will leaves "my household furniture, plate, linen and books entirely to my wife's disposal."[18] Thus, Mason seems only to err in his foolish, exaggerated insistence on the Woodyates Robert's "having cultivated tastes for literature and indulging then, a love for poetry" (pp. 14-15). Cyrus himself even adds that his grandfather objected to "the study of literature as an unprofitable pursuit" (p. 64). Seemingly this Robert came to London with a sound, thoroughly middle-class and provincial education; once there, he immersed himself in his bank job and probably indulged himself only in his taste for popular literature current among middle-class Church of Englanders.

Robert of Dorsetshire was, all in all, a most successful middle-class man: he secured an appointment as clerk in the Bank of England through the influence of his father's landlord, the Earl of Shaftsbury, when only a Woodyates lad of not quite twenty; he climbed the promotion ladder to become Principal Clerk of the Bank Stock Division at age thirty-four, probably as high a position as native ability alone could achieve for him;[19] he served as a

---

16. See pp. 59-60.
17. *Browning's Youth*, p. 24.
18. Furnivall's "Ancestors," p. 40.
19. Furnivall's "Ancestors," p. 34, quotes Robert Shergold Browning regarding this position:

> The position of Principal of the Bank Stock office, while my Grandfather held it, was a much more important one in the City than it is now, as Bank Stock was then one of the few stocks for speculative Stock-Exchange bargains; and my Grandfather, was, by his position, brought into contact with the leading financiers of the City.

Lieutenant in the Honourable Artillery; he placed all four of his sons in banking positions (albeit Thomas's was abandoned and Robert's was not much desired); and he left behind three sons— Robert, Reuben, and William—who were liberally educated, had literary inclinations, and were safely established in banking careers. And, perhaps most firmly implanted in Cyrus Mason's memory, Robert of Woodyates ultimately earned a salary of £561—"an amount in that time which easily placed him in buying power, if not in hereditary dignity, among the comfortable gentry."[20]

For Reuben of Woodyates, the elder Robert's brother, Cyrus Mason asserts much: not only did he implant in his nephew, Robert Senior, the tendency toward Methodism, but he also was responsible for the liberal, literarily inclined education received by the poet's father.[21] Reuben's interest in and conversion to Methodism Cyrus attributes to his marriage to the widow Mason; Reuben's educational aptitude seems natural for a man who "with his pen or by teaching [was able] to provide a comfortable maintenance" for himself and his wife and stepson.[22] According to Cyrus Mason, "the literary world owes a debt of gratitude never yet acknowledged to the Dorsetshire learned Reuben Browning" (p. 16), for Reuben first employed the educational techniques with Robert Senior that Robert Senior in turn used with his son the poet. Reuben's "method of teaching" (pp. 65-6) seems to have been mostly liberal encouragement, inspiration,

---

Maynard's *Browning's Youth*, p. 21, refers to his "prestigious position, tantamount to being head of one governmental office." Contemporary references to him as "Gentleman" and "Esquire" corroborate his relative importance as a middle-class bank officer (see Afterword, I).

20. Maynard's *Browning's Youth*, p. 21.

21. Mason's comments about this Reuben center in Part Three; Maynard also evaluates Reuben's importance in *Browning's Youth*, pp. 356-7.

22. Mason's hint here (see p. 53), his disclosure of Reuben's association with a publisher of "educational publications" (pp. 45-6), and his impression that "one of the brothers when residing in Dorsetshire, was associated with educational pursuits" (pp. 46, 32) all point to the idea of Reuben's having been a teacher; Cyrus, his step-grandson, seems somewhat unsure and is therefore reluctant to say so categorically, and, indeed, no evidence exists to support this impression. In London, in fact, this Reuben followed his elder brother into the Bank of England where he served from 1790 to 1819 when he was pensioned off (see Maynard's *Browning's Youth*, p. 357).

perhaps even example, and certainly sympathy for his nephew's study of the arts: he "encouraged" Robert Senior's "literary and poetic tastes," humored "his habit of wandering book in hand about the fields and in the woods," "taught" him "to really love books," and "fostered in the lad's mind a desire to acquire knowledge" (pp. 55-6). And, probably most significantly, he "comforted the boy" against the father's harsher judgment regarding such impractical studies (p. 56). This Reuben—who was also responsible for the education of his stepson, John Mason—was obviously a favorite of Cyrus Mason. "As proof of the affectionate regard felt in the family for the Woodyates Reuben Browning," Cyrus notes that his Christian name has been preserved through three generations—"my uncle, my Brother, Cousins, and one of my own sons, were all given the name of Reuben" (p. 58).

No other account of the character of this Reuben exists. Though Cyrus certainly exaggerates his importance in order to fit the pattern of his history, Mason may well be correct in his general picture of the understanding, encouraging uncle's providing his nephew with something of a pattern as a broad-minded paternal figure. Thus, this Dorsetshire Browning seems to have introduced into the London clan a strain of liberal appreciation of the arts and an adherence to a nonconformist method of worship.[23] Mason's sketch of Reuben of Woodyates adds a unique portrait to the Browning family gallery.

Reuben's nephews, the sons of Robert of Woodyates, comprised the first generation of London-born Brownings. With the exception of the temperamental Thomas, these sons appear to have been well-educated, articulate, literary-minded bankers. In his opening section Mason enumerates their talents and accomplishments as he wonders why none of them ever compiled a family history. William Shergold Browning, second oldest son of the Woodyates Robert (and oldest son by the second marriage), carried on a successful banking career with the Rothschild house in Paris, wrote several historical novels, and published "a very

---

23. It must be noted, however, that Robert Senior's own temperament was the most significant factor in the development of his own educational "techniques" and that Sarah Anna Wiedemann Browning's Congregationalism was the profound dissenting religious influence upon the poet.

acceptable *History of the Huguenots*,"[24] "a work of considerable scholarship and intellectual detachment."[25] According to Mason, Uncle William "cordially received" the poet as his guest in Paris, wrote a poem in praise of Browning's early works, and planned to include young Robert in a trip to St. Petersburg;[26] yet the poet, in a letter to Elizabeth, "slightingly" refers to William's daughter, Louisa Jane, who was visiting London on her honeymoon trip (pp. 84-5)—one of several real, exaggerated, or imagined instances of the poet's disregard for kinsfolk cited by Cousin Cyrus.

The second Reuben, uncle of the poet, served Nathan Rothschild in the London house and wrote several pamphlets on financial matters, sometimes "using the *nom de plume* 'Brutus Britannicus'" (pp. 11-12). This Reuben was close to the poet, "showed a keen interest" in the poet's work, and advised and generously assisted whenever needed (p. 12). Reuben allowed the poet to ride his horse, York, and even—according to Mason—unwittingly supplied the money for Robert's honeymoon.[27] Robert was not the only nephew to benefit from "ever generous" Uncle Reuben, for he also supplied tickets for Cyrus and another nephew, Robert Shergold Browning, to attend a performance of *A Blot in the 'Scutcheon* (pp. 81-3). Reuben's sense of humor, however, presents a slight hint of contradiction: Mason early portrays the uncle as most sympathetic to the poet and keenly interested in his nephew's work, while he later pictures Reuben and John Mason "laughing heartily" and joking over a copy of *Sordello*.[28] His sense of humor must have been taxed, however, when a thief made off with his clothes while he enjoyed his morning swim in the New River (pp. 75-6)!

Cyrus's presentation of William and Reuben Browning pic-

24. Griffin and Minchin, p. 7; William Browning's publications are listed above in Part One, n. 12.

25. Maynard's *Browning's Youth*, p. 114.

26. See pp. 8-10, 84-5.

27. See pp. 85-6, 93; Mason, it must be noted, was probably wrong in portraying Reuben as a source of financial aid to the poet. Though Browning certainly relied on Reuben for financial *advice* until his death, the poet's father probably forwarded to his son the £100 necessary for the elopement: see Part Four, n. 54.

28. See pp. 77-8; Mrs. Orr, I, 115, also relates that "an irreverent remark on 'Sordello' " originated with Uncle Reuben, whom she describes as not appreciating Young Robert's poetry.

tures two generous, helpful uncles who were successful bankers and who had successfully published. Uncle William, Cyrus probably did not know well; Reuben, however, was one of Cyrus's favorite relatives: Mrs. Scarlett, his granddaughter, relates that her "Grandfather had great love for Uncle Reuben B."[29] Cyrus again seeks to establish the Browning family as educated, talented, and literarily inclined. Trimming away Cyrus's more exaggerated claims, one can conclude that Browning's family background was "the solid and educated middle class," and that his uncles, while not men of genius like their nephew, were certainly middle-class men of "considerable talent and accomplishment."[30] Otherwise he adds little to what is already known of his uncles: only the personal anecdotes—such as Reuben's swimming in the New River—and the imputations that young Robert was indebted to them—William entertained him in Paris and planned to take him to St. Petersburg while Reuben is supposed to have financed the poet's honeymoon. Mason's treatment of their brother, his Uncle Robert, is not so clear-cut.

Toward Robert Senior, nephew Cyrus expresses somewhat ambivalent feelings. The predominant picture he draws portrays an almost helpless simpleton—"singularly diffident and inclined to eccentricity"—who, nevertheless, was "possessed of much learning" and was a "most loveable old man" (pp. 8, 89). At least a portion of this mixed attitude seems to derive from Mason's high regard for the Woodyates Reuben who plays such an important part in this version of the family history: ". . . had it not been for the kindly natured gentleman, Reuben Browning; a peculiar temperament and eccentric manner would have drifted my Uncle Robert into . . . an aimless wandering life . . ." (pp. 15-16). Thus it is that Mason can write of the "dreamy eccentric" Robert Senior with "such a simple childhood nature" (p. 80) having "assisted in the production of the early Browning poems" (p. 81): when Cyrus gives credit to Robert Senior for training his son to be a great poet, he is, in effect, praising the elder Reuben for

---

29. Mrs. Scarlett to Mrs. Armstrong, August 29, 1955, Baylor.
30. Chesterton's *Browning*, p. 3; Maynard's *Browning's Youth*, p. 114.

educating Robert Senior in such a way as to produce a great poet.

Cyrus Mason throughout emphasizes what he repeatedly refers to as Robert Senior's "eccentricity." Poor Uncle Robert became so absorbed in his interest in anatomy and dissection that he kept his puzzled wedding party waiting while he cut up a duck, and once caused a ruckus at the Bank by keeping a dead rat too long in his desk (p. 65). Though his artistic talents were original and interesting, they were inexplicably "ungenteel" (p. 87). After his wife's death, the poet's lonely father was tyrannized over by his daughter, Sarianna, and fell into a complicated court-ship with the widow Von Müller in an attempt to gain relief from his "simply mechanical" existence (p. 99). As Mason progresses through his Part Four and into Part Five his sympathy for the simple dotard builds as his wrath against the poet mounts: because of the poet's letter to the widow, Robert Senior lost his court case and was banished from England to live out his remaining years in exile in Paris.[31]

Robert Senior, however, was not alone in his eccentricity: Margaret, his sister, Mason pictures as even more strange. Aunt Margaret crooned mysterious "prophecies over her Nephew" and was seen "mostly at family funerals" (pp. 14, 112). "Margaret Browning was as eccentric in her ways and as simple minded in her behavior as her brother Robert," Mason records (p. 112). From Robert Senior and Margaret—the two children of the Woodyates Robert's first marriage—the poet "inherited eccentricity" which, with "Browning pride," "dominated" him to the extreme of feeling only "antagonism" toward his kinsfolk (p. 14).

Cyrus Mason, influenced by his grandmother, pictures sister Sarianna Browning as having " 'stuck up manners' " and as tyrannizing over her simple old father (pp. 97-9). The kindest words Cyrus can muster for Robert Senior's daughter are that she "devoted her life to forward her brother's literary ambition" (p. 115). Here again, however, the poet must bear the expense of the kindness to his sister: he is the pampered child of the household who is catered to as he is trained to be a poet. Though brief,

---

31. For a particularly sympathetic treatment of Robert Senior, see pp. 87-9.

Mason's treatment of Sarianna is one of the harshest in his manuscript.

About the poet's mother, Sarah Anna Wiedemann Browning, Cyrus has little to say.[32] "Aunt Robert," as he calls her, receives only bare mention and then in regard to her constant self-absorption—"ever mindful of her garden or busy arranging some household punctillios" (p. 80).

Cousin Cyrus reserves for the poet, however, his strongest venom. The main charges leveled at young Robert are twofold: he was trained to be a poet and this training "obliterated natural affection" causing "The Poet's aloofness from kinsfolk" (pp. 115, 81). According to Mason, both Robert Senior and his Uncle Reuben of Woodyates, "at the birth of this infant Browning at Camberwell, actually planned that he should be reared and educated to become a poet!" (p. 65). The same educational process used by Reuben on Robert Senior was to be employed on young Robert (pp. 65-7); his training and teaching were "with only the one object in view"—to make young Robert Browning into a poet (p. 14). The entire London clan was involved in this momentous undertaking, writes Cyrus, for "from his birth at Camberwell Robert Browning's swaddling clothes were wrapped around his little body with a poetic consideration—he was rocked in his cradle rhythmically by his father—his Aunt Margaret prophecied in her dark mysterious manner his brilliant future—my mother, when a girl, lulled her nephew to rest by whispering to him lines of poetry!" (p. 66). No one "ever suggested that his superior brain should be trained to do anything else but to write poetry" (p. 69). While "it will have to be admitted that his kinsfolk greatly assisted in the making of the child Robert Browning into a Poet" (p. 14), it was primarily Robert Senior who decided—"as some atonement for the suppression of his own mental gifts and as some recompense to himself for the stoppage of his own literary career" (pp. 69-70)—that his son should be made into a poet.

Mason's motivation in such assertions seems to be to give

---

32. This lack of information about the poet's mother is in keeping with most of what has been written about Browning's life and background.

kinsfolk, especially Reuben of Woodyates, as much credit as possible while allowing the poet as little superiority as possible. The imputation seems to be that any child—perhaps even Cousin Cyrus?—born into Robert Senior's household would, with the Woodyates Reuben's superior techniques and the father's single-minded determination, have been "made" into a poet. Was Robert Browning a homemade poet? Edmund Gosse argues that Browning was "trained to be a poet," and implies that the family readily accepted young Robert's choice of career.[33] Betty Miller, however, disagrees, contending that "There is a tradition, sponsored by Edmund Gosse, that this choice received the unqualified approval of Browning's parents. . . . But there is evidence that the acquiescence was by no means as prompt or as willing as Gosse suggests"; Miller proceeds to cite what she regards as "conclusive proof that the son's mode of life evoked some very real opposition in the family circle."[34] Mrs. Orr records "an idea of his father's that he should qualify himself for the Bar" and also writes that Browning "played with the thought of becoming an artist"; she concludes, however, that a diplomatic career was the only "active career" which really appealed to the youthful Browning.[35] William Sharp portrays the father as having "practically left the decision as to his course of life to Robert himself," and, he adds, "there was of course but one way open to him."[36] Maisie Ward feels that Browning's parents readily accepted the choice of a poetic career by their son, but, "it seems likely that Reuben and the Silverthornes and Masons disapproved, that it was with aunts and uncles that the battles were fought to which he alludes in the Love Letters."[37] Robert's own ambiguous remark in the Love Letters refers to "this absolute independence of mine, which . . . I have fought so many good battles to preserve."[38]

It is, of course, ridiculous to claim that anyone can simply be

---

33. Gosse's *Personalia*, pp. 19, 25-6.
34. Miller's *Portrait*, pp. 19-21.
35. Mrs. Orr, I, 69-72, 92.
36. Sharp's *Life*, pp. 34-5.
37. Ward, I, 48-51.
38. *RBEBK*, I, 200; see also I, 193: "I even convinced the people *here* what was my true 'honorable position in society'. . . ."

"trained" to be a great poet. That Browning was encouraged and indulged in his poetic interests there can be little doubt, but the stuff of genius obviously was there to be encouraged and indulged. The type of education he received, however, did play an important part in the type of poet Browning became. At about age five Browning attended a local Peckham dame's school from which he was dismissed because his precociousness brought him both special treatment and "the jealousy of the parents of other pupils."[39] From the age of eight or nine to fourteen he attended a Peckham preparatory school presided over by the Reverend Thomas Ready and his sisters, an experience which Browning later insisted "taught me nothing." But the poet was there introduced to "the old classical system" of education, probably studied both Latin and Greek, and received a "quite solid and very conservative" childhood schooling.[40] He was later enrolled for a term at the London University in Greek, German, and Latin after further private tutoring in such areas as French, fencing, boxing, and music.

Mason, as one might suspect—and, indeed, as Browning's biographers have too frequently done—minimizes Browning's formal education by noting that he attended "a day school in the neighborhood, the main purpose being to get the boy away from home during the time that his father was in the City" (pp. 68-9).[41] Cousin Cyrus typically exaggerates family importance when he claims that Robert Senior was "his son's sole teacher" in Greek (p. 92). But, again, his main thrust seems correct. For, as Griffin and Minchin acknowledge, it is to Browning's home "that one must look for his early education, and not to his school" (p. 29). More gifted and more learned than Thomas Ready, Browning's father provided "deft and sympathetic teaching [which] spoiled him for other schoolmasters."[42] Even Maynard concludes that "a very large part of his education obviously had nothing to do with

_____

39. Griffin and Minchin, p. 31; their discussion of Browning's education includes pp. 29-33. See also Maynard's *Browning's Youth*, pp. 241-86.

40. Maynard's *Browning's Youth*, pp. 249-50.

41. Among Browning's biographers only Maynard makes a point of the significance of Browning's formal schooling.

42. Irvine and Honan, pp. 5-6.

schools and formal study," that his educational standards differed from those of his family primarily "in the degree of his commitment and the seriousness of his aims," and that "much of his education was literally home education, with supervision by his father and special tutors."[43] And the type of home education Browning received has been most convincingly and most simply pointed out by William Lyon Phelps: "it is interesting to remember that Browning's education was simply the elective system pushed to its last possibility. . . . His education depended absolutely and exclusively on his own inclinations; he was encouraged to study anything he wished. His father granted him perfect liberty. . . ."[44] Thus is a Robert Browning "trained to be a poet."

Mason's second "charge" against the poet ranges from young Robert's having "never evinced much regard for kinsfolk" (p. 14) to, finally, "an absence of that affectionate sentiment from which flows the purest source of delight found in most poetry" (p. 113).[45] Throughout, Cousin Cyrus castigates Browning with the general charge of "aloofness from kinsfolk" (p. 81). Mason creates the impression that the poet had no close ties with relations outside his immediate household, and he feels that in Browning's poetry and "throughout the two volumes of letters, the Poet's kinsfolk are almost ignored" (p. 85).

Cyrus more specifically alleges that young Robert wronged Uncle William—who had hospitably received him in Paris—by "slightingly" referring to his daughter who was honeymooning in London (p. 85); that Uncle Reuben was not given due credit for allowing the poet generous use of his horse York (pp. 85-6); that

---

43. *Browning's Youth*, p. 241; Maynard even notes that "though the foundations of Greek were probably laid at Ready's," probably "the main inspiration for his progress in Greek" derived from his father (p. 250). A footnote to Maynard's discussion of the poet's schooling admits that "It is also possible that Greek was not offered at Ready's and that Robert Browning studied it only at home with his father, as 'Development' seems to imply" (p. 440, n. 42).

44. Phelps's entire discussion in *Robert Browning*, pp. 4-6, is incisive; Maynard also discusses this aspect in great detail (see *Browning's Youth*, pp. 37ff.).

45. An interesting allegation in view of the fact that Robert and Elizabeth have been called "the immortal lovers" and that many of Browning's poems deal with love in its varied forms. "Love" is also one of the more frequently used substantive words in Browning's poetic vocabulary.

Robert's secret courtship of and subsequent elopement with Elizabeth Barrett demonstrated selfishness and insensitivity toward
his immediate family and caused them much unnecessary pain;[46]
that he offended family members who called on him after his
return to London, particularly Jane Eliza Browning Mason
(Cyrus's mother) who was "made aware by her reception that she
was not wanted" (pp. 112-13). Mason further asserts that after his
marriage Robert "stopped communication" with all kinsfolk,
friends, and acquaintances except "Arnould, a lawyer, useful in
arranging the money affairs of the poet's wife" (p. 96).

Despite Mason's accusations, Browning did without doubt
cultivate some deep and lasting family ties. Reuben Browning,
for instance, was "the poet's favorite uncle and but nine years his
senior"; he gave to his talented nephew several noteworthy gifts,
including "an exquisite edition of the *Encheiridion* of Epicte-
tus."[47] Browning later reciprocated by sending Reuben copies of
his own published works. In further contrast with Mason's picture, the two men became so close that Reuben has been characterized as the poet's kindest and best friend, "as much an older
brother as an uncle."[48] Browning came to rely on Reuben for
financial advice throughout his adult life, and the two carried on
what seems to have been an extensive correspondence.[49] The
poet's regard for his uncle and, one might suspect, his gratitude to
him are evidenced by a complicated request in his will that Sarianna should include "the children of my uncle Reuben" in her
final division of his bequest to her.[50] With another uncle, William Shergold Browning, Robert also maintained a warm relationship, "even to the point of honoring him by keeping a plaster

---

46. Parts Four and Five, passim: e.g., p. 112.
47. Griffin and Minchin, pp. 6-7.
48. Maynard's *Browning's Youth*, pp. 115-17.
49. The poet's correspondence with his Uncle Reuben has been partly published
in *New Letters*, though most of it remains unpublished in the Boston Public Library
and the Armstrong Browning Library, Baylor. Some of it is known only through
listings in the Sotheby Sales Catalogue of April 5, 1894 (see Maynard's *Browning's
Youth*, p. 117—especially n. 190). See also the two letters to Reuben in Baly,
"Talking of the Brownings," pp. 14-16.
50. The poet's will has been published as an Appendix to Furnivall's "Ancestors,"
pp. 37-8.

bust of him after his death."[51] At a much later date, Robert
Jardine Browning, William's grandson, "was also intimate with
the poet and his sister, who liked him very much."[52] Mrs. Orr
also refers to William Shergold, after Reuben, as "another favorite uncle" (I, 117), while Maynard deduces that "with both
uncles Browning was on friendly, even close terms" (p. 210).
Family tradition even hints that young Robert was at one time in
love with their sister—his aunt—Jemima; Elaine Baly reports
that Jemima, only one year older than the poet, and Robert "were
very close to each other all their single lives."[53] She further refers
to close relations between the poet and William Shergold's family, and the poet and Reuben's family; in fact, according to Mrs.
Baly, family tradition assigns to the *Masons* the role of feuders
with both Robert Senior's family and Reuben's family.[54]

Among his maternal kinsfolk the younger Browning also developed some close relationships. James Silverthorne, his cousin,
was one of the two witnesses at Browning's secret marriage
ceremony, and his death was commemorated by the poet in the
1852 poem "May and Death."[55] James's mother, Christina Silverthorne (sister to Sarah Anna Wiedemann Browning), furnished her poet-nephew with £30 to pay for the printing costs of
Pauline, Browning's first published work.[56] Just as Browning
requested that Sarianna include Reuben's children in her will, so
did he ask that the children of his cousins James, John, and
George Silverthorne be benefactors.[57] More generally, Griffin
and Minchin have recorded that the poet's "affections, according
to universal testimony, were remarkably tenacious, equally
within the four corners of his own family and the large circle of
his friends" (pp. 284-5). But Mason's feelings—and possibly
those of some other family members, one may surmise—were

51. Maynard's *Browning's Youth*, p. 114.
52. Mrs. Orr, I, 117, n. 1.
53. "Talking of the Brownings," pp. 6-7.
54. "Talking of the Brownings," pp. 6-7, 10, 16; see also Maynard's *Browning's Youth*, p. 458, n. 71.
55. Griffin and Minchin, pp. 54-5; see also Mrs. Orr, I, 69; Maynard's *Browning's Youth*, pp. 96-7; Irvine and Honan, pp. 19, 292.
56. Griffin and Minchin, p. 57.
57. Furnivall's "Ancestors," pp. 37-8.

wounded because the poet did not choose to laud kinsfolk in print or to praise their talents and accomplishments in letters (which were, of course, published posthumously). As Maynard has concluded, "Mason seems only right in his general view that Browning chose not to center his life upon the extended and extensive Browning family."[58]

The household of Robert Browning's immediate family Cyrus Mason regarded as "genteelly dreary" with each of its four members "constantly self absorbed" (p. 80). "Uncle Robert's family," writes Mason, "to me seemed enveloped in a misty pride which clung about it's members, overflowing the home and communicating to visitors, a feeling of dampness" (pp. 80-1). Ironically, their single unifying concern—to develop a poet of genius—Mason cites as the factor which "obliterated natural affection" within the family and which caused their drifting apart (p. 115).

John Maynard's intense study of Browning's early life and environment has led him to regard the household as "both warm and lively" and its members as "hospitable and open," especially to young Robert's friends.[59] Even after Browning's marriage and elopement to Italy, his friend Joseph Arnould writes of visiting New Cross and spending "a most delightful evening there . . . one of the old evenings."[60] Maisie Ward even "suspects that the Brownings were bored to death by the Masons, and it might be refreshing to hear the Silverthorne opinion of both families and their mutual relationship!"[61] Perhaps the most famous evaluation of the New Cross household, however, comes from another Browning friend, Alfred Domett: "Altogether, father, mother, only son and only daughter formed a most suited, harmonious and intellectual family, as appeared to me."[62]

Perhaps it is the "intellectual" which causes Mason to remark

---

58. *Browning's Youth*, p. 363.
59. *Browning's Youth*, p. 35.
60. Donald Smalley, "Joseph Arnould and Robert Browning: New Letters (1842-50) and a Verse Epistle," *PMLA*, 80 (March, 1965), p. 95: J. A. to R. B., Dec. 6, 1848.
61. *Browning*, I, 11.
62. *The Diary of Alfred Domett*, ed. E. A. Horseman (London: Oxford Univ. Press, 1969), p. 213. Phelps similarly comments that Browning "could hardly have selected a better father and mother than were chosen for him" (*Robert Browning*, p. 1).

on their self-absorption; Maynard feels that their "concern for cultivation" prompted Cyrus to record both their self-absorption and their "misty pride."[63] Mason's own immediate family circle, seemingly dominated by the Dorsetshire Robert, may well have been more concerned with middle-class practical, material, and social successes than the household of the dreamy, eccentric Uncle Robert. The poet's immediate family—father, mother, son, daughter—were all allowed great freedom to grow individually and to cultivate their own interests: Robert Senior with his art and his anatomy studies; Sarah Anna with her garden and her music; young Robert with his poetry and, for a short time, Elizabeth; and Sarianna with her chapel interests and, probably more than anything else, her devotion to the family.[64] What Cousin Cyrus labels self-absorption may well be termed, from a more sympathetic vantage point, self-realization and self-fulfillment. Surely Robert Senior was a somewhat dreamy, eccentric character; Sarah Anna was engrossed by her house and garden; Sarianna was something of a "petty snob"; and young Robert did not lard his letters and verse with references to kinsfolk. But the New Cross household still seems to have been admired and visited by friends and family, and Browning certainly cultivated important and lasting friendships among both his acquaintances and his kinsfolk. However, Cyrus Mason's complex motivations—especially envy and disappointment, the influence of grandfather Robert of Woodyates, and a smoldering family feud—prompted him to report unfavorably and sometimes unfairly on his famous cousin's immediate family, while at the same time praising the clan and other kinsfolk from Grandfather Robert's second family.

---

63. *Browning's Youth*, p. 35.
64. See Maynard's *Browning's Youth*, Chapter 3, passim, for a discussion of the individual interests within the family group.

III

ATTITUDE

> He was so many-sided that there may be room for any picture
> of him that is quite sincere and personal, however slight it
> may prove; and in the case of Mr. Browning, far more than
> most men of genius, the portrait may be truly and boldly
> drawn without offense.
>
> Edmund Gosse, *Personalia*, p. 80

The central dichotomy which characterizes "The Poet Robert
Browning and his Kinsfolk" involves its author's attempt to
elevate the Browning family status while simultaneously trying
to demean Robert Browning and his immediate family. Three
major factors seem to motivate Cousin Cyrus's ambivalent attitude: personal jealousy, the family search for a patriarch, and a
long-standing intrafamily feud. Maisie Ward characterizes Cyrus's "obviously disliking his cousin, perhaps envying his good
luck" as the reason behind "Mason's rather spiteful account of
the Browning family."[1] John Maynard takes only a slightly
different tack when he refers to Cyrus being "smitten with
mingled feelings of envy and inferiority" (p. 35). The fourth child
in a ten-member family, Cyrus was certainly not supported by his
parents well into his thirties as his favored cousin was. Also,
Mason's artistic interests were almost certainly not indulged and
encouraged to the extent that the poet's were. Young Robert's
intellect and accomplishments were probably held up—or at least
stood as their own advocates—before the younger cousins; Cyrus,
about sixteen years the poet's junior, remembers the cousins as

---

1. *Ward*, I, 6, 309 (Chapter 1, n. 2).

"Having always been accustomed to consider 'Young Robert' as the very superior individual in the family" (p. 97). As the favored only son of what must have appeared to the second family of Robert of Woodyates as a favored son, Robert the poet stood as a natural target for the envy of all his cousins. As they grew older and were forced to go to work to support themselves, they must have been provoked as they watched their over-thirty cousin, still without gainful employment, becoming a celebrity. His secret marriage to a famous poetess and their departure to live in Italy could only have added more gall to an already distasteful situation. That Cyrus Mason should feel jealousy toward his more talented and more successful older cousin seems only natural. But there is more involved in Cyrus's attitude than mere cousin's jealousy.

At several points in the manuscript Mason hints at the tradition of and the desire for a patriarch figure among London Brownings. The dominant Robert of Woodyates was obviously such a figure until his death in 1833. Mason records that his own family moved from the south to the north side of London in the 1820s—after the death of the Woodyates Reuben, stepfather to John Mason—to settle in Middlesex, "situated within walking distance" of his Grandfather Robert's house (p. 71). Grandmother Jane Smith Browning, after the death of her husband, the Woodyates Robert, moved her family again to the south side of London, this time to New Cross where "Uncle Robert, his wife, his son the Poet and daughter had resided for sometime" (p. 77). About 1840 Cyrus's "parents also removed to New Cross and resided near Uncle Robert Browning" (p. 78). In both moves the Mason family seems to have sought out and followed the family head; [2] more interesting—and perhaps more revealing—is the move by Jane Smith Browning to reside near her *stepson*, Robert Senior. The bad feelings between the two families sired by Robert of Woodyates were of long standing; such a move by one of the

---

2. Maynard's *Browning's Youth*, p. 363, concludes that the Masons were "somewhat in the position of poor relations and, following the family wherever its center seemed to be, were rather envious onlookers of the more prominent members of the family. . . ."

primary instigators of the family feud, therefore, seems remarkably inconsistent.[3] Inconsistent, that is, unless regarded in the light of the family's seeking out its new patriarch.

In his closing pages Mason remembers that the poet "was waited upon, as *head of the family*, when in Italy and in London by kinsfolk" (p. 113, italics mine). Much as the eldest son was traditionally named Robert, so he traditionally was expected to assume the position of family patriarch. Perhaps at least a part of Mason's quarrel with the poet and his family is attributable to the lack of interest by both the poet and his father in serving as "head of the family." Such abdication on their part must have seemed "eccentric" to a young Cyrus Mason reared in the shadow of Grandfather Robert, and as "aloofness from kinsfolk" to a family used to a dominant Robert at its head. How much more strange must Robert Wiedemann Barrett Browning—"now the *head of the family*" (p. 114; italics mine)—have seemed to his Browning kinsfolk? This last Robert, according to Cyrus in 1908, "remains as much a strange foreigner to all his kinsfolk as any lighthouse keeper stationed on the shores of the Meditteraenan [*sic*] Sea" (p. 114). Neither Robert Senior nor the poet—nor indeed the poet's son—had the least inclination toward assuming his inherited mantle as patriarch of the London Brownings.

But probably the most pervasive cause influencing Cyrus Mason's attitude toward his cousin and his cousin's family involves the complex, long-standing feud which grew up between Robert of Woodyates and Robert Senior. To begin with, in Mrs. Orr's words (I, 6), "no two persons were ever more unlike": few people have even been more impractical and unbusinesslike than the son of the eminently practical, businesslike Dorsetshire Robert; conversely, few people have ever been more unartistic and illiberal than the father of the artistic, liberal Robert Senior. The notorious St. Kitt's episode seems only to have been the final blow to the everwidening wedge which drove the two men apart.

---

3. Mason suggests that one possible cause for the Woodyates Robert's initial move from Peckham to Islington was "the objection indulged by the second Mrs. Browning [Jane Smith] to the proximity of her step-son Robert" (p. 67). Mrs. Orr, I, 113, also notes that the widow moved to New Cross "in order to be near her relations" and thus had "friendly contact" with Robert Senior's family "for the first time."

Jane Smith Browning, the second wife, contributed heavily to the split. Natural jealousy of the first wife and first family of the Woodyates Robert unfortunately resulted in a more than naturally harsh stepmother. For instance, she persuaded her husband to prohibit his first son from pursuing a formal education at a university—in spite of Robert Senior's income through a maternal inheritance—because "they could not afford to send their other sons to college."[4] Such a great influence did she exert over her usually dominant husband that he was even induced to move from south to north London at least partially because of "the objection indulged by the second Mrs. Browning to the proximity of her step-son" (p. 67).

As has been noted, the liberal education received from the uncle as well as the Methodist influence exerted by the Woodyates Reuben were factors which furthered the widening gap between father and son. Chesterton acknowledges the major part played by religious differences in his statement that Robert Senior "completed his severance from his father by joining a dissenting sect."[5] Cyrus somewhat unwittingly points to what must have been another matter for contention between the two—politics. Though Mason claims that the Brownings "always have been pronounced Tories" (p. 36), Robert Senior seems to have been as much a liberal, or Whig, as his father must have been Tory. Thus, two men with basically different temperaments were further divided by family (a second marriage), religion, and politics: the result, as Browning has recorded in a letter to Elizabeth, was that Robert Senior's father "continued to hate him till a few years before his death."[6]

Jane Eliza Browning Mason, Cyrus's mother, was daughter to Robert of Woodyates by his second wife, Jane Smith; as such, she was probably more sympathetic with father than with half brother. And it is from Jane Eliza that Cyrus garnered most of the

---

4. See Mrs. Orr, I, 6-7.
5. Chesterton's *Browning*, p. 10.
6. Letter 523, *RBEBK*, II, 1003 ff. One is tempted to wonder if some of Robert Senior's reluctance to talk of the St. Kitt's episode might have derived from the father-son split which ensued (as well as the distaste for slavery to which it has been attributed).

family gossip and tradition as well as much of the opinion which he injects into his family history. Also, Elaine Baly, herself a descendant of Robert Senior's half brother Reuben, has written: "I gathered from my grandmother [Elizabeth Browning Deacon] that there was a family feud between the Masons, Jane's family, and the Browning family at New Cross [Robert Senior's family]. . . . Cyrus Mason was only a lad in those days and would have grown up with the feelings of antipathy held by his mother towards the poet."[7] While Mrs. Baly remembers that family tradition reports "that Jane was jealous of the close relationship between the poet and [her sister] Jemima," the long-standing feud between father and son, between first family and second family, must have been felt strongly among the patriarch-minded Masons. For Robert Senior, his children (the poet and Sarianna), and his sister (Margaret)—all members of the Woodyates Robert's first family—are the only kinsfolk whom Mason attacks.

Jealous of his favored and famous cousin, puzzled and hurt by both uncle's and cousin's denial of patriarchal rights and responsibilities, and reared in the shadow of an old family feud, Cyrus Mason seeks to demean the poet and his family while at the same time exalting the clan of which both he and they are a part. The instinct to defend family—Faulkner's "old, fierce pull of blood"—runs hot through Mason's veins, but the prejudices of a lifetime keep clogging its free flow: Cyrus probably just could not like young Robert enough to allow his defense to proceed smoothly. Cousin Cyrus Mason thus defends family, claims kinship with a famous poet, and yet at the same time vents his true, largely hostile feelings for Browning. Though biased and somewhat bitter, Mason's unique inside testimony can be helpful if examined carefully and warily: "The Poet Robert Browning and his Kinsfolk" is most valuable as an unparalleled personal glimpse by a contemporary relative—albeit a jealous and feuding one—into the family history and early life and environment of the poet.

---

7. Baly, "Talking of the Brownings," pp. 6-7.